HOW TO BECOME A

RADIO

DISC JOCKEY

By Hal Fisher

TAB BOOKS

Blue Ridge Summit, Pa. 17214

FIRST EDITION

FIRST PRINTING—JULY 1971

Copyright © 1971 by TAB BOOKS

Printed in the United States
of America

Library of Congress Card Number: 74-162407

Preface

"Everybody wants to get into the act," quips comedian Jimmie Durante. And why not? Why shouldn't today's talented young people want to express themselves in some phase of the performing arts? Some youngsters want to "do their thing" on radio, others prefer the sight-and-sound medium. Either way, it's show business, and that's good! I got into "the act" years ago and I have never regretted my decision. Ask the Hopes, the Bennys, the Skeltons and other famous names in show biz. They'll concur that this is a soul-satisfying profession. And broadcasting, of course, is a very real branch of show business.

Could YOU, perhaps, be one of the thousands of talented young persons with a happy attitude and natural aptitude to spin and chat, flip switches and twist knobs for a livelihood in this fascinating world of instant communication? You could!

Following the publication of my two broadcast handbooks, it was suggested that I write another volume, a book expressly formulated to serve a dual purpose: a lesson-by-lesson course for classroom instruction and a self-teaching guide for the student disc jockey who prefers to go it alone, with his tape recorder, in the privacy of his own home. This comprehensive volume, "How To Become a Radio Disc Jockey" is the result of that suggestion. It follows the outline I use for my tape-recorded correspondence course. The classroom instructor will notice the inclusion of easy-to-copy line drawings and diagrams for blackboard-illustration purposes. The sections on production practices, timing etc., may be directly applied to students' on-the-job training in a school's campus broadcast station.

Finally, let me say this to the serious-minded reader. Ahead of you lies a boundless dimension to explore, a challenging world to conquer—a populous region called show business, with its lights and shadows, gags and gimmicks with commercial overtones, and literally, old-fashioned fame and fortune. Yes, broadcasting is a powerful combine, abundant with opportunities for the worthy. Herein lies the essential technology peculiar to our zany profession, to which I have added a few personal pros and cons and a recounting of my experiences as guidance on your goal-searching adventure. I will at all times be greatly interested in your progress.

HAL FISHER

Contents

We believe:

That radio broadcasting in the United States of America is a living symbol of democracy; a significant instrument for maintaining freedom of speech, as established by the First Amendment to the Constitution of the United States. . . That it is our obligation to serve the people in such a manner to reflect credit upon our profession and to encourage aspiration toward a better estate for all mankind by making available to every person in America such programs as will perpetuate the traditional leadership of the United States in all phases of the broadcasting art. . .

(Excerpted from the NAB Radio Broadcaster's Creed)

Introduction

Broadcasting spells **BIG** business for those who **dare** to think big. Do you? We have big thinkers in this mighty montage of art, science and craftsmanship who earn close to $1 million a year! They are the energetic artistes, the human dynamos, who sweat through their make-up under the blazing lights of Hollywood's TV-film sound stages, and they do this for 50-plus hours a week. These performers revel in popularity and prestige; they bask warmly in the glamour and idolatry accorded the Hollywoodian image; they are securely anchored in the financial happiness of movie stars.

Preferred artists, they are, because of their talents and training, and because of their showmanship and experience gained while playing to the eagle eye of the television camera. Importantly, they are where they are because they didn't fear to think big. You, the radio disc jockey, should not hesitate to visualize your goal way up on top of the broadcast heap. Remember, this is show business, and it's not mere lyricism when I say, "there's no business like show business for a career of rare fulfillment!"

DOES IT PAY?

Charlton Heston, President of the Screen Actors Guild, recently stated, "Income from members of the Guild breaks down like this: $25 million a year from making films, $31 million from making entertainment television and $53 million from making television commercials." In Hollywood's TV-commercial studios, photogenic Thespians sing and act, sip Cokes, munch on potato chips, flash their "whiter-than-white" dentures, or simply look pretty fro the TV camera. They do this thing at the rate of a "starving" $125 for an 8-hour-day's work; off-camera work pays a "measly" AFTRA scale of **only** $90 a day. A salary figure of $25,000 a year is not at all uncommon. A chosen few boast of incomes amounting to $50,000 (and I wouldn't doubt them), while a half-dozen or so "preferred" ones demand and receive as much as $60 for an hour's work on a commercial, which when timed will run exactly 60 seconds on the tube.

One of the profession's highest paid off-camera announcers, a man with a "thousand" voices, has proved that he can do any type of commercial in any dialect required of him. For this reason, it's said, the "king of commercials," as they call him on Madison Avenue, earns between $500,000 and $750,000 annually. He's one of the industry's preferred artistes, and rightly so. His is not raw talent, but a highly skilled voice. Allen Swift is his name, and you never see the fellow.

About those cute baby commercials, in which a little one may do nothing more than goo goo, or reach for some toy out of grasp, or gurgle for the microphone, the child earns as much as $139 a day. When you add residuals to a baby's earnings, some tiny actors clock an annual income of $20,000. Of course, there are rules and regulations which apply exclusively to baby actors; one of them stipulates that babies may be worked only 10 minutes at a stretch. What do the tykes do in between takes? Why, they nap, naturally. More on TV-commercial making later.

Speaking about preferred artistes, as you probably know, DJs enjoy the enviable popularity and prestige, as well as the fabulous earnings of Hollywood's finest. Salary figures of famous disc jockeys are not readily available, but I did learn that a most personable jock by the name of Hal Lewis, better known as Aku to his thousands of radio fans in and around Honolulu, recently was signed to a long-time contract at an annual salary of $400,000. His 6 to 10 AM show is the preferred one on the Islands. Lewis—I mean, Aku—is considered the highest paid disc jockey in the United States. I would guess that broadcasting's number-2 man-about-LPs might be WOR's John Gambling, but it's difficult to say for sure; too many deejays wallow in dollar signs.

EMPLOYMENT POTENTIAL

The employment outlook for radio and television has never appeared more promising! Let me substantiate that statement by quoting a few statistics from a United States Department of Labor bulletin: Broadcasting employs more than 90,000 full-time artists and craftsmen. According to the latest report, about 21,000 part-time workers find broadcasting a highly profitable field. It's an excellent means of supplementing their incomes from other sources, and it helps students to pay for four years of college. Here's an important point: More than 55 percent of the figures I have just given you apply to persons employed in radio broadcasting, and less than 45 percent do things in the sight-and-sound medium. In

9

addition to staff employees, there are the free lancers (many of them), musicians, writers, office personnel, and the others—top-name announcers, narrators and commentators. There are overseas news correspondents who work on special assignments for the network and press-wire services, and broadcast journalists and camera crews who on a moment's notice are flown to the war zones of far-off Asia, to the tinderbox in the Middle East or other areas of global conflict, for firsthand, graphic accounts of battle and bloodshed.

This is a vast industry, and your field of operation lies before you. Almost every community of 10,000 or so, supports at least one broadcast station, usually radio, of course. It should be of interest to you that about one-third of all radio stations serve broadcast areas of less than 10,000 population; most of these are one-station markets. That's good news for the young broadcaster who seeks a start on the local level. We find television outlets in communities of more than 25,000, but three-fourths of the TV stations are located in areas of 100,000 and more. In contrast, over 60 percent of all **radio** stations serve areas of less than 100,000.

Now, let's examine the employment outlook in this business of broadcasting. More than 14,000 men and women work behind mikes, most of them in radio stations. Over 20,000 supervisory technicians busy themselves in both radio and television. The weekly salary figure of broadcast personnel breaks down to an average $155 on a 40-hour-per-week basis. In addition to base salaries, announcers in larger operations are paid talent fees for special commercial assignments. Starting salaries vary according to station size, local market conditions, etc. They run from the minimum hourly rate of pay as stipulated by law (usually observed by only a few, very small local outlets) to perhaps $75 to $100 weekly for newcomers and broadcast-school graduates with some experience.

The radio profession reports an annual turnover of about 33 percent and the visual medium about 28 percent. As evidenced by the above percentages, there's a constant ebb and flow, a going and coming, of radio and television personnel—a healthy situation. In my opinion, the above turnover is due to a steady up-hill climb to the top of the heap by the ambitious and talented. This advancing trend should prove interesting for the beginner. The men and women who move up, up and away to greater broadcast heights clear the way for the advancement of talented and trained newcomers to the profession. After you read this book, I suggest that you write for a copy of Bulletin 1150-115, **Employment Outlook for Radio** and **Television Broadcasting**. Order it for ten cents from the Superintendent of Documents, U.S. Printing Office, Washington, D.C. 20402. The information is priceless.

Getting back to statistics, there are more than 6,000 commercial AM and FM stations on the air today and applications for new construction permits flow into the Commission's office with regularity. About 600 television towers beam signals across this great land. That's your field of operation. In an industry the magnitude of broadcasting, you may be sure that there is, and will continue to be, a real need for qualified broadcasters to keep abreast of the profession's phenomenal expansion. It must be remembered, however, that it's the **trained** engineer, the **developed** disc jockey, the **schooled** broadcast journalist who is wanted and to whom the industry will gladly pay premium salaries. Raw talent won't do.

Student counselors continually put the emphasis on two factors conducive to success in any trade or profession. Because a youngster likes to spin discs on his record player, or because he has collected a stack of choice rock tunes, in itself, doesn't indicate that he possesses the essential attitude and aptitude for a successful broadcast career. The aspirant, for his own good, should realize that his life's work is at stake, and the occupation he chooses must be followed over a 30- or 40-year period. That's a long time to grind away for a mediocre living in a profession for which he is unsuited. If he lacks artistic talent, maybe he's the scientific type, basically equipped for an exciting career in that wonderful world of electronics. And the commercially minded chap may find advertising salesmanship an exceptionally profitable field. You see, there's something for all of us to do in broadcasting.

We can't all be captains—some must be crew.

There's something for all of us to do.

—Anon.

THE MODERN DJ

Let me give you a brief profile of the modern disc jockey and what he must do to make a living. Today's successful jock is a hard-working, energetic, fast-thinking, resourceful chap of several talents. He must be all these things to properly function in the complexities of today's control room. What does he do between chatter? Too many things. He must pull, spin and file away his own recordings. He is plagued with every imaginable type of telephone call. At a most confusing moment someone will call to inquire, "Was that an explosion?" The jock is supposed to know. And this kind of thing goes on throughout his entire working day. The jock must take half-hourly transmitter-meter readings and, in keeping with FCC rules and regulations, make notations on as many as three logs. Besides rehearsing copy and reading commercials, spinning records and such, the jock prepares his own newscasts, unless he is fortunate enough to have a news editor on duty.

In case of equipment or power failure, a civilian defense alert or other emergency, or should fire break out in the transmitter room, the DJ must know what to do and do it pronto! He must be resourceful. Just about anyone can be taught to spin records; therefore, the jock would be a surplus commodity if it weren't for his talent and training in the techniques used in professional announcing and authoritative newscasting. I have watched personable chaps with pear-shaped tones in their voices fail miserably as disc jockeys simply because they failed to cope with the mechanics of the business or because they were the lethargic type—plain lazy. Yes, today's deejay is a complex personality with rapid-fire reflexes.

In broadcasting there's little margin for error, no allowance for tardiness, and plain laziness cannot be tolerated. Lethargy is taboo in this split-second business. There's never a dull moment in a control room, and the DJ must constantly be on his toes. To keep tension under control, and to keep himself mentally and physically alert, the broadcaster should cultivate sensible living habits. More on this later. The jock who opens up in the morning is called the "morning man"; the earlybird who must rise and shine at 5 AM, perhaps earlier, if he lives in the suburbs. Sign-on at six sharp means 6:00:00, not a second earlier or later, and that's precisely how it must be entered on the logs: "**On the air at 6:00:00.**" If the station is what is known as a "daytimer," the jock's hours will vary with the seasons.

A daytimer is licensed to operate from average local sunrise to local sunset. During the wintertime with its short days, such a station leaves the air in the late afternoon; its broadcast days are lengthened with the approach of spring and summer. A definite FCC daytime operational schedule is (or should be) posted on the control room wall and must be strictly observed. Daytime operation calls for half-hour to 45-minute adjustments, from month to month, in keeping with average local sunrise and sunset, with a standstill in mid-summer and again in midwinter. But it seems the control room clock never holds for the DJ; he fights it eight hours a day, five days a week. The going may become rough at times, but I have yet to know a disc jockey who didn't like his work behind the mike. Maybe that's because it's show business. More on the DJ and his control room in Lesson 18.

By the time you complete work on this book, you'll have to answer four questions. Think about the four A's as you read: Aspiration, Attitude, Aptitude and Action.

1. Do I really aspire to a career in broadcasting, or am I only superficially interested in the work?

2. Will I be able to maintain the necessary mental attitude over a long period of time as a broadcast careerist?

3. Do I have the necessary, basic qualifications (talent, educational background, etc.) for a broadcast career?

4. Am I in a position, financially or otherwise, to carry through on long-range plans to reach my goal? Do I have the determination and perseverence required for success?

The more you know, the farther you go! You are fortunate, indeed, if your high school offers its student body a comprehensive course in communication and practical experience as gained behind the mike in a campus radio station. Insofar as a general educational background is concerned, I may safely say that a high school diploma is the minimum requirement. Some college training is preferred; if possible, a liberal arts education should be sought. Your school may be considering a course in communication and the inauguration of a campus radio station, hence the following information material about educational broadcasting may prove extremely interesting, and for the educator, encouraging.

EDUCATIONAL RADIO

The advantages offered to the talented and ambitious by educational radio are many and varied. Increasing numbers of high schools across the land, in classrooms and in campus broadcast stations, busily prepare precollege-age students for the day when the freshmen, on a new educational level and with great aplomb, will take their places in commercial radio stations near their campuses to ease up on the rising cost of their four years of college life. More on this later. If reaching

WRHS 540 KC

The Voice of Robbinsville High School

P. O. BOX 576, ROBBINSVILLE, N. C. 28771
PHONE 479-3919

STA ID	ON	OFF	PROGRAM TITLE/ANNCMT	SPONSOR	TYPE	ON	OFF
	7:55	7:57	Sign On				
	7:57	8:00	Headline News		N		
	8:00	8:25	Musical Interlude		E		
	8:25	8:30	News		N		
	8:30	8:55	America Emerges		ED		
	8:55	9:00	News		N		
	9:00	9:25	Exploring Science		ED		
	9:25	9:30	News		N		
	9:30	9:55	A World of Brothers		R		
	9:55	10:00	News		N		
	10:00	10:25	Famous Moments in History		ED		
	10:25	10:30	News		N		
	10:30	10:55	Growing Up		O		
	10:55	11:00	News		N		
	11:00	11:25	Careers Unlimited		ED		
	11:25	11:30	News		N		
	11:30	11:55	When Men Are Free		O		
	11:55	12:00	News		N		
	12:00	12:25	Meet the Music Masters		E-I		
	12:25	12:30	News		N		
	12:30	1:00	Information Unlimited		ED		
	1:00	1:25	A Pocketful of Tales		E		
	1:25	1:30	News		N		

Note half-hourly news policy.

Typical campus radio station program log. Notice the half-hourly news policy.

14

for a college diploma lies beyond your grasp, and the cost of a higher education seems out-of-bounds for you, a high school communications course and some campus broadcast-station activity may well prepare you for part-time employment as a deejay, newscaster or in some other capacity in a commercial operation to help you earn that doctorate or lesser degree.

Incidentally, it's generally supposed that a college degree or even a college diploma is essential for success in this profession. In all fairness let me put it this way: A diploma and a degree are admirable and applausive achievements and undoubtedly impressive in appearance on a job application, but from what I have learned from personnel managers, a diploma or a college rank is no longer necessarily accepted as "proof of performance" as it were. So don't overemphasize the importance of acquiring a degree. A high school education and graduation? Yes, by all means, as I have, complete your general education before you start specialized training. It also bears repeating that the industry cannot use raw talent; it must insist upon talent plus technology and training. Most certainly, educational radio with its campus stations should be applauded and encouraged to continue bringing broadcasting and its techniques into the classroom. How we broadcasters of the old school could have used such preparatory instruction! for us it was swim or sink, trial and error, but then, it's said that experience is the best teacher. I wonder.

The steadily growing interest in and, understandably, the nationwide expansion of educational radio and TV, as I see it, represents a truly remarkable contribution to commercial broadcasting. Our industry is duly aware of the great strides being undertaken on broadcasting's scholastic level; the profession proudly extends a welcoming hand to the classroom-trained neophyte. High schools all over America are emulating colleges and universities by inaugurating campus broadcast-station operations, expressly to ready able students for communications work during their 4-year stay in institutions of higher learning.

Educational radio and television has come a long way over the years. The National Association of Educational Broadcasters, founded in 1925, today has a membership of 3,000 and the National Educational Radio Network has 170 affiliate stations. At present 180 colleges operate campus radio stations and 116 maintain television facilities. Additional information on educational broadcasting may be obtained directly from the National Association of Educational Broadcasters, 1346 Connecticut Avenue, N.W., Washington, D. C. 20036.

15

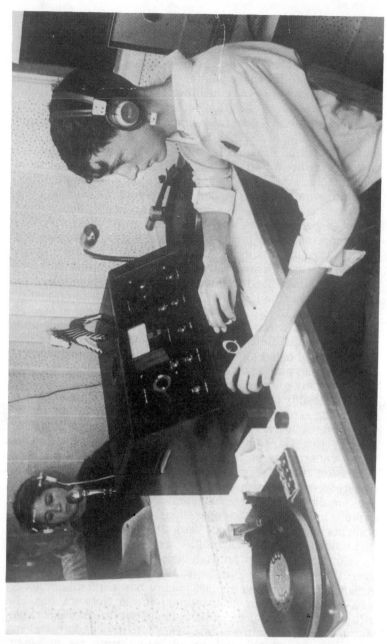

Young deejay at the WRHS console. Students assisted the school's electronics instructor in constructing the equipment (Asheville (N.C.) **Citizens-Times** photo.)

16

The first educational radio station to go on the air was WHA, at the University of Wisconsin at Madison in 1919. In 1925,—171 stations were beaming signals operated by educational organizations, and currently there are more than 400 educational radio stations licensed or with construction permits. The scope and limits of educational radio today are clearly controlled by the medium's economic base. It's interesting to note that almost half the stations operate on budgets of less than $20,000 per year. "Educational radio has begun at last to respond with a budding aggressiveness to the almost overwhelming challenge of television. Like its commercial counterpart of a decade earlier, it is awakening to the realization that no one medium can be all things to all men all the time, and that there is a legitimate, important role that it, too, can play in this complex, changing American society. Educational radio is the Hidden Medium," concludes the NAEB.

To reinforce the concept of practical application in school radio and television workshops, educators parallel such actual on-air activity with comprehensive classroom courses in the areas of speech, electronics, personality development, writing and related subject matter. Students learn the basics from textbooks and classwork, then, under the guidance and direction of instructors expressly trained in teachers' colleges for this highly specialized phase of broadcasting, they gain practical, behind-the-mike experience under simulated, professional broadcast conditions. On the air in a fully equipped control room, the neophyte develops the intricate techniques conducive to professional announcing, newscasting, board work and production. The scientifically minded youth is able to investigate, first-hand, the intriguing mysteries of electronics. Students achieve the essential know-how of expertly handling and operating sensitive and costly professional broadcast equipment found in the "workshop" of the budding disc jockey. At graduation time, the precollege-age student is prepared to advance another step in the direction of commercial broadcasting. He is sufficiently acclimated and adjusted, both physically and psychologically, to the broadcast environment; he has developed that human quality of self-confidence to a point where it will lend itself favorably to success on a higher level. The student is well versed in good and proper broadcast proctices, and in all probabilty, he has studied the National Association of Broadcaster's Creed and its code of ethics, as well as the fundamental rules and regulations of the Federal Communications Commission. Hence, the graduate is ready and

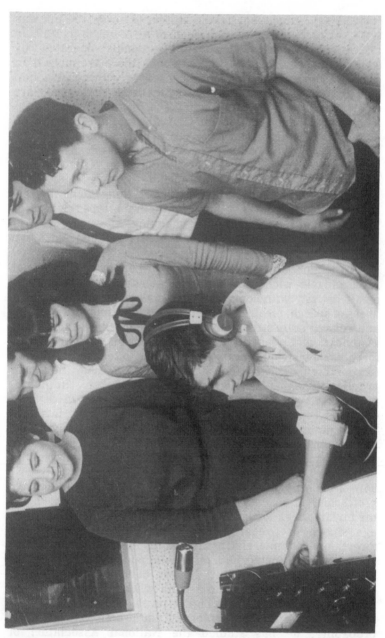

Students get on-the-job training at the WRHS Campus radio station control board. (Asheville (N.C.) **Citizens-Times** photo.)

able to accept his first job in a commercial broadcast station. Incidentally, my remarks, here and throughout this entire book, are equally directed to women of talent. Broadcasting is a woman's world, too. Milady's place in this profession will be discussed in a later section.

School boards wince when educational radio is suggested. Some educators are of the opinion that the cost of construction, operation and maintenance of a campus broadcast project comes excessively high. Actually, the expenditure for such an installation and its operation need not run out of bounds. Let me cite a striking example: Radio Station WRHS, owned and operated by Robbinsville High School, in Robbinsville, North Carolina. The WRHS success story is an extremely interesting and long one; I can but touch on it here. It seems that Henry W. Lamb Jr., Robbinsville's band-radio teacher and Walter Denton, electronics instructor worked out a plan to inaugurate a campus radio station in a spare room of the school. "That's way out, man!" was the cry, but for the two pioneers of educational radio in North Carolina, the idea was in. It wasn't wishful thinking for Lamb and Denton; these men had cold facts to prove that it could be done. Armed with a handful of facts and figures, they approached the Robbinsville School Board and won their case. How? By uttering the phrase, "It can be done on a shoestring," and so it was done on a shoestring!

A free-for-all construction project, students pitched in with saws and hammers to get their campus radio station on the air without delay. Lamb and Denton made their point: In modest proportions, a campus radio station can be put into operation at an amazingly low cash outlay. Quite unique is the fact that the station's special programs are piped into classrooms where such group instruction coincides with the educational material being broadcast over the area's power lines. "It's great experience for the kids," said Lamb, "gives them 'on-the-job' training, you might say." As you will notice from the WRHS program log, the station features half-hour newscasts. Mr. Lamb told me recently that he will gladly send any interested educator or school board a comprehensive fact sheet showing, in dollars and cents, how Robbinsville High School did it "on a shoestring," and, as he put it, "Anyone can do it."

Today's commercial world, as I'm sure you know, is educationally minded, and rightly so. True, the accent is on youth and we welcome the new thoughts they bring the profession. Yet the overzealous youth who drops out of classes to prematurely seize a business opportunity, to jump the gun on his colleagues, for what he considers a headstart, will surely regret his hasty decision; in fact, he may have to retrace his steps. If you believe you have certain talents, natural aptitude, which may qualify you for a career in broadcasting—excellent! But get all the general education you can before you seek specialized training in the broadcast arts. It's the same, old advice: Stay in school; don't drop out. As I said, broadcasting spells big business for those who dare to think big. To think big you need something worthwhile with which to think, and that would seem to indicate the need for a solid education in its related ramifications.

I don't want to go overly statistical here, but you do have big things to think about—the industry as you will know it in 20, 30 and 40 years from now. In 1970, broadcasting celebrated its 50th anniversary; the business has come a long, long way. For the record, let's go back to 1958. Department of Commerce, Office of Economics reports, show that broadcasting's national income during that year totalled $769 million. "Unbelievable," we said. Only seven years later, in 1965, national advertising billings jumped to a walloping $1 billion, 228 million, and we thought that was insuperable. Recently, Advertising Age released the information that the world's ten largest advertising agencies reported estimated total billings for 1969 in the staggering amount of $4 billion, 62 million, 900 thousand dollars for handling the nation's radio and television accounts. What will the figure be in 1980? And in 1990? Advertising billings in the future may well zoom to $8 and $10 billion as new towers of steel keep shooting skyward. That's what I call Thinking BIG. What a promising career you have chosen!

How to use this book.

To expedite progress, this book is arranged in three main sections: Technological, Consultative, and Operational. The informational material which accompanies the technical portion of each lesson may be read verbatim for instruction en masse. The material contained in the third category, e.g., production practices, timing, how to seek work etc., may be applied directly to students' training in campus broadcast stations, or it may be used for lecturing purposes. The student working in the privacy of his room may read and study the operational information at leisure, and use it as a refresher during his early days as a working jock.

As you will notice, each week's lesson concludes with a suggested practice schedule. The group instructor may copy schedules on the blackboard for notation. The home-study aspirant who must be his own teacher, as it were, should try to adhere to a minimum, one-hour-daily practice session, five or six times weekly. Rest on Sunday. Unless you are able to devote full time to your self-improvement program, your schedule, in time, may become top heavy. Should this happen, simply decrease the allotted time of each segment of your schedule, or you may, for example, alternate pronunciation with enunciation. Also in your daily practice session, include from five to fifteen minutes for the reading of news accounts. This reading should be done aloud to an invisible listener to develop a story-telling style.

Lessons 6 through 15 deal with the seven basic techniques conducive to professional air work. Starting with Lesson 6, devote one full week (read instructional text daily) to each lesson and its drills, etc., then proceed to the next lesson. Be sure that you carry forward the technique acquired to each succeeding lesson; lessons must merge. By the time you reach Lesson 15 you may already, automatically, employ all accumulated techniques. Their merging, as it is sure to happen, will result in that professional sound. Listen for it. Make a convincing test. Today, before you read Lesson 1, record one or two of the commercials in the book. Then, after you have completed Lesson 15, again record the same announcements. You'll be amazed at the improvement in only fifteen weeks of study.

Incidentally, use your tape recorder with discretion—it's a sound mirror. As you well know, a person may become appearance conscious if he habitually criticizes his reflection in a mirror. By the same token, it's possible that you may become voice conscious—become over-critical of your abilities—if you make it a practice to constantly tear yourself apart via tape. Please follow this tried-and-tested advice on the matter of using your tape recorder to its utmost advantage: At the end of each day's practice session, record the commercials or some news—the day's finished product. Avoid use of your tape recorder during your study period. At the close of your daily practice session, when you do record the finished product, don't judge your work harshly, but listen for your improvement to help build up that important self-confidence. Notice errors and try to correct them the next time around. Introjection must be avoided, so if you wish to monitor your tape on headphones, fine, but wear them only on playback, never during your practice session and when recording. This is explained in Lesson 6 where we discuss projection, the opposite of introjection. Relative to the mechanics of broadcasting, flipping discs, cueing in LPs, twisting knobs and pushing buttons—you'll learn all that quickly enough. If your school maintains a campus station, you'll grasp the mechanics long before you make commercial broadcasting.

For classwork, students may practice the vocal exercises and relaxation drills as a group. Illustrations and diagrams, as suggested, may quickly be copied on the board. Of course, a tape recorder should be available in the classroom. To fill the average school term, the 25-lesson series may be arranged as follows: 1st week, blend Lessons 1 and 2. Lessons 3 through 17 will require one week (three hours) each. The consultative material contained in Lessons 18 through 25 may be used as lecture subject matter, for blackboard notations, or in any other way the instructor sees fit. Insofar as press wire news copy is concerned, your local radio station will probably be willing to supply students with discarded wire copy, unwanted public service announcements and other scripts which eventually reach the copywriter's wastepaper basket. Students may be asked to clip newspaper and magazine advertising for home-study purposes and subsequent classroom reading and teacher critique.

Think about your vocal apparatus as a wonderful instrument, the highly sensitive equipment with which humans—and only humans— communicate their thoughts to others. Remarkable is its construction, with resounding chambers, echo spots, some call them. You'll learn all about them later. There are the delicate vocal cords and the air supply. Actually, your vocal apparatus encompasses the entire area from the top of the head down to the solar plexus. Please remember that as a speaker or singer, you play upon your instrument in much the same way as the musician plays on his violin, trumpet or clarinet. As the result of years of tedious practice devoted to bowing, pizzicato and the other techniques, the violin virtuoso produces soulful passages or displays technical dexterity. The artist who plays a wind instrument worked diligently and tirelessly on sustained tones, scales and other uninteresting exercises to develop his endurance and a flexible embouchure for the production of a pleasing tonal quality. As the musician becomes expert in the various techniques of his specific instrument, so must you, the deejay, endeavor to work ceaselessly on your vocal apparatus. Strive to develop an effective, easy-to-listen-to, yet convincing and forceful, sales instrument behind the mike. Take care of your marvelous voice as the virtuoso preserves his priceless Stradivarius. Your instrument is priceless, too. The observance of sensible living habits will keep your vocal instrument sounding youthful and vibrant.

I have repeatedly affirmed that announcers are **not born** (as some people seem to think). They are **made**! Talented, yes; but a gift in the rough won't do in our highly competitive field. The untrained and frustrated deejay, despite his pear-shaped tones, simply piddles his way as a mere **speaker** through a career of mediocrity. Expertly trained and watchfully guided by a professional instructor, he may have become a premium product—the **artiste**.

You now know how to use this book. It contains the knowledge, wisdom and understanding applicable to the various areas in which you may find yourself as you travel to the top. Serious application to the studies, as I have outlined them, will bring you the finesse of the professional. Richly rewarding experiences will follow.

Lesson 1

Stop, Think, Relax!

Couéism, which embraces the faith that mind supercedes matter, like metaphysics, hypnosis, Yoga and other life sciences, is no longer dubiously viewed with tongue in cheek as the hocus-pocus machination of a philosophizing crackpot. We now know for sure that autosuggestion works! And we shall put it to good use during this course of study. Couéism has ceased to be considered a shallow, speculative philosophy. Actually, the 19th century, French psychologist, Emile Coué gave the world an **active** philosophy—a **practical** psychology. M. Coué proved, unequivocally, that the superconscious, or the subconscious, is insuperable. The French psychotherapist's comprehensive findings have been accepted by the scientific world and hailed as sweeping and brilliant research in the field of psychological therapy. It was a phenomenal success, a statement with which any ardent student of psychology will concur. His technique is exceedingly simple. It is impossible, in a self-teaching volume such as this book, to delve any deeper in the subject of Couéism, however, the interested reader may check, "How To Use Autosuggestion Effectively" by John Duckworth. Mr. Duckworth covers the psychological principles thoroughly and expertly explains M. Coué's teachings. Because it has repeatedly been proved, and many times during my own broadcast career, that mind **does** rule matter, that our mentality effectively dominates the physical. Consequently, I place the **mental** aspect of relaxation first.

The serious-minded student will do well to develop, to the best of his ability, the art of relaxation, and it is an art. So, let's get started on a tried-and-tested way to induce mental relaxation, and, subsequently, physical reaction. Remember: thoughts are things. The title of this lesson is a three-step formula, namely: **stop** (thinking wild thoughts), **think** (about relaxation) and you'll **r-e-l-a-x**. Simple? Yes, it is. Your subconscious mind is your obedient servant. Very much like an electronic computer, you may feed it what thoughts you wish—good, bad, constructive or destructive thoughts. Don't be deceived. Your servo mechanism will accept whatever you feed it; it doesn't know good from evil, negative from positive. Your subconscious will materialize the condition, your thought pattern. Let me put it this way: thoughts become things. Yes, think success and in some mysterious manner, success will be yours. Think failure, and you'll fail. (See "Psycho-Cybernetics," an excellent treatment of the subject matter, by Maxwell Maltz M.D. This book is now available in a paperback edition.)

To produce complete relaxation of mind and body, we will work with the monosyllable, pen, which is a contraction of the states of mind we wish to attain, namely: Poise, Ease, and Naturalness. Concentration on the word pen and its meanings, with practice, will produce that very comfortable feeling of complete relaxation. Relaxation may also be induced by means of self-hypnosis, but for our purposes, autosuggestion coupled with your imagination will do. Poise is defined as a suspension of motion, an absence of activity; ease refers to freedom from tension, restfulness; naturalness is characterized by friendliness, sincerity, calmness, and unaffected behavior.

Psychotherapists say that every person is "suggestible" to some degree, at least. Obviously, this is true. To be awakened in the middle of the night by a telephone ring gives some folks the jitters; their imaginations run wild. In city housing developments where the cry is: muggers, rapists, burglars, an unfamiliar knock on the door or stealthy footsteps quickly panic a lone woman occupant. Try to get some much-needed sleep after you "program" your mind with, "I hope I can sleep tonight. I'm not a bit tired." You won't. If we can mentally create fear and panic, and cause psychosomatic illnesses and sleepless nights by overworking our power of imagination, why can't we put our thinking to good use—to produce complete, mental and physical relaxation? We can! Here's how it's done.

Seated in a comfortable chair or in a reclining position, loosen all tight clothing, belt, collar, tie, etc. Close your big and allow your imagination to soar. Visualize your body as weighted down with concrete, or imagine that your body is being deflated by a heavy, stone slab. Try to "see" this in your mind's eye. Get that "sinking-in" feeling. To completely relax your body in preparation for the mental exercise which follows, start with the scalp, then the ears, facial muscles, throat, shoulders, chest and so on down to your toes. As you concentrate on each part, say to yourself, "relax!" At first you may not be able to relax as easily as you want to, but make it a daily ritual, and before long you'll condition yourself, as psychologists term it, for **reflex action**. That is, when you **think** about relaxation, you'll r-e-l-a-x completely. It's mind over matter, of course, but Coué proved that autosuggestion will work for anyone who'll sincerely and properly apply the required suggestions. Try it. Now, to the second part of this exercise.

Remain relaxed. Close your eyes and imagine that you're watching a white motion picture screen. Visualize, on that screen, some restful scene such as, the calmness of a mountain lake, a grazing herd of cows in a pastoral setting, or a lonely cowboy on his horse slowly making his way across the sands of a desert. Allow the quietude of it all to become impressed on your subconscious mind. Then, think about the word PEN and the meanings as I have given them to you. Keep sensing that very comfortable feeling of mental and physical relaxation. Next, devote 10 minutes, later 15 minutes, to reading aloud from your newspaper to an invisible listener. Don't read words; tell him the news story. (News technique is thoroughly explained in Lesson 15.) After your news "reporting," practice the commercial announcements which follow. The techniques will come later. For now, be conversational and friendly in your delivery to acquaint you with standard forms of commercial radio copy. Carry this routine over into your second week. (See this week's practice schedule.)

Relax mind and body completely. Take an informal, conversational style.

There's only one headache remedy . . . aspirin . . . and the finest aspirin is made by WHITEHALL. Yes, with the flu season here and for fever due to colds and for the relief of muscular aches and pains, reach for your bottle of WHITEHALL aspirin. There's no finer! You see, WHITEHALL aspirin is **all** aspirin . . . no fillers. That's why WHITEHALL aspirin goes to work so fast . . . that's why WHITEHALL aspirin so effectively relieves the pains and discomforts that usually accompany colds. So when you get the feverish feeling, don't wait! Take two WHITEHALL aspirin tablets every four hours, get plenty of bed rest and drink plenty of water. Because WHITEHALL aspirin is the world's best, there's no better, no quicker way to get rid of that annoying cold than to take time-tested WHITEHALL aspirin. At all druggists.

There's nothing that tastes quite so good on a cold winter's day than, SMITH'S New England style clam chowder. Hearty and gusty, SMITH'S New England clam chowder is nutritious, too. Besides being downright good eating, SMITH'S New England clam chowder contains all the natural vitamins and iron to build strong bodies in many ways. For a tasty and satisfying snack or lunch for the children make it a bowl of steaming clam chowder, but be sure it's SMITH'S New England clam chowder. Add a hefty sandwich, and presto! you have a nutritious and taste-tempting lunch for the hungry. Either way, SMITH'S New England clam chowder is a quick heat-and-serve treat whenever anyone says, "I'm hungry, Ma!" At your supermarket.

There's a special technique we use to do a commercial of this type. Try to acquire that quiet, confidential tonal quality in your voice.

Your youthful complexion can grow lovelier day after day if lavishly nurtured with a new, remarkable face cream called FLUFF. FLUFF is water soluble, that means it's not greasy. You apply FLUFF to the face before you retire, wash it off in the morning . . . that's all. In weeks, you'll notice those aging lines disappear. Your skin will glow and the precious bloom of youth will again be yours. The reason this new FLUFF works wonders, is because it goes deep down into the skin to remove impurities and collected dust particles that even soap and water cannot reach. Yes, new FLUFF is guaranteed to do just that. If it doesn't . . . if after only two weeks of faithful application you don't see some improvement in your complexion, if by then you aren't convinced that new FLUFF is a miracle skin conditioner, return the unused portion of the jar and receive a complete refund of your purchase price. We want you to try new FLUFF . . . Get the trial size jar of creamy, non-greasy FLUFF **today** then watch how new FLUFF puts its skin-cleansing powers to work for a more youthful **tomorrow**. FLUFF promises you skin beauty. Try FLUFF. It works!

Also practice this commercial almost whispering the words as though you were conveying a secret process to new skin beauty to your listener.

Again, feel your mind at ease and your body completely relaxed. Take a moderate rate of speed and speak in a friendly, conversational yet convincing voice.

Now, restful sleep can be **yours** on the newest, most comfortably designed mattress **ever**! Yes, CUSHION, in your choice of twin or full-size mattresses and box springs at only $59! Here are fabulous values for you. Fine quality innerspring mattresses and box springs at their lowest prices in our store's history. See these CUSHION mattresses today . . . fine quality bedding at down-to-earth budget prices. You'll find deep, resilient spring construction in these fine CUSHION mattresses. . . . heavy durable ticking. And the innersprings are hand-tied for lasting sleeping comfort. Matching box springs are included. CUSHION also makes foam mattresses in all the popular sizes, tastefully covered with heavy-duty ticking. Same price, for both mattress and box spring . . . only $59! And that's for both pieces, mind you! Yes, use your convenient credit card at CUSHION FURNITURE, 1677 Delaney Road, across the street from the post office in Allentown. CUSHION FURNITURE is open from 9 to 9, and on Saturdays until 10 PM. CUSHION FURNITURE will never be undersold. You **can't** do better elsewhere. See CUSHION **first** for bedding of every description . . . they're bedding **specialists** . . in the furniture business for over 65 years! CUSHION FURNITURE MART 1677 Delaney Road, opposite the post office, in Allentown. Open tonight until 10 PM. Plenty of free parking space.

PRACTICE SCHEDULE—1st WEEK

1. **RELAXATION** Untense yourself before starting each day's study period as explained in this lesson. Allow about 10 minutes for this.

2. **READING ALOUD** Make newspaper reading aloud a daily practice. Tell an invisible listener about the news. Work for a factual, reportorial style. The techniques will be explained later. Start with five minutes.

3. **COMMERCIALS** Each lesson, up until Lesson 18, contains commercial announcements or other exercises.

From Lesson 18 on, you will work with fresh copy daily, advertisements clipped from newspapers and magazines, to develop versatility. The techniques conducive to professional announcing will follow in a few lessons. For now put the mental attitudes or states of mind to use in the commercials. Assume a poised mental attitude, feel at ease and work for naturalness—conversational delivery. Allow about 20 minutes a day for this.

4. Read lesson test daily, when possible.

5. Sometime during this week review briefly the section "How To Use This Book"

6. When your week comes to a close, take time out to indulge in a bit of retrospection. This survey of the past week's activities—especially noting your improvement—will tend to build your much-needed self-confidence. Tomorrow you will benefit from today's trials and errors.

Lesson 2

How To "Roll" Your
Way to Relaxation

This exercise will quickly loosen up the muscular area surrounding the vocal cords to prepare you for the drills which follow. It should be done daily and should always follow the suggestions given in Lesson 1. Use it any time when relaxation is indicated, before going on the air, for example, in conjunction with some deep breathing to r-e-l-a-x you.

Standing or sitting, dangle your arms. Loosen the shoulder muscles by making circles with them for 10 or 15 **seconds**. Feel your scalp, eyes, ears, facial muscles **completely** relax. Allow your jaw to drop of its own weight. When you feel that comfortable loosened-up sensation, you're ready. Without force of any kind, allow your head to slowly drop forward onto your chest until you feel your chin make contact with your breastbone. Manipulate your body by bending slightly from the hips so that your head, of its own weight, will roll s-l-o-w-l-y clockwise over your right shoulder, across your back, over the left shoulder back to the starting position. Repeat. Then pause for a minute and repeat the entire exercise in a counter-clockwise direction. Two revolutions in each direction will suffice.

Don't force the head rolling, guard against using the neck muscles to move your head. This would tend to exercise them and **strengthen** such muscles, when actually we want to get them to r-e-l-a-x. Before you start the humming exercises in the next lesson, test with your fingers to see if your gullet is flexible and relaxed. You should be able to jiggle it from side to side. Breathing should be effortless and quiet.

Because of the ultrasensitivity of today's microphones, care should be taken to breathe silently. It can be done; there's no special trick to breathing inaudibly. When the soft palate is properly raised during speech passages (as explained in detail in Lesson 3), breathing is an easy and quiet process, as you will note in Fig. 2-1. When a person suffers from a cold or a sinus condition, the voice takes on a nasal quality, because the soft palate, swollen and irritated, drops toward the tongue, allowing the vocal vibrations to escape into

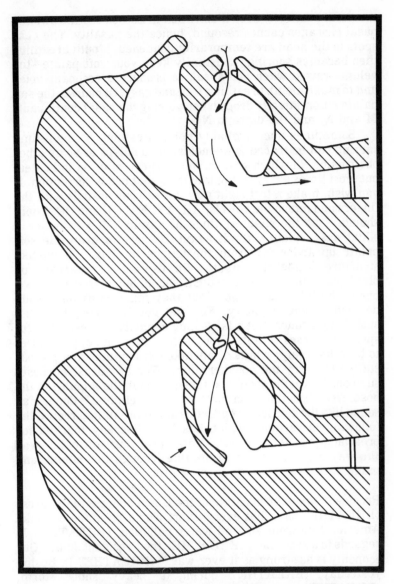

Fig. 2-1. CORRECT AND INCORRECT BREATHING.
The illustration at the left shows the soft palate **lowered**—
tongue **raised.** Notice how an obstruction at the entrance
to the throat (arrow) causes noisy breathing. Illustration
at the right shows the soft palate **raised**—tongue
depressed. An open, unobstructed throat makes mouth
breathing effortless and silent.

the nasal passages. (See illustration in Lesson 3.) The swollen nasal passages cannot resound, hence the nasality. The echo spots in the head are temporarily deadened. Mouth breathing then becomes snoring. Constantly keep your soft palate—the velum—raised when you speak to produce a resonant voice and to make mouth breathing free and easy. Of course, the soft palate automatically drops when voicing the nasal continuants M and N, and the digraph NG.

Sometimes uncontrollably noisy breathing or night-time snoring can be traced to adenoids, or to polyps or some other obstruction, in which case minor surgery may be indicated, but most times a lazy soft palate is all that needs correction. If you wish, make a test right now. Close your nostrils with the fingers and intone the vowels, AH, AY, EE, OH and OO. There shouldn't be the slightest tinge of nasality. If you notice a slight nasal quality, try it again. Be sure to draw the soft palate up and away from the tongue to form a dome-like structure inside the mouth. Be especially observant on playback of the close-formed EE sound. Some students labor under the false impression that they must cultivate a well-developed lung capacity. For the vocalist, yes; he must sustain long tones. But a large lung capacity is unessential for speech purposes with its clippy articulation and opportunities to breathe freely; whiffs of air taken at commas and periods suffice to carry the speaker along. For broadcast purposes such quick breaths should be taken through the **mouth**, not the nose. Nose breathing, no matter how carefully it's done, may sound like the sniffles. To practice silent breathing, record the following news item, which has been liberally marked for breathing-practice purposes. Now, raise your soft palate—**all the way up**. Remember to breathe through the **mouth**, and make such breaths very short whiffs.

President Nixon, in his State of the Union address to Congress (BREATHE) said that every effort would be made to make America free from air and water pollution. (BREATHE) In regards to a recession, (BREATHE) the President said: "Our economy is as strong as it ever was." (BREATHE) In Boston yesterday (BREATHE) during a heavy snow storm, (BREATHE)...

Listen closely. Was your breathing inaudible? When you start out with a moderate air supply, a whiff per line should carry you through a commercial as well as a long newscast. Never build up an uncomfortable excess of air which you must expel noisily. Avoid breathlessness and gasping. To allow your lungs and diaphragm to function freely, sit up straight—don't slouch. Keep chest and shoulder muscles relaxed, the soft palate raised. If you wish, insert vergules (/) between phrases as breathing cues in your copy, or be guided by commas and periods. If you take short whiffs of air through the mouth, breathing will become a comfortable, effortless and noiseless achievement.

Keep your soft palate raised. Listen for resonance. Mark in breathing spots using the vergule (/).

Let me ask you a question. Why shouldn't your hands look as lovely as your face? Well, they will, if after washing dishes with today's strong detergent, you pamper them with a quick beauty treatment. I'm speaking about DREEM, a new kind of hand cream. You see, we put expensive face-cleansing oils into DREEM. Your lovely hands deserve the same, fine treatment you give your face. DREEM makes your hands feel silky and smooth...like they used to feel, remember? DREEM is a moisturizing agent, that restores the natural oils which strong dishwashing detergents remove. If your hands aren't as smooth and silky as your face...DREEM is your answer. Give it a try.

The next time you get the kids together and smiling, reach for your SNAPIT automatic camera and press the button. It's that simple to take pictures with a SNAPIT automatic camera. We made it simple to operate. No need to adjust the shutter speed...it'll take care of itself, and there's a built-in electric eye to give you perfect pictures every time! The SNAPIT loads instantly. No threading. Drop in the cartridge and you're ready to shoot picture after picture. You'll be amazed at the professional touch in picture making with SNAPIT. A SNAPIT kit, including camera, film, flash bulbs and instruction book costs under $20. See it at your nearest SNAPIT dealer. What a Christmas gift for the whole family!

PRACTICE SCHEDULE—2nd WEEK

1. **RELAXATION** Mental and physical as explained in this lesson.

2. **BREATHING** Devote a few minutes, each day, to silent breathing, as explained in this lesson.

3. **READING ALOUD** Read aloud from your newspaper or magazine. Increase the time to 10 minutes. Sound factual, yet friendly. Visualize a listener.

4. **COMMERCIALS** Use your commercials this week to practice inaudible mouth breathing. See Fig. 2-1 again, and review the instructions on proper breathing. 20 minutes.

5. Review the entire Lesson 2 each day if time permits.

6. Your practice period should run at least 50 minutes this week.

Lesson 3

How To Develop a Forceful Speaking Voice

If you have the basics with which to work, humming exercises—if properly practiced—will surely result in a resonant, convincing and forceful speaking instrument. As differentiated from the untrained speech apparatus of the nonprofessional, you will command attention and admiration, so essential in professional broadcasting circles.

With the soft palate raised to prevent that throaty quality, hum the 5-tone scales. Start in your middle register, then move up one tone at a time. Also practice hums in your **lower** register. The neck muscles and gullet should always be relaxed. The inside of the mouth should resemble a dome-like structure (Fig. 3-1). If privacy permits, sing aloud short scales using the vowels: AH, AY, EE, OH, OO. Alternate the above humming drill with the following. Sing the four words listed below. Dwell well on the M, N and NG. Like this:

> **meaning**—MM-ea-NN-i-NNGG
> **mining**—MM-i-NN-i-NNGG
> **moaning**—MM-oa-NN-i-NNGG
> **mooning**—MM-oo-NN-i-NNGG

As you develop, you'll feel strong vibrations evident in the forehead, neck and chin and in your upper chest area. Like loudspeakers, these echo spots amplify the lower, medium and upper registers of your voice. When you speak, sing or hum, project to the front of the head, to the lips, cheeks and forehead. **Keep the soft palate raised.** Make a before-and-after test. Record a brief reading today **before** you start to practice any of the techniques presented in this book. Then, one month from today repeat the reading. Notice the improvement in the quality of your speaking voice! (See Fig. 2-1 in Lesson 2, proper breathing.)

EXERCISE

Start on middle C. Hum up and down the 5-tone scale six times. Repeat, starting on D, then to E, until a comfortable

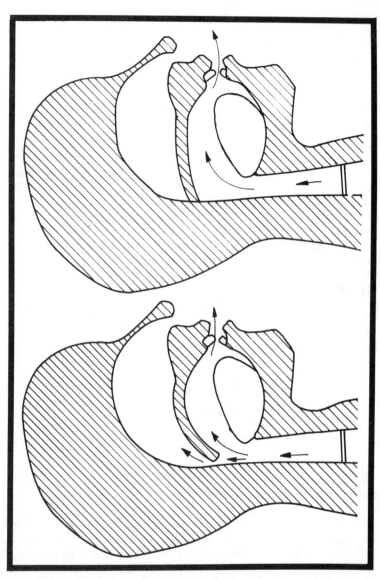

Fig. 3-1. CORRECT AND INCORRECT WAY TO VOICE
DEVELOPMENT. Illustration at the left shows the soft
palate **lowered.** Vibrations escape into the nasal area,
causing nasality and impairing resonance. Illustration at
the right shows the soft palate **raised**—tongue comfortably **depressed.** Produces dome-like structure inside
the mouth for full, resonant vocal quality. Vibrations are
shut off from the nasal area.

limit in register has been reached. Also practice hums in the lower register.

```
              G mm
        F mm        mm F
       E mm         mm E
      D mm            mm D
    C mm                mmmmmm C
```

Key of C

```
              A mm
        G mm        mm G
     F     mm         mm F
      E mm            mm E
    D mm                mmmmm D
```

Key of D etc.

Alternate humming exercises above with the singing drill below. Instead of 5-tone scales, practice on 4-tone chords as illustrated. Repeat each chord six times, then move one tone higher. Also sing the vowels in lower register.

```
        ah                           ay
     ah    ah                     ay    ay
    ah        ah                  ay        ay
   ah          ahhhhhhh           ay          ayyyyyy
```

Key of C   Key of D

```
        ee                           oh
     ee    ee                     oh    oh
    ee        ee                  oh        oh
   ee          eeeee              oh          ohhhh
```

Key of E   Key of F

```
              oo
         oo        oo
       oo              oo
     oo                    oooooooh
```

Key of G

The soft palate must remain raised at all times for resonance. Test with your fingers. Close your nose. If a nasal, stuffy tone results, the soft palate is **not** raised.

Be patient. A cultured voice, as any schooled singer knows, results from days, weeks, and years of diligent practice. Even those persons to whom we refer as "naturals" must take specialized training to qualify them for professional broadcasting. A pleasing, cultured voice is only one of the numerous qualifications demanded by a critical profession. Today's standards are high: resourcefulness, attractive personality, a good general and specialized educational background, indisputable references, etc. In television they also stress the importance of a photogenic quality and the ability to quickly memorize.

Seemingly, the baritone voice is preferred, but there are numerous good deejays who are tenors. If your voice is unusually high-pitched, the relaxation exercises in Lessons 1 and 2 and the humming drills in this lesson may very possibly help to relax it and subsequently lower it. Sometimes an abnormality causes an exceptionally high-pitched voice.

A college student who telephoned for a lesson appointment surprised me when he called in person the following week. I expected to meet a girl. In regards to his high-pitched voice, I suggested that he consult a laryngologist, or that a speech therapist might be able to help. A talented person with a high-pitched voice may not be chosen for air work, but there's much to be done in other areas of broadcasting. This is a multifaceted industry. Those with speech disorders and voice difficulties should write to **The American Speech and Hearing Association**, 9030 Old Georgetown Road, Washington, D.C. 20014, for free information on help and services available in their communities.

Keep your soft palate raised when you practice these announcements. Listen for resonance on the words containing N, M and NG.

If you don't believe there's anything new under the sun...see the new 1970 WHEELER washer-dryer. The WHEELER is unique! You wheel it about, wherever you want it, and it stores in almost any closet. Listen! The new WHEELER washer easily rolls up to a sink and is quickly attached to a mixing faucet. That's all there is to it. Plug in the cord, and you're all set for your first load of clothes. Takes only seconds to hook up. Takes only six minutes per load...four to wash, and two to spin dry. If you live in a mobile home or in a small apartment...the WHEELER is for **you**! But don't take my word for it. Your local WHEELER dealer will gladly do a test run for you to prove how efficient, how simple this new WHEELER washer operates. See him soon. Look for his name in your telephone directory under...appliances. WHEELER's the name...a **famous** name in home appliances.

Dry skin your problem? Well, I have news for you. Good news. Do you know that there's a skin lotion on the market today called SHEEN which guarantees to heal any dry skin problem within one month, at the longest, or the makers will refund twice the price you paid for it? Yes, unbelievable, but it's true! SHEEN goes to work instantly...it goes down deep into the under layer of the skin and heals even cracked skin due to dryness. Shouldn't **you** investigate new SHEEN? Ask your doctor. He knows! He has probably recommended SHEEN to his patients. S-H-E-E-N at your druggist.

You may also clip advertising from newspapers and magazines for additional practice material. Another reminder that your local radio station may be happy to furnish you with unwanted announcements and press wire news copy.

PRACTICE SCHEDULE—3rd WEEK

1. **RELAXATION** Mental and physical. 10 minutes.

2. **BREATHING** Devote a few minutes daily to proper breathing. If necessary review "proper breathing" in Lesson 2.

3. **VOICE DEVELOPMENT** Hum short scales. Alternate with singing the vowels, as instructed. 10 minutes.

4. **READING ALOUD** Increase your reading time to 15 minutes. Always picture an invisible listener. Imagine that

your microphone is a miniature TV screen upon which you see a listener to whom you speak.

5. **COMMERCIALS** Strive for noiseless breathing. Mark in breathing spots. 20 minutes.

6. Review lesson material daily, if possible.

7. Study the diagrams in this lesson. Notice the functioning of the soft palate.

8. Don't overlook your weekend review of accomplishments. Give yourself a mental pat on the back when you deserve it.

9. Your study period should now run approximately 60 minutes.

Lesson 4

How To Acquire Impeccable Pronunciation

Be careful how you pronounce it. Watch your enunciation. Pronunciation and enunciation are easily confused. To properly pronounce a word means to speak the word correctly; to properly enunciate a word means to speak the word distinctly. When we hear the word, **library** voiced, "liberry" or "libree," or when someone speaks about a "television progrum," when the viewer refers to a **program**, we wonder if his pronunciation is faulty, or if he has a lazy tongue—or both.

No one can become perfect, but we should work toward perfection as our goal, without becoming a perfectionist. To actually achieve impeccable pronunciation would require a lifetime of study devoted to the subject, orthoepy, the art of correct pronunciation. When I started in broadcasting, I bought a pocket-size notebook in which I jotted down, phonetically, any words of which I was unsure as to either pronunciation or meaning. I worked with a good dictionary at my side. It was a daily ritual to run down the increasing list of words until I felt absolutely certain of a word. Only then did I cross it off the list. The two pages of words frequently mispronounced will get you started on your personal list of words. I suggest that you read Chapter 11, "Pronunciation and Enunciation" in **The Man Behind the Mike**. This study of pronunciation, articulation and enunciation is a very interesting and essential one for the serious minded student.

Keep a good dictionary by your side for ready reference. Only a good edition carries a complete pronunciation guide, list of foreign names and places, a pronouncing gazetteer, and other valuable information you should have at your finger tips. In the pronunciation guide, for example, you'll notice that the word, **dog**, sometimes pronounced "dawg" is erroneous. The 'o' in dog should be boiced midway between the vowel sounds in the words, **dock** and **dark**. The word, **half**, should not be pronounced "haaf" or "hahf" but in between the vowel sounds in the words, **ham** and **harm**. Here is a brief rundown on the vowels and their variations:

a — ATE	i — FIN	oo — FOOT
a — BAND	i — FINE	u — USE
a — LAUGH	o — BOAT	u — BUT
a — AIR	o — NOT	u — URN
e — END	o — ORBIT	oi — COIN
e — EAT	oo — FOOD	ou — HOUSE

Do some of the following belong to you?

TELEPHONE not tulluphone
LEND not lind or lund
AWFUL not awrful
ISN'T not ain't
TIME not tahm or tam
AMERICA not Amurica
WILL not wahll
CAN not kin or kaan
LEARN not loin
BEAUTIFUL (BEW-tih-ful) not bewdeeful
MONDAY (MUN-dih) not Monday
SAYS (sez) not says
AGAIN (agen) not agin or agane
GENUINE (jen-yu-in) not gen-you-wine
MY not mah
LAUGH not laaf or lahf
MAN not main or maan
YES not yeah
HALF not hahlf
MA not maw
NEW not noo
BILL not beel
FINE not fan
FARM not fam
FAST not fahst
TWENTY not twenny
TURN not toin
DOG not dawg
PA not PAW
TIMES not tams
CAN'T not cain't
WATER not wadder

FINE not foin
SUBDUE not subdoo
ENGINE not ingine
YET not yit
CAN'T not cahn't
LAW not lah
FIVE not fav
FAST not faist
HARM not ham
TOMORROW not tomahrow
TEN not tin
OIL not earl
GETTING not gedding or gettin'

How about these?

Do you say "BACON" when you mean — **baking?**
Do you say "SANE" when you mean — **saying?**
Do you say "WEDDING" when you mean — **wetting?**
Do you say "PUDDING" when you mean — **putting?**
Do you say "COIL" when you mean — **curl?**
Do you say "WOOL" when you mean — **will?**

And watch these, too. Don't drop them!

WH in when, who, why, where
ING in going, saying, making
D in sand, land, band
STS in tastes, wastes, lasts, masts
TT in getting, letting, meeting
CH in much, such, lunch

I know of an excellent book which covers the subject of grammar, spelling and everyday pronunciation for the secretary, letter writer and public speaker. Ask your bookseller for **Grammar and Spelling Simplified** by Edward C. Gruber (ARCO Publishing Co. N.Y.) A student brought this publication to my attention and it looks good to me. Wish it had been available when I started in the business!

Occasionally, a student encounters difficulty when voicing sibilants, the S as in the word, **sun,** for example. The result is an annoying hissing which sometimes resembles a whistle. This is possibly due to ill-fitting dentures or to the improper placement of the tongue and formation of the lips. The latter causes of this vocal disturbance may easily and quickly be corrected with a few interesting exercises. There are differences in opinion on the placement of the tongue: (1) against the upper teeth, (2) against the lower teethridge. The pronunciation guide of the dictionary gives both placements. I think you'll agree that placing the tongue against the **upper** teethridge all too easily produces the interdental fricative TH, making the word **this** sound like **thith**, as does a speech defect. If your Ss hiss, try this: With your lips relaxed and spread in a smile, place your tongue flatly against your **lower** teethridge. Guard against curling the tip of your tongue and withdrawing it. **The tongue should not flutter freely between the teeth!** It is precisely the cause of hissing when the S is voiced. To clarify this point, notice that when voicing the SH the **opposite** formation of the lips and the tongue placement should be observed. Lips are **rounded**, and the tongue is **withdrawn**. Notice in the following exercises how easily the lip formation and tongue placements of S and SH may become confused. Smile and place your tongue against the inside of your **lower** teeth.

so — show	sack — shack
sane — shame	sell — shell
assume — assure	sin — shin
sop — shop	sewer — sure
sue — shoe	seen — sheen
sign — shine	subtle — shuttle

Now, **round** your lips, and slightly **withdraw** your tongue:

mush, much, chicken, chin, check, jog, jungle, jerk, stretch, jingle, China, shrug, shriek, snatch, match, lodge, dodge, judge.

To produce agility, practice the following set of words slowly. Increase the tempo as the ease of tongue and lip movements is noted.

situation	persuasion
conscientious	station
suspension	selfish
emancipation	satisfaction
sludge	insatiable
sensation	succession

44

Now, give the following tongue twisters a try:

1. Sister Susie's sewing silk shirts for sick soldiers.

2. She sells seashells by the seashore.

3. Some shun sunshine. Do you sometimes shun sunshine?

4. Shiny silk sashes shimmered when the sun shone on the shop signs.

Check the next lesson for additional tongue twisters. Consult the section on microphone technique. Also check the pronunciation guide of your dictionary.

How do you pronounce the following words?

> Cuisine (kwee-ZEEN)
> acumen (a-KEW-m'n)
> program (PROH-gram)
> news (NEWS not NOOS)
> acclimate (a-KLY-mat)
> elite (ay-LEET)
> attache (at-a-SHAY)
> corps (KOHR)
> address (ad-DRESS)
> curator (KYOO-ra-tor)
> joust (just)
> harass (HAR-ass)
> apricot (AY-pri-cot)
> crises (CRY-seez)
> harbinger (HAR-bin-ger)
> gondola (GON-doh-la)
> sacrilegious (sack-re-LEE-jus)
> fungicide (FUN-jih-side)
> pro rate (pro-RAY-ta)
> strata (STRAY-ta)
> dacron (DAY-cron)
> incognito (in-COG-nih-to)
> retroactive (ret-tro-ACK-tiv)
> bronchial (BRONG-kih-al)
> Pago Pago (PAHNG-o PAHNG-o)
> incomparable (in-COMP-ar-abl)
> culinary (KEW-lih-ner-ih)
> charge d'affaires (shar-SHAY-de-FAIR)
> coup d'etat (koo-day-TAH)

discharge (dis-CHARGE)
ignominy (IG-no-min-ih)*
hiccough (HIK-up)*
inextricable (in-EKS-tric-a-bl)
orchestral (or-KESS-trl)
cupola (KEW-poh-la)
quintuplets (KWIN-tu-plets)
tarpaulin (tar-PAW-lin)
diabetic (di-a-BET-ic)
indict (in-DITE)
victuals (VIT-ls)
says (sez)
data (DAY-ta)
controversial (con-troh-VER-shal)
sacrosanct (SACK-roh-sahnt)
ration (RAY-shun)
frugal (FROO-gl)
architect (AHR-kih-tect)
associate (a-SOH-shee-ate)
clique (KLEEK)
equitable (ECK-wih-ti-bl)
comptroller (con-TROHL-er)
New Orleans (Nyew OHR-le-ans)
Terre Haute (Ter-a-HOTE)
February (FEB-ru-er-ih)
genuine (GEN-you-in)
raspberry (RAZZ-berry)
suite (Sweet)
ignoramus (ig-no-RAY-mus)
exquisite (EKS-kwih-zit)
despicable (DES-pic-a-bl)
lamentable (LAM-en-ta-bl)
preferably (PREF-er-ab-lih)
precedent (PRESS-ih-dent)
superfluous (syew-PER-flu-us)
grimace (grih-MAYS)
naphtha (NAF-tha)
Worcester (WOOS-ter)
chiropodist (ky-ROP-o-dist)
rebuttal (ree-BUT-l)
Chicago (Shih-KAW-go)
diptheria (dif-THEER-ih-a)
err (ur)
Thames (Tems)
arctic (ARK-tic not AHR-tic)
radiator (RAY-dee-ay-tor)

mercantile (MUR-kan-till)
engineer (en-jih-neer)
Puget Sound (PYEW-git Sound)
Louisville (LYOU-ee-vile)
chasm (KAZ-um)
absolutely (AB-soh-lyut-lih)
hospitable (HOS-pih-ta-bl)
mischievous (MISS-chih-vus)
precedence (pre-CEED-ens)
damask (DAM-sk)
finance (fih-NANS)
exemplary (ex-EMP-lar-ih)
exigency (EK-ih-jen-sih)
Gloucester (GLOS-ter)
bona fide (BOH-na FYE-dee)
depot (DEE-poh)
coupon (KOO-pon)

Now, you have an excellent start for your list of words frequently mispronounced. Keep adding to your list as you encounter words with which you are unfamiliar as to pronunciation and-or meaning. You'll soon be admired for your impeccable pronunciation.

Speaking of correct pronunciation, I want to touch briefly on something which has bugged radio announcers right from the start, namely, the correct pronunciation of foreign names of people, places, foreign musical titles, etc. Insofar as news is concerned, the press wire news services are quite aware of the problem and liberally furnish phonetic spellings to aid the newscaster or deejay in that respect. At least once a year press wire services furnish broadcast stations with phonetic spellings on not only foreign places but the correct pronunciations of people who make the news, such as sports figures, internationally famous persons, etc. Despite the universal usage of the correct pronunciation of say, Vietnam (Vee-et-NAHM), it is voiced as "Vet-nam" by people who should know better. Of course, an erroneous pronunciation of some foreign place isn't a crime, yet you should make every effort to learn the correct pronunciations of foreign places and people. It adds distinction to your work and lends authority to your newscasting.

In regard to concert programs, the announcer on the evening trick of a middle-of-the-road or a good-music station is supplied, as a rule, with scripts which also give the phonetic spellings to aid the deejay. For example:

One of the first compositions of Johann Strauss (YOH-hahn SHTROWS) was his Wein, Weib und Gesang (Vine, Vipe oont ge-ZAHNG). Rimsky-Korsakov (REEM-skee KOHR-sah-kuff) on the other hand came into...

Top good-music stations must choose announcers for their linguistic abilities, or at least because of their fluency and accomplished working knowledge of several foreign languages in relation to music and composers. I can safely tell you that top good-music stations make auditions real tough, indeed. One time I auditioned for WQXR in New York, a good-music operation which I consider one of the best, if not THE top station in its class. The reception room was packed with tensed announcers. Each applicant was handed a mimeographed audition script. Besides French, German, Spanish and Italian names, with which many announcers are generally familiar, the script included Hungarian and little-known Dutch names of musical compositions and composers. It was the roughest audition ever; in fact, I was surprised to be chosen one of three finalists. We were asked if we wanted to compete in a deciding test to eliminate two of us. That wasn't necessary. The job was only a summer replacement assign-ment, so two of us bowed out. In case you're wondering, WQXR's audition material does not contain any phonetic spellings. Either you know your languages or you muff it. You get it right the first time, or you get the Don't-call-us,-we'll-call-you treatment.

Be conscious of your pronunciation. Watch the endings of words, the final 's', the 'ing', and the 't' in beauTify, ferTilize. Make it LUCKurious, not LUGurious, etc.

thickest, most luxurious lawn ever. If it's something for the home garden or farm, you'll find it at NELSON'S GARDEN SUPPLY, 110 Mullberry Road, in Claremount. Look for the famous NELSON greenhouses; just outside town.

Get set for party time... the holidays are on the way! Spruce up your home **now** with new traditional or modern furniture, whichever your taste dictates. WILLIAMS FURNITURE MART now offers the public the greatest money-saving sale ever! Listen to this. Living room groups from only $189! Regularly $298, you save $100! A four-piece contemporary bedroom set, in choice hardwoods and beautifully hand rubbed must go for only $189...you save $50! Bookcases, recliners, platform rockers, desks—all must go this week end at WILLIAMS FURNITURE MART on route 102, Millersville. Store opens at 8 tomorrow morning. Hurry!

PRACTICE SCHEDULE—4th WEEK

1. **RELAXATION** Mental and physical. 5 minutes.

2. **VOCAL DRILLS** Humming exercises and singing of vowels. 10 minutes.

3. **PRONUNCIATION** Each day this week check the list of words frequently mispronounced. Study six words daily for correct pronunciation. Also this week start your own collection of words frequently mispronounced. 10 minutes.

4. **READING** Become a storyteller, not a reader of words. 15 minutes.

5. **COMMERCIALS** Follow the special instruction preceding the announcements. 20 minutes. Reread this lesson daily if time permits.

Lesson 5

How To Attract and Hold Listeners

The disc jockey with a well modulated voice, enhanced by a striking personality, needs only a well articulated delivery to be easily understood, to attract and to sustain audience interest.

In the example exercise illustrated below, start mouthing the word very slowly, accentuate the lip and tongue movements to develop articulation (Fig. 5-1). Increase speed gradually until you can pronounce the word rapidly yet clearly and distinctly. For a test, record the finished product in a whisper. On playback, if every syllable is audible and crisp, the desired improvement is evident. Become syllable conscious. Speak toward the lips, not down in the throat. Make the lips work to form vowels and consonants. Form the three tongue-point stops—the voiceless t, d and n—distinctly. Round the mouth well when pronouncing the sh sound, as in the words, tension, shop, shark. The lip nasal continuant m should be voiced with the lips tightly squeezed closed (for practice purposes) to accentuate the articulation. Also check the pronunciation guide in your dictionary for other details.

Pronounce the following word at the varying speeds indicated, six times in each case.

tran ... scen ... den ... tal ... is ... m

tran . . scen . . den . . tal . . is . . m

tran . scen . den . tal . is . m

transcendentalism

Watch out for these and other similar words in everyday use:

    poem - POH-em (not pome)
    different - DIF-er-ent (not DIFrint)
    interesting - IN-ter-est-ing (not IN-trist-ing)
    Athletic - ath-LET-ic (not ath-a-LET-ic)
    film - film (not FILL-um)

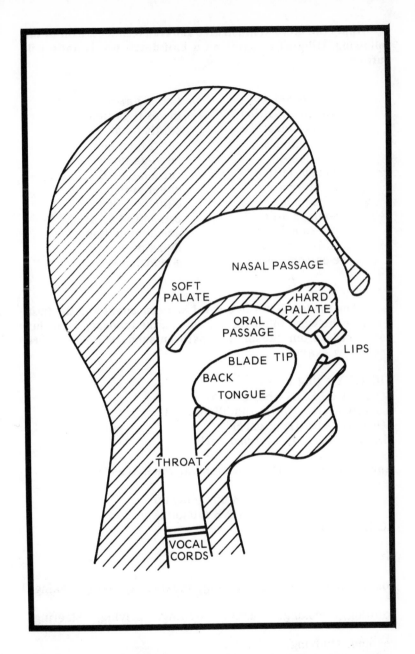

Fig. 5-1. YOUR SPEAKING INSTRUMENT. These are the articulators with which you produce distinct, easy-to-understand speech.

Apply the method illustrated for transcendentalism to the following. Diligent practice on a half-dozen words daily will suffice.

Cal-i-for-ni-a
pro-nun-ci-a-tion
del-i-ca-cies
re-or-gan-ize
ep-i-dem-ic
con-sul-ta-tive
de-lib-er-ate
ir-reg-u-lar
e-nun-ci-a-tion
per-so-nal-i-ty
sim-i-la-ri-ties
e-co-nom-i-cal

Lou-is-i-an-a
in-ves-ti-ga-tion
sta-tis-ti-cal
cer-ti-fi-ca-tion
na-vi-ga-tion
cer-e-mo-ni-al
di-ver-si-fied
e-lim-in-a-tion
con-sti-tu-tion-al
ac-cu-mu-la-tion
dy-na-mite
e-lec-tric-i-ty

When the last letter in a word is a consonant and the first letter of the word following is a vowel, the tendency is to slur both words, often causing a drastic misunderstanding. Here are a few examples:

BIG GUYS (big eyes)
BORE A GASSET (boric acid)
A DISH AND A LAID (additional aid)
LONG GEARS (long ears)
MARRY DURLY (married early)

Another bad speech habit is sounding the ING as INK:

GOINK up (going up)
SINGINK (singing)
LOOKINK (looking)

Exercises:

going, seeing, looking, wanting, making, speaking, taking, painting, cooking, baking, writing, driving, steering, reading, studying.

Now, to multisyllable words, to be practiced, six a day, as illustrated previously.

totalitarianism	materialization
individualization	constitutionality
transilluminate	meteorological
democratization	ophthalmologist
superserviceable	individualization

How do you pronounce these?

engine not INgine	which not witch
going to not gonna	when not wen
get not git	whether not weather
had to not hadda	while not wile
got to not godda	can not kin
doing not doin'	just not jist
going not goin'	new not noo
what do you not whatdya	suppose not spose
getting not gedding	really not reely

And there are hundreds more. Avoid dropping syllables and adding them. Peculiar to our language, there are stressed and unstressed forms of certain monosyllables. Under the condition of sense stress, these words may require any degree of stress, from the lowest to the highest. This subject of strong and weak forms, which create a naturalness in your speech, is fully explained in the pronunciation guide of your dictionary. I urge you to check on it. Here are some of them: **at, for, from, to, am, are, has, must, he, your, me, her,** etc.

The strong form of a monosyllable is always used when the word stands alone, I **shall.** We weaken it when it becomes a part of the context, I **sh'll not.** The stressing and weakening of words should not be confused with slovenly enunciation, as when the careless speaker pronounces the word, **can** as **kin,** or when the word, **get** is provincially voiced, **git.** Incidentally, the unstressed form of the word, **can,** is **c'n,** but not **kin.** "Unstressed words make for a rhythmic succession of monosyllables to produce a natural flow of speech, without which, the announcer would sound stilted and amateurish." (**The Man Behind The Mike,** page 129) Example:

AS WRITTEN: Give him the benefit of the doubt
AS SPOKEN: Give 'm th' benefit 'v th' doubt

Here's an illustration of how the preposition, **to,** in one sentence, appears in both the strong and weakened forms:

AS WRITTEN: It began to move to and fro from the east to the west.

AS SPOKEN: It began t' move to 'nd fro fr'm th' east t' th' west.

Keep your vocabulary under control. You see, in broadcasting we speak blindly to listeners of many intelligence levels with diverse educational backgrounds. We must also consider the ethnic angle, the multilinguistic group in our audience with a limited understanding of our language. Strive to speak distinctly. Devote a few minutes daily to enunciation drills. Undoubtedly, an attractive speaking voice and striking personality are powerful assets, yet, basically, you must be **easy and effortless to understand** to attract and hold listeners. Try the technique on the following commercials. **The underscored monosyllables should be weakened as explained previously.**

Springtime is paint-up time. And MORRISON'S, **the** house of colors, **has a** complete line **of** paints **and** varnishes, stains **and** enamels, exterior **and** interior paints **to** give your home that fresh, new look. Now, during MORRISON'S April-sale days, stock up on exterior latex paints **at** only $3.96 a gallon. This is top-quality paint, one-coat guarantee, regularly on sale **at** $4.74 a gallon. And **to** help you do **the** job better, get yourself **a** new wooden or aluminum ladder, tray **and** roller set, brushes, drop cloths...everything **to** do **a** professional job. MORRISON'S also carries famous names in wallpapers in **the** season's newest patterns. If you have **a** special decorating problem bring it to MORRISON'S PAINT AND BUILDING SUPPLY on Fairmont Drive in Sunland. **The** folks **at** MORRISON'S **have** been helping their friends **and** neighbors **for** more **than** forty years. For paints, wallpapers, home-decorating tools **and** supplies, see MORRISON'S PAINT AND BUILDING SUPPLY in Sunland. Open **from** 7 to 9 PM, Monday through Saturday. Plenty **of** free off-street parking.

Take **a** load off **your** mind **and** off **your** budget! If those monthly bills **are** getting you down, stop paying **them!** What I mean is, go to **your** nearest FAMILY BUDGET office **and** borrow **the** money you **need to** pay **ALL your** bills at once. Then pay back your loan **to** FAMILY BUDGET in easy monthly payments plus **a** small interest charge. Everybody's doing **it!** Why not you? Your nearest

FAMILY BUDGET office wants **to** serve you. See your local FAMILY BUDGET office...today!

After rehearsal, record this announcement. Listen for clear enunciation. Check if all underlined monosyllables were properly weakened. Try it again.

A classical example of confusing articulation is the childish prattle which goes:

"Mairsey doats and dosey dotes and lillamsy divey..." (Mares eat oats and does eat oats and little lambs eat ivy)

This is another example of how consonants slur over into vowels unless we are especially vigilant and conscious of our enunciation. Tongue twisters have long been used by public speakers and in classrooms as excellent material for the development of a nimble tongue. Included here are several of the popular ones. We are not interested in speed; rather, in clarity and distinctness of pronunciation. Relax the tongue and lips. All them to function freely. Start very slowly, then gradually increase speed. Repeat each six times.

1. Peter Piper picked a peck of pickled peppers.

2. She sells seashells by the seashore.

3. Theda and Theodore thought that the athletes were enthusiastic.

4. Ethel's thread and thimble were thrown straight through the thatches thicket.

5. The whale wheeled, whirred and whirled in the whirlpool.

6. We whispered while the whale wheezed and whimpered.

7. Shiny silk sashes shimmered when the sun shone on the shop signs.

8. Thrice six thick thristle sticks thrust straight through three thrushes.

9. Amidst the mist and the coldest frosts with stoutest wrists.

10. Some shun sunshine. Do you shun sunshine sometimes?

11. The old scold sold an old school coal scuttle.

12. The seething sea ceaseth to seethe and it sufficeth me.

13. She shrilly shouted when she saw the shining shark near the shore.

It is suggested that you include a few of the above exercises, repeating each at least six times, in future lessons. Start very slowly. Don't hurry.

PRACTICE SCHEDULE—5th WEEK

1. **RELAXATION** Mental and physical. 5 minutes.

2. **VOCAL DRILLS** As per previous instruction. 10 minutes.

3. **PRONUNCIATION** Check the list of words frequently mispronounced. Study six words a day. Have you started your own list of words yet? 10 minutes.

4. **ENUNCIATION** As instructed, practice on three multisyllable words daily. Also practice on three tongue twisters a day. When your schedule becomes too heavy, you may alternate tongue twisters with multisyllable words, or alternate pronunciation with enunciation. 10 minutes.

5. **WEAK AND STRONG WORDS** Study this section well. Check your dictionary for detailed explanation on the use of stressed and unstressed monosyllables. Did you obtain a good standard dictionary? Five minutes.

6. **READING** Continue your daily reading to an invisible listener. Your local radio station will gladly furnish you with discarded teletype news copy. 15 minutes.

7. **COMMERCIALS** Observe carefully your articulation, the endings of words, etc. 20 minutes.

8. Do a daily review, whenever possible, of the week's lesson.

Lesson 6

Developing A
Person-to-Person Approach

There are two types of theatrical productions—presentational and representational. They are opposites. The presentational production is so called because the speaker **presents** **something to** the audience. In the representational production the performer **represents something for** the audience. The presentational type of production may be referred to as the **personal** approach, the representational as the **impersonal** theatrical approach. Let's discuss them individually.

In the **presentational** category we find the public speaker, deejay, politician, auctioneer, school teacher, salesman, newscaster, etc., who **present** something **to** the audience— instruction, news, campaign issues, merchandise, etc. These persons make and maintain contact, eye-to-eye contact—with their listeners. To lose such contact will sever their invisible lines of communication. This is the person-to-person approach that has to be developed for effective communication through word power. Speak to **one** listener. It's impossible to address more than one person at a time. Even in a group of three, you must shift your gaze from person to person. The podium speaker scans his audience; he cannot address his audience as a unit. Your radio approach, in every respect, should parallel the method you use when you chat over the telephone with a **personal friend.**

In the **representational** theatre, we find the motion picture, TV film, panel show, actor and the others who **represent** something **for** the audience. Let's take a stage play as a working example. The audience, through an invisible fourth wall, impersonally, views a tragedy affecting the lives of the actors on stage. The onlookers take an **objective** view of the story because they are not participants. The DJ speaks **to** an individual. The stage actor performs **for** a **group.**

Projection is the number-one technique to be mastered (Fig. 6-1). In radio it may be likened to the eyeball-to-eyeball treatment of the TV announcer. The jock who habitually wears phones while he speaks does not project, he **introjects**; he speaks to himself and for his own benefit (Fig. 6-2). Some jocks may not admit it, but they wear phones to monitor and

NO PROJECTION
NO IMPRESSION

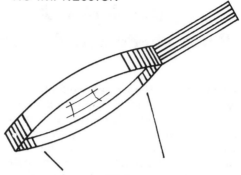

SUBCONSCIOUS MIND

Have y' had y' soup today?

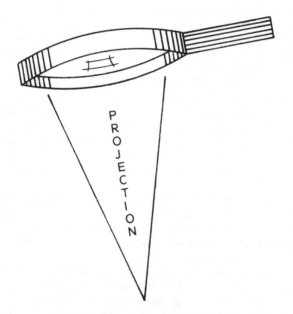

P
R
O
J
E
C
T
I
O
N

SUBCONSCIOUS MIND

Have you . . had **YOUR** . . soup . . **TODAY**?

Fig. 6-1.

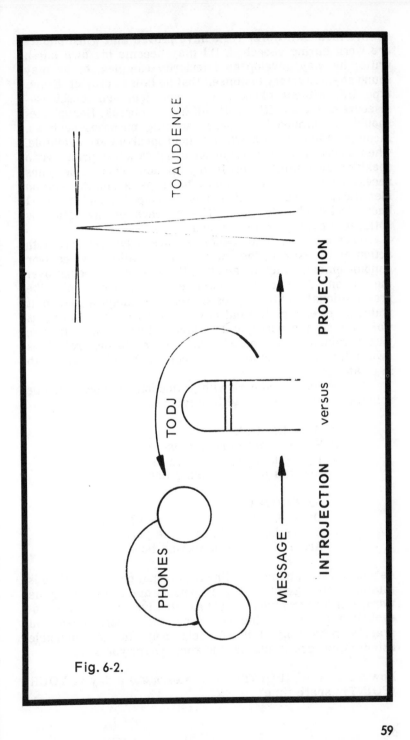

Fig. 6-2.

TO AUDIENCE

PROJECTION

TO DJ

PHONES

versus

MESSAGE

INTROJECTION

admire their own work. Tests have proved that when phones are worn during speech, a DJ may become his own harsh critic; he may develop an inferiority complex, or he may sound so satisfactory to himself that he fails to project. Either type DJ, without phones, may well feel self-conscious— insecure on the air. It's a difficult habit to break. Headphones should be employed to serve specific purposes such as, monitoring the network, when no loud speakers are available, when inserting a local tie-in on a network program, when speaking over music, etc. In my opinion, when it becomes necessary to wear headphones to speak a simple, station identification, the announcer has developed a bad habit. (I know jocks who do this.) The absence of projection is noticeably evident to the listener.

When a television announcer's voice is synchronized with action on the screen, the commercial is called a voice-over announcement, which means that the announcer speaks over the action. A voice-over commercial employs both the presentational and the representational techniques; hence, it is doubly effective. The old proverb applies: One picture is worth a thousand words, and TV knows it well. The radio disc jockey, minus video to assist him, must create and project his own pictures, word pictures, a subject which will be dealt with in a later lesson.

We are concerned here with projection and how it can be achieved. Let me illustrate briefly:

> **AS WRITTEN**
> So you want to save money?
> Here's how you can take part.
> Are you tired of waxing floors?
>
> **AS PROJECTED**
> Do YOU...want to save money?
> Here's how YOU...can take part.
> Are YOU...tired of waxing floors?

As you can see, an invisible line of personal communication is established using a cleverly placed pause and gently lifting the word, you. The technique is just as effective as the eyeball-to-eyeball approach of the television announcer. When you practice projection, if it will help, point to your invisible listener when you emphasize the word, you or yours etc.

How would YOU (POINT)...like to earn $20 a day in YOUR (POINT)...spare time?

Make your ONE listener feel that you are addressing only HER and no one else in your audience. That's true communication.

Here is a list of exercises to develop the person-to-person approach. A student of mine devised a gimmick to still further help him get the picture. He stood in front of a full-length mirror, then as he spoke the line, he pointed to his image to feel the person-to-person contact. Try it. I usually suggest a mental exercise to produce the same effect. The deejay should mentally picture one listener looking directly at him from his microphone, as if his mike were a miniature TV screen.

EXERCISE

1. Are YOU...wondering if it's YOUR...bad breath that's at fault?

2. Are YOU...tired of waxing floors? Let me tell YOU...about GLOSS.

3. Have YOU...received this year's Christmas Seals yet? YOU'LL...like them.

4. How many times have YOU...said, "I wish I could play the piano."?

5. Taste it just once...then YOU...be the judge. YOU'LL...like it.

6. If money is YOUR...problem, I have good news for YOU!

7. Have YOU...had YOUR...soup today? YOU...should try some soon.

8. Now, YOU...can pour yourself a vinyl floor. Saves YOU...work.

9. Money problems got YOU...down?

10. What do YOU...do when a headache strikes?

11. Stop wasting YOUR...money.

12. Here's how YOU...can be a winner.

13. Will YOU...know what to do?

14. Are YOU...a modern thinker?

15. What is it worth to YOU?

16. Do YOU...know what to think?

17. How can YOU..help?

18. YOU'LL...be surprised!

Note: the pauses which follow the lifted word, YOU or YOU'LL, are momentary in duration, for about as long as it takes you to snap your fingers. The longer the pause, the more emphatic becomes the word preceding it. Now, practice the presentational approach—the person-to-person technique—on the following commercial announcements.

Yes, a headache can get you down, feeling low and miserable. If that's the way **YOU** feel—don't wait! Reach for that blue and white bottle of BLUE CROSS aspirin, for quick, long-lasting relief. You see, BLUE CROSS aspirin offers you fast flaking action. That means that YOU get immediate relief from the nagging ache or pain. It's comforting to know that YOU have BLUE CROSS aspirin handy in YOUR medicine chest. Can YOU afford to be without BLUE CROSS aspirin? Of course, not! Here's another important thing: BLUE CROSS aspirin cannot upset YOUR stomach because it contains a special buffering agent to give YOU gentle, fast relief every time. So, for the fast relief from the agonizing pain of neuritis or arthritis always reach, first, for YOUR bottle of BLUE CROSS aspirin, world's best aspirin. YOU'LL find BLUE CROSS aspirin at drug counters from coast to coast, but be sure to ask for it by name...BLUE CROSS aspirin.

Here's another:

Only YOU can prevent forest fires. Yes, a thoughtless flick of a cigarette butt...a smoldering campfire...little things like that may destory millions of dollars of America's valuable timberland. YOU can play it safe. Because only YOU can prevent forest fires by using precaution. It's YOUR America...preserve it!

Project on the bold typed words:

If YOU'RE particular about YOUR taste, you don't have to shout from the rooftops to prove it! No sir! Simply smoke WALTON cigarettes. Why? Well, sir, WALTON'S natural mildness give YOU **smooth**, pleasing flavor. What a smoke! You see, when YOU smoke a **longer** cigarette, YOU smoke a cigarette that's long in **taste**, too. Sure! Shouldn't YOUR smoke be WALTON? Outstanding and mild, WALTONS are the smoke for YOU. Wherever you find particular folks you'll find WALTONS. Again I ask YOU...shouldn't YOUR smoke be...WALTON?

Now, repeat the above announcement. This time smile broadly; try to look off into space using the eyeball-to-eyeball technique of the television announcer. Point sharply with your free hand every time you use the word **you** or **yours**, then take the same approach on the following announcement. These announcements should be repeated **several** times **each day** for one **full** week before proceeding to Lesson 7. Smile and now **PROJECT!**

Have YOU had YOUR soup today? Good! Yes, MORELL soups are **all** downright good eating. Mmmm. Delicious. MORELL soups are good and good **for** YOU. Fifteen garden-fresh vegetables, just the right amount of seasoning to give MORELL soups that old-world flavor, and YOU'LL enjoy those old-fashioned egg noodles, **oodles** of noodles in MORELL soups. MORELL offers twenty-three kinds of delicious soups. YOU'LL find one YOU like, that's for sure. So, the next time YOU'RE in your favorite market, look for MORELL soups...they're the greatest!

In the following announcements the words to be projected have been left unmarked. PROJECT!

Have you heard about the new DICKENSON way to smoother, effortless shaving? For a shave without drag and pull, two things are needed. A good, keen blade and a DICKENSON ultra-smooth blade holder. What counts is the angle at which the blade is held by the razor, and that's exactly what DICKENSON has perfected...a razor expressly designed to hold a blade just **right** for smooth shaving. Furthermore, the ultra-keen blades made by DICKENSON are engineered to work perfectly in the **new** DICKENSON razor. It's a combination you just can't beat! The new DICKENSON razor is a precision instrument, featherweight, and so easy to handle. It lets you stroke across your face with no pressure at all. Now you know why the DICKENSON way of shaving has caught on so fast. Yes, men find shaving a pleasure and not a distasteful chore. Try a DICKENSON shave tomorrow morning. What a surprise you'll get!

Now—for the first time in ten years—TV CENTER proudly announces a giant money-saving sale on all name black-and-white and color TV sets. Take your pick of famous names, Zenith, RCA, Sylvania, Eureka...name your favorite brand, we **have** it! See the entire line of famous TRUETONE TV sets in rich, handcrafted cabinets in ten elegant stylings to enhance your living room, and TRUETONE'S 1970 models feature that exclusive **set-it-forget-it** color adjustment. That's all you do, adjust your set only **once**, then forget about it. The adjustor automatically tunes in a beautifully color-balanced picture on all channels every time. TV CENTER'S money-saving sale starts today!

PRACTICE SCHEDULE—6th WEEK

1. **RELAXATION** 5 minutes.

2. **VOCAL DRILLS** 10 minutes.

3. **PROJECTION** Person-to-person drills. Six lines a day. 10 minutes.

4. **PRONUNCIATION** Continue your daily check on six words frequently mispronounced. 10 minutes.

5. **ENUNCIATION** Continue work on multisyllable words. Alternate with tongue twisters if time is limited. 10 minutes.

6. **READING** Continue indefinitely as instructed. 15 minutes.

7. **COMMERCIALS** Apply the presentational approach as explained in this lesson. Carry all techniques forward from less to lesson. They will merge. 20 minutes.

8. Give this lesson a daily reading, if time permits.

9. Keep up your weekly survey on your progress. Don't become over-critical of your work. Learning is a process of trial and error. You cannot become perfect. Do the best you can—that's enough. Disregard those "off days." We all have them.

Lesson 7

Analyzing A Commercial Announcement

Every commercial follows a special style, one chosen by the copywriter to best sell the advertiser's product or services. To do a good selling job from a piece of copy, a simple analysis, sometimes referred to as "interpretation," is in order. To do this, three points must be taken into consideration: the nature of the product or service, the sex group to which the product will appeal and the average age of the group—potential purchasers of the product. Here are a few examples of what is meant by selling style.

Male listeners won't be offended if you laughingly shout, "Five o'clock shadow! You've got to shave, man!" But you can't take the same approach with a product for women: "Gray hair? It makes you look old, lady!" So the copywriter adopts a special style to sell hair dye. "Tired of gray hair? Well, wash it away. Look and feel your youthful, lovely self again." Of course, a cosmetic announcement takes a soft-spoken, almost whispering tone of voice, as for the following: "New Swan soap will keep your skin so **soft**, so **baby** soft, so kissable, so caressable..." For the commercial slanted to teenagers, take a light and lively tack, "Hey, kids! Enjoy fun in the sun this summer with a Coke. That's good, man—**real good!**" If it's a medical product, your potential purchasers may be quite mature folks who seek relief from some discomforting illness; therefore, drop the smile and speak in a conversational, friendly voice, as a pharmacist or the family doctor would. You must be versatile. If you have a copy of **The Man Behind The Mike**, read Chapter 7 "The Art of Interpretation."

Analyze the following sample commercials. Try various types of deliveries. Decide on the one which would best sell the product.

1. Has a headache got you down? Feeling low and miserable? Don't wait! Take BLUE CROSS ASPIRIN for fast-acting, **long-lasting** relief.

2. Have you had **your** soup today? Good! Yes, WAGNER'S make twenty-three kinds of soups, and they're **all** downright **delicious** eating.

3. Worried about graying hair? You **needn't**! Wash that gray away with GLOSS for a more youthful, **lovelier** you. It's so easy and quick, too.

4. Are you smoking **more** now but enjoying it **less**? Then switch today to PIEDMONTS, for **smooth** smoking pleasure. A **satisfying** smoke.

5. Today is your last chance to take advantage of SMITH'S bargain days. Everything must go at 30 to 40 percent off! Don't wait! Act **today**!

6. Wherever young folks gather, there you'll find ice-cold, **refreshing** POP COLA. In summer, what could be better at the beach or picnic than POP COLA?

Number 1 sells a medical product; therefore, it requires a friendly, factual voice. Number 2 should carry a very definite smile to reflect satisfaction and to stimulate the listener's appetite. For number 3 use a subdued, between-us-gals type of delivery. Number 4 takes the same voice as does number 2. On number 5 become very enthusiastic and emphatic. Number 6 calls for a lively, brisk tempo and plenty of smile and highly colored words. The technique of characterization and color is explained in Lesson 9. Practice analysis on newspaper and magazine advertisements.

Before you start practicing these commercials, analyze each one of them. What style (conversational, informal, confidential, enthusiastic, etc.)? What age group? What sex?

Stainless steel has been around for a long time...nothing new, but it's what the makers of KEEN blades have done to stainless steel that makes shaving a pleasure, well, **almost**. Ah, man! What a smooth, no-drag shave **you'll** get with these new, stainless blades by KEEN. Try 'em tomorrow morning. You're in for a surprise! Believe me!

Did you smile with satisfaction on that one? Did you take a moderately fast, a bright pace, with an enthusiastic approach? Try it again.

Ladies! Are you tired of gray hair? Does it make you look older than you really are? Well, confidentially, do something about it. Rinse that gray away with KOLOR. Sure, it's so easy. Shampoo your hair as you usually do, rinse it with KOLOR. That's all! Look forward to a brighter and more youthful tomorrow. Be your former youthful self again. Rinse away that aging gray **today**! Get new, **easy-to-use** KOLOR. Your druggist has it...now!

If you took the whispering, between-us-girls tone of voice, you were right. When you do this type of sotto voce delivery, work closer to the microphone, the lighter the whisper, the closer. The harder the sell, the farther from the mike.

Now! Yes, now you save dollars and dollars on home furnishings during WILSON'S big, **big** fall clearance sale. Everything must go! Prices slashed to the bone...unheard-of buys for the economy-minded homemaker! All sales final! WILSON'S big fall clearance sale is now on, so hurry, hurry, hurry to WILSONS, home of fine furniture for more than fifty years!

How will you handle this commercial?

For a wonderful and bright spirit, say, KOKE! Yes, KOKE is **still** America's number-one drink for the young and for those who **think** young. You see, wherever you find happy, carefree people, there you'll find that friendly bottle of COKE. Folks just naturally love that ice-cold goodness...that satisfying **light** taste...that thirst-quenching goodness that only a bottle of KOKE can give you. For that weekend party, at home, for the picnic, at the seashore...take along a carton or two of frosty, delicious taste-tempting KOKE. Now in family-size bottles and in cartons of a dozen. At your market, now, But be sure you say, KOKE, please. You bet there's a **difference**!

Come back to these commercials for practice when you study Lesson 9, Characterization and Coloring.

Are you smoking more than you should? Well, it could be that you're simply tired of your present cigarette. Maybe a change to MENTHOS will enliven your taste buds. You see, MENTHOS are made with the world's best domestic and imported tobaccos, plus just the right amount of menthol to give you the coolest, most satisfying smoke...ever. You've got to try a pack of MENTHOS to really know how good a cigarette **can** taste. MENTHOS with the pure white filter, in king and extra-long sizes for better, more satisfying smoking. Yes, those in the know changed to MENTHOS when **they** smoked more than they should. Shouldn't **you** change, too?

PRACTICE SCHEDULE—7th WEEK

1. **RELAXATION** 5 minutes.

2. **VOCAL DRILLS** 10 minutes.

3. **PROJECTION** As instructed in Lesson 6. 10 minutes.

4. **PRONUNCIATION** Continue daily check on six words frequently mispronounced. 10 minutes.

5. **ENUNCIATION** Multisyllable words. Alternate with tongue twisters. If necessary, alternate enunciation with pronunciation 10 minutes.

6. **READING** 15 minutes.

7. **ANALYSIS** Work daily on the exercises on interpretation. Also devote some time daily to advertisements in newspapers and magazines. Notice the different types of commercials. 10 minutes.

8. **COMMERCIALS** Analyze each message before reading. Apply the person-to-person technique of projection. Carry techniques forward. 20 minutes.

9. Read the text daily. Pay no attention to "fluffs," as errors are called in broadcast jargon. A name announcer on a major network once introduced President Herbert Hoover as "Hubert Heever." Another famous voice called the A & P Gypsies, the "A & G Pippsies" and a nationally known newscaster read a bulletin: "An English battleship was left stinking in the English Channel!" Are you still concerned about an occasional error? We all make them. Make them— forget them.

Lesson 8

Putting Your Imagination To Work

You now know that to do an effective selling job on the air, some interpretation is necessary. To be able to project a commercial announcement with genuine enthusiasm and believability, the various aspects of the message (its character, mood, etc.) must firmly be established in your mind. You, primarily, must be convinced of the worthiness of the product or services as presented in your copy. Your listener will believe you in proportion to how much you believe yourself. It is for this very reason that sponsors quite frequently supply announcers with samples of their products. For instance, while in New York, I was assigned to the production staff of a program sponsored by the Lambert Pharmaceutical Co., manufacturers of Listerine antiseptic. Through its advertising agency, the sponsor sent me a carton containing his entire line of products.

Most professionals take their advertising seriously. Frankly, I dislike superlatives in commercials. Such words as, amazing, astounding, incredible and other strong modifiers sometimes tend to overrate a product. One of the most conscientious performers in our midst, veteran radio and TV personality., Arthur Godfrey, in a public statement not too long ago, said he ceased to recommend a certain washday soaker. "It's a good product, and all that," he said, "but, now I am told it contains a polluting agent." Mr. Godfrey felt it was against his principles to speak highly about a product unless he could personally vouch for its merits. I admire his candid action. Undoubtedly, he'll again sing its praises when the offending ingredient is removed.

Yes, we have performers in this profession who take a very strong stand on ethics and personal principles, and Mr. Godfrey is one of them. As a longtime conservationist, he acted precisely as his conscience and common sense dictated. There are many professionals, who act likewise when they harbor any doubts as to the efficacy or integrity of a product or if they can't seem to whip up enough enthusiasm about it. To mask negative feelings about a product, and yet rave and shout in glowing terms about its outstanding qualities, requires the performance of an actor. I firmly believe that to do justice to a sponsor, his product and to an audience, the deejay should feel a profound respect for whatever it is he is selling. The store owner proudly displays samples of his line of merchandise because he, too, believes in the worthiness of his inventory. Ethics and principles in this business of broadcasting are important.

Some years ago, the Mentholatum Company sponsored one of my newscasts. Knowing that Mentholatum was (and still is) a high-quality cold remedy, I felt pleased to be commercially associated with the product. That winter I developed a bad cold. When our program director heard me on the air through sniffles telling the audience about the efficacy of Mentholatum, he called me to his office. "How do you expect your listeners to believe what you say about Mentholatum as a cold remedy when you, yourself, struggle through wheezing and sniffling on the air?" He was right. I had never thought about it that way. A substitute took over for a week, while I used Mentholatum to clear up a stuffy nose and congested sinuses.

Speaking of principles, when the Debbie Reynolds show bowed in during the Fall of 1969, cigarette advertising appeared on the screen that first evening. Quite upset about it, Miss Reynolds flatly stated that she disapproved of the practice and demanded deletion of such commercials, or else. It seemed that the star simply did not wish to be associated with a production which promoted the sale of tobacco and encouraged the smoking of cigarettes. Incidentally, as I write this, cigarette advertising has been banned from the broadcast scene. The industry reports this will cost it a loss in advertising revenue of about $250 million a year, about one-eighth of its current national billings.

You see, this is an unpredictable business, maybe zany is the better word. During my very early days in the profession, I was assigned as announcer to a band show which originated in a hotel just outside town. The show clicked and I looked forward to the following week's program, until a colleague informed me that the "hotel" had a local reputation of being a swanky, hanky-panky establishment. And I had actually invited our listeners to "put fun in your life—come on over..." I quit the assignment. If you feel a lack of moral soundness or dishonesty about a product or service, and yet wish to accept the assignment, you'll have to be a good actor to sound convincing. To register sincerity and believability, I think an announcer should feel that he's telling the truth, and that he is

70

not merely mouthing a conglomeration of words, the handiwork of an ingenious advertising-agency writer.

To develop the ability to mentally see, hear, smell, taste and, in your mind's eye, closely examine a product or a service, I devised a certain exercise to be used for practice only. I have found the eye closure method, as used in the development of ESP, very satisfactory. It helps you stimulate your imagination. In other words, close your eyes and on an imaginary white screen, visualize the product or services in action. It's the next best thing to actually seeing and using the product.

Don't become confused at this stage of your progress. Analyzing a commercial, determining its mood and character, activating the imagination, conjuring up mental pictures—in other words, all the steps preparatory to doing a good selling job from a piece of typed copy—will very soon become a one-step process. That is, you will be able to quickly read through a commercial, then, in a flash, determine the fitting and proper manner in which to handle the account. A few readings or two, a few markings to guide, you and you'll be ready to send those mind pictures out to your listener. As I said in the beginning of the book, all techniques will merge. For practice purposes and to simplify instruction, we must necessarily study and develop the techniques one at a time.

The deejay or commercial announcer must sound just as believable as does the play-by-play sportscaster, yet this techniques differ slightly. Let me explain. The sports announcer has the advantage, he is able to SEE the action on the field, in the ring, at the track, on the court. He simply converts the action he SEES into WORDS; he makes word pictures. The sports fan listening to his radio, via his imagination, recreates the sports event, as though he were observing the action on the TV tube. You might say the listener is seated on the 50-yard line through the eyes and ears of the play-by-play announcer. While announcing, the deejay cannot see his product in action as does the sportscaster, yet he, too, must create lifelike word pictures. The announcer sees only a piece of paper with words typed on it, symbols which he must convert and use as building blocks to construct his word pictures. That's precisely why the power of the imagination is of utmost importance to the deejay or commercial announcer. When the deejay's projected word or mind picture is well defined—clear, distinct and believable—the listener is "sold," convinced! Lesson 10 explains this in detail. On one hand the sportscaster SEES what he is describing, while the announcer or deejay uses his IMAGINATION to "see" what he describes. Both project word or mind pictures; the effects are identical. The sports fan eagerly watches the scoreboard, the passes and fumbles and the bargain-conscious homemaker observes the day's market buys, all via the magic of mind pictures.

Now, to a well-tested method to develop your ability to "see" in your mind's eye. Relaxation is important; so is a quiet atmosphere. Be patient. Results may not be forthcoming on your first try, but daily practice will do it. First, read one of the groups of descriptive words several times. Then, close your eyes, relax completely in a comfortable chair, imagine that you are sitting quietly in a motion picture theatre, looking at the blank screen waiting for the picture to begin. Allow your imagination to create a picture—a moving picture—in accordance with the descriptive words you memorized. For example, when you visualize the mental picture of a creamy dish of chocolate ice cream in all its tasty goodness, just waiting to be scooped up, your mouth should water. When it does, you are mentally conditioned to do a good job of selling ice cream; you'll sound **believable** because you "experienced" tasting its goodness. All right, let's try mind picture number 1:

1. This is the picture of a bowl of **steaming-hot,** home-cooked, **hearty,** old-fashioned **chicken** soup with oodles of noodles. It has that **rich, tantalizing, chickeny flavor.**

2. This description depicts a **mouth-watering** helping of delicious chocolate ice cream, overflowing with **thick marshmallow topping,** like lava cascading down the sides of an erupting volcano. On top sits a **bright-red, sweet** maraschino cherry.

3. Here is a **murky and gloomy** torture chamber **deep** down in the **musty dungeon** of a crumbling, medieval castle, dank and **moldy** with age.

4. This time visualize the **bone-chilling, frozen wasteland** of the Arctic. Look out upon a **desolate icebound** horizon.

Because Lessons 8 and 9 are so closely related, include the exercises in this lesson in next week's work. Carry this imagination technique over into your next lesson.

PRACTICE SCHEDULE—8th WEEK

1. **RELAXATION** 5 minutes.

2. **VOCAL DRILLS** 10 minutes.

3. **PROJECTION** 10 minutes.

4. **PRONUNCIATION** 10 minutes.

5. **ENUNCIATION** 10 minutes.

6. **IMAGINATION** Work daily on the exercises as instructed. 10 minutes.

7. **READING** 15 minutes.

8. **COMMERCIALS** During this week apply all the techniques you have acquired so far to the commercials contained in Lessons 1 through 7. You may now check on your original recording and make a comparison. 20 minutes.

9. Reread this lesson carefully. It has a very definite bearing on your next lesson.

10. Notice that your schedule now runs 90 minutes. If you must limit yourself to one hour, decrease numbers 2, 3, 4, 5, 7 and 8 by 5 minutes each.

Lesson 9

Words Have Character

Make it real—speak in living color! It's easy. The technique with which we are concerned in this lesson, I call **coloring**, which sometimes is referred to as characterization. Shun the monotony of black and white. The world is color-conscious. So, color your speech for interesting conversation and believable reception. On the street, on radio or TV, you communicate thoughts, and such thoughts, to be properly translated in the subconscious of your listener, must be transmitted alive in living color! When you practice imagination as explained in Lesson 8, apply coloring, then simply speak descriptive words as you see them. It's that simple! Don't over color, though. When a TV set is not properly adjusted, blues become too deep, greens, muddy, and a picture becomes unbelievable. Tint your words. Here's an example: The word **smooth**, should be characterized as, **smooth** but **not** smooooooth, the word grip, as you would see a tire grip the road when brakes are applied, would appear to **grrip** but not **grrrrrrrip** the pavement, and ice cream would be described as **creeamy** but not **creeeeeeamy**.

When using coloring words, such as, white, black, muddy, dismal etc., pitch plays an important part in the technique. In your mind's eye see the color **white** as spoken in an upper register, and the word, **black**, voiced on a lower level. The words **cold** and **hot** are both spoken in your lower register **but** to make the word cold sound **collld**, a slight shiver in the voice should be evident, and the word, **hottt** should sound slightly breathless and "perspiring." Yes, words **have** character—make them live!

EXERCISE

soothing	sooothing
smooth	smoooth
long-lasting	lonngg-lasting
quick	(say it quickly)
slowly-cooked	slowwwly-cooked
delicious	deeelicious

striking	(strike it hard)
amazing	amayyyzing!
gripping	grrripping
exploding	(explode it)
crash	(make it crash)
tremendous	tremmmmenndous!
millions	milllions!
clean	(make it sound clean)
fresh	(Make it sound fresh)
new (not noo)	(Make it sound new!)

It has that fresh taste.
Your mouth feels clean.
Here's something brand new!
What delicious food.
That's remarkable!
An amazing invention.
It's a smoother smoke.
What a cool day.

What an easy life.
Do it instantly!
Tires grip the road.
A wonderful world.
It's ice-cold.
New exciting!
Very refreshing.

IN YOUR LOWER REGISTER

dark	gloom
black	murky
dismal	foggy
brown	down
murder	cold
tomb	frozen
depths	clammy

IN YOUR HIGHER REGISTER

airy	cool
brisk	bright
white	snowy
dainty	filmy
light	fluffy
lacy	gay
frilly	frivolous

In addition to the announcements here, include the exercises in Lesson 8. You are now working with projection (the person-to-person) technique, characterization and coloring. Use your imagination to KNOW your product. Analyze each commercial to determine the treatment. To assist, the words to be characterized appear in bold face.

Now, there's a **brand new** tire with a **broader** tread, NO SKID! Yes, NO SKIDS are **unconditionally** guaranteed for life. When other tires skid on slippery pavements, NO SKIDS **grip** the road...bring your car to a safe, **fast** stop. See this **new,** this **amazing** NO SKID tire, the last word in automotive development. . . Today!

Did you make the word NEW sound **new**? Did you make the guarantee sound **unconditional**? Did you make your listeners "see" a tire GRRRIP the road? Were your listeners "amazed"? They were if you pronounced the word, "aMAYYYYzed!" Here's another:

The Danes know good beer. . .they cherish the old. That's why PRIDE OF DENMARK is still the **finest, thirst-quenching** brew in the world today. They still brew it today as they did over a **hundred** years ago. PRIDE OF DENMARK has that **old-world flavor,** the **cooling, smooth taste** found only in a **premium** beer like PRIDE OF DENMARK. **Creamy, golden-amber** PRIDE OF DENMARK hits the **hot spot** on a **sizzling-hot summer's day**. Try PRIDE OF DENMARK...You'll see what I mean when I say, PRIDE OF DENMARK is **still** the **tastiest** brew in the **world**.

Don't fail to go back to the announcements in Lessons 6, 7, and 8 for characterization practice. Fig. 9-1 shows a student's markings to insert inflections, pauses, and characterization.

For practice purposes, descriptive words which should be characterized will be left unmarked in the following commercials. After analyzing the announcements, underscore the proper words.

Hurry..Hurry..Hurry! This is your last chance to buy a 1971 Hudson for the low, low price of only $2250! That's right! Every car on our showroom floor must go immediately! Hardtops, sports models, sedans...They're all here! For smooth riding qualities, for the utmost in automotive convenience and traveling comfort, test drive the new 1971 Hudson. Feel how easy it steers, how quickly its brakes bring it to a stop, how economical Hudson is to operate. See this new, 1969 Hudson, on display at all BISHOP showrooms..now!

Did you mark them all? Hurry, last, low, only, right, immediately, all, smooth, utmost, new, feel, easy, quickly, economical, now. The line should read; "Feeeel how eeeeasy it steers...how **quickkkly** its brakes.." Pronounce the word quickly—QUICKLY!

Have you tasted new, KRISPY TOAST! You haven't? Lady, you're really in for a surprise! Nutritious? Yes! Delicious? Yes, again! KRISPY TOAST snaps and

Smile ↖ _project_

<u>45 Seconds</u>

It's sheer magic what a drop of EYELO can do for red, tired eyes. Yes, EYELO quickly clears up that irritated look in your eyes due to fatigue and overwork. EYELO works amazingly fast, too. Makes your eyes look bigger, / younger, / brighter. And the effect last and lasts for hours! EYELO is non-staining and absolutely safe to use. Clear up your eyes tomorrow morning. EYELO brings sheer magic to morning eyes. Get / EYELO in two sizes, the convenient pocket-sized bottle and the larger, // family-sized plastic container for your medicine chest. EYELO . . . at druggists / everywhere! /

<u>35 Seconds</u>

If it takes you more than fifteen minutes to get to sleep, then take two / DROWSE tablets for a night of safe and restful slumber. DROWSE tablets are non-habit forming . . . cannot upset your stomach. No hangover, either. . . . just natural sleep. If business tension or everyday nervousness keeps you awake, take / DROWSE. Next thing you know / it's morning. // Why twist and turn half the night when two DROWSE tablets will quickly bring on blessed sleep? DROWSE / D-R-O-W-S-E . . . at all drug counters / now! /

COLOR

Fig. 9-1. Copy markings to denote inflections, pauses and characterization.

crackles. It's sweet and tasty. The kids'll love KRISPY TOAST and they're downright good for them, too. What an idea for a midnight snack! You'll say they're great! Try KRISPY TOAST tomorrow morning. KRISPY TOAST at grocers and supermarkets...everywhere!

PRACTICE SCHEDULE—9th WEEK

1. **RELAXATION** 5 minutes.

2. **VOCAL DRILLS** 10 minutes.

3. **PROJECTION** 10 minutes.

4. **PRONUNCIATION** 10 minutes.

5. **ENUNCIATION** 10 minutes.

6. **READING** 15 minutes.

7. **CHARACTERIZATION** Devote as much time as possible on this important subject, also called coloring. Work well on the drills. Also review the process of imagination and development. 10 minutes.

8. **COMMERCIALS** Your commercials should now begin to reflect that professional sound. 20 minutes.

9. Try to do a daily reading of the lesson text.

Lesson 10

YOU — The Living Slide Projector

Is there an analogical relationship between the process of projecting a colored image on a screen and on-the-air broadcast techniques? Yes, definitely! Because this is a truism, I say PROJECT! Don't **introject**! When you wear phones you introject. Forget about yourself and how well or poorly you sound to your own ears. Instead, concentrate upon one listener and communicate a believable **word picture** to her. If you can't feel a genuine interest in your product, or if it's difficult to believe in the product's merit or proof of performance, be an actor! (The successful announcer must be a good actor.) Make what you say **sound** believable.

It's imperative that the serious student relaizes that there is a relation of likeness between a slide projector and himself, a correspondence of function, as it were. Whether you, the disc jockey, create and effectively communicate word or mind pictures, or whether you use a projector to show colored slides on a screen in your living room, the process is basically the same and the result is identical. A living image in lifelike color is registered and impressed upon the viewer's (listener's) subconscious. It may be different, **structurally**, but you can't change the resemblance one iota. Mentally, the communication is tantamount. A comparison should prove instructive and interesting.

The Slide Projector	The Broadcaster
The colored slide	This is equivalent to well-written copy from which the DJ reads and speaks—the original.
The electrical current	Controlled breathing in well-spaced places for an ample air supply, taken in whiffs.

The illumination	This may be likened to a cultured, resonant speaking voice, forceful enough to register clearly.
The lens	The human "lens" is the mouth through which pass the vowels and consonants as formed by the lips and distinctly articulated.
The focusing device	Think of this as technology: the person-to-person approach, the use of attention-getting devices etc., to project a clearly-defined word picture.
The screen	The listener's subconscious mind.
The projected image	The projected (word) picture, an effective sales message.

By now you should be convinced of one thing: you're in show business—you're an actor!

Here's an example of a poorly projected word picture. Let's assume that the announcer read too quickly; that he failed to use any attention-getting devices; and that his articulation was slovenly. His delivery impressed the listener's subconscious with little more than a poorly-formed, "washed out", blurred image. It sounded something like this:

"Hizzaboggin ywoon wanna miss.
Yikingit toofiti pricea one.
Gitchaintri blan' 'day."

Exaggerated? Not too much. I heard something quite similar on radio last week. Here's how a **trained** jockey, using the various techniques conducive to professionalism, would deliver the same lines:

Here's a **bargain**...you **won't** want to **miss**!
You can get **two**...for the price of **one**!
Get yourself an **entry** blank...**today**!

This jockey obviously took a **moderate** tempo to do a selling job with color and characterization. He made the word **bargain** sound like a BARGAIN! He used pauses and inflections, the techniques of which will be explained in later lessons. You might say, that he cleaned the lens, removed the finger smudges from the slide, turned the illumination up full and focused the picture sharply to project a living image of his product. Yes, in a very real sense you are a projector of pictures.

Following is a test for clarity and projection. Watch the endings of the words, dressing, advertising, according, etc. Observe the WH in the words, why, where, when and what. Notice the momentary pauses and color the words, smoothly, clean, free, greasy, pleasantly scented, etc. Get a smile into your speech and project on you, your, and you'll. In other words, apply all the techniques learned thus far. When you record these commercials, listen on playback for a well-defined, understandable message.

According to the advertising one reads these days, one brand of hair dressing will get you a girl...the other...will get you that job you've always wanted. It makes one wonder what's a hair dressing for in the first place? Well, the way I look at it, a hair dressing is made to keep your hair neatly in place, smoothly groomed, all day long. Right? Sure..and that's why you should use STAYKREEM. You see, this new STAYKREEM won't leave your hair greasy looking. STAYKREEM conditions your hair...keeps your scalp feeling so clean..absolutely free of annoying dandruff. Why don't you try STAYKREEM? Yes, it's a real, he-man's hair dressing without that strong, smelly perfume, but pleasantly scented with a masculine freshness. STAYKREEM comes in two sizes...the trial and regular sized tube as well as in attractive plastic jars. Ask for...STAYKREEM wherever drugs are sold. You'll like...STAYKREEM.

Did you give each of the words, first, right, sure, greasy, he-man's, without, perfume, freshness, like, a gentle emphasis—a lift? Inflections, upward inflections, they are called. More on inflection in Lesson 14. Please record the STAYKREEN commercial again. This time add another touch of professionalism. Plant (as it's called in show business) the product's trade name or the name of the sponsor in the subconscious mind of your listener. You'll make a lifelong friend of an advertiser if you give his name prominence in the commercial, or if you highlight the trade name of his product. How do you do it? Simple! Use the attention-getting device, the pause, but do it subtly. Pause momentarily before, and lift, the name of the product or the name of the sponsor, like this:

1. This new...STAYKREEM ╱ is non-grasy!

2. For the lowest prices in town...MILLER ╱ is the name!

3. Only...OAKLAND MOTORS╱ can make you a deal like that!

Notice also the brief pause after the name of the product or advertiser. There's a very definite rule for use of the pause to be explained in Lesson 13. The use of pauses, inflections, coloring and the other professional techniques give top name announcers that finesse. Deejays speak about finesse, but they don't know how to acquire it. They know it sounds great, but how to get it? That's the question. You are acquiring it right now. By the way, I think now's a good time to start clipping advertisements from newspapers and magazines. From Lesson 18 on, you'll practice with fresh copy every day to develop your skill at analyzing, and working with, various types of commercials—a seasoning process. You may, if you wish to put variety into your practice sessions, add a few magazine and newspaper advertisements as I suggested in an earlier lesson.

PRACTICE SCHEDULE—10th WEEK

1. **RELAXATION** 5 minutes.

2. **VOCAL DRILLS** 10 minutes.

3. **PROJECTION** 10 minutes.

4. **PRONUNCIATION** 10 minutes.

5. **ENUNCIATION** 10 minutes.

6. **CHARACTERIZATION** 10 minutes.

7. **READING** 15 minutes.

8. **COMMERCIALS** 20 minutes.

9. Daily reading of the lesson.

Lesson 11

Sales Points & Customer Benefits

A sales point, itself, may arouse the potential customer's attention, but to actually sell the product the announcer must place importance on **how the customer will benefit** from the sales point. Of course, a good copywriter will see that both appear in the copy. The sales point in an aspirin commercial may read, "It has **fast flaking action!**" To clinch the sale the customer benefit must be emphasized: "That means that BLUE CROSS aspirin goes to work **fast** to relieve your headache in **seconds!**" Here's another example: To exclaim: "Yes, BREEZE is **different** from other deodorants...it's **better!**" won't tell the customer much. You must still tell her why it's better, and in which way it's **different** by "selling" this line: "BREEZE gives you **long-lasting** protection—48-hour protection; that's why it's different from **old-fashioned** kinds of deodorants." Now, you've answered both questions. You have stated a sales point and bolstered it with a customer benefit.

Another sales point may be the fact that this new BREEZE deodorant now comes in an **unbreakable plastic bottle**. Of course, everyone knows that a plastic bottle won't shatter; still, the customer benefit must be strongly indicated, "Yes, no more messy spills to mar your dresser tops..." Let me give you a BREEZE commercial. Notice the many customer benefits in the message.

Does your present deodorant give you 24-hour protection? If not, you owe it to yourself to give **new** BREEZE a trial. BREEZE is **different...entirely** different! BREEZE is **guaranteed** to kill the germs that **cause**..body odor. BREEZE gives you **long-lasting** protection. You get that fresh...**clean** feeling all over. No stickiness...BREEZE dries **immediately!** And BREEZE lasts, and **lasts**...and LASTS! **New...improved** BREEZE is now at your druggist's.

Notice that the sales point, "new BREEZE is entirely different," is established first, then the balance of the message clarifies the sales point with four customer benefits: (1) it kills germs, (2) it's long-lasting, (3) it leaves a clean, fresh feeling, (4) it isn't sticky, but dries immediately. Then, the sales point is further strengthened and illustrated with the line, "It lasts, and lasts and LASTS," which is spoken, "It lasts...and lasssts...and LASSSTS!" Also notice the two adjectives which both describe the same word, "fresh.. clean feeling." When two adjectives describe the same word, pause, momentarily between them, and lift the second modifier in pitch...an upward inflection. Inflections will be dealt with in another lesson, but here are a few examples of this technique.

> It's a cool...smooth smoke
> A light, and airy atmosphere
> This is a cold...dismal day.
> A cool, and refreshing drink.

The professional copywriter makes the second modifier the stronger of the two; actually, that's the purpose of doubling up.

Let me illustrate a few sales points and their related customer benefits. Notice the characterized readings of the customer benefits to create an action word picture of the product in the commercial.

1. FREESTONE TIRES now have new and wider treads! Yes, FREESTONE TIRES grip (GRRIP) the road when ordinary tires skid on slippery pavements.

2. Now, THE AMERICAN INSURANCE COMPANY offers you the family-group policy which insures every member of your family—protects all of you in one, single policy. You save money because there's only one premium to pay! That's economy for you!

3. The new FREEZEALL refrigerator is finished in gleaming coppertone. It looks good?...Yes, and so easy to keep clean. A damp cloth will keep this beautiful, permanent finish sparkling clean and immaculate! (Make it sound eaaasy, beauutiful and sparrrkling)

4. At last! Now, you can pour yourself a beautiful, shiny floor with new GLOSS. No need to slave each week with a polishing cloth to keep your floors clean and shiny. You see, new GLOSS is self-shining. Saves you precious time and money, too. Takes only five minutes to dry to a hard, durable

and tough shine... and it lasts for weeks and weeks. (Make the floors sound clean, shiny and beautiful. Make the finished job sound harrd, durrable, touggh.)

The serious-minded student will understand that copy should never be read "cold," that is to say, without analyzing it, rehearsing it and learning how it should be handled as explained in Lesson 7.

PRACTICE SCHEDULE—11th WEEK

1. **RELAXATION** 5 minutes.

2. **VOCAL DRILLS** 10 minutes.

3. **PRONUNCIATION** 10 minutes.

4. **ENUNCIATION** 10 minutes.

5. **PROJECTION** 10 minutes.

6. **CHARACTERIZATION** 10 minutes.

7. **READING** 15 minutes.

8. **COMMERCIALS** Observe the sales points and customer benefits as indicated in this exercise and announcements. 20 minutes.

10. How is your list of frequently mispronounced words coming along? Have you asked your local radio station for discarded teletypewriter news copy? Also ask the copywriter for government and other public service announcements they no longer use on the air. If you can't handle a 90-minute study period, decrease the time as suggested previously.

Lesson 12

How To Develop a Dynamic Personality

No single factor will probably do more to promote a magnetic personality than will self-confidence. The happy and contented disposition of a well-balanced deejay is brightly reflected in what he says and how he says it. When he sounds off with, "Well, how are you out there?" he comes over as a sincere and believable friend. Such a personable jock is said to possess a dynamic personality. In this lesson let's briefly discuss the human quality, self-confidence and its relationship to personality.

How can we best define the word, **personality**? For one thing, personality is that quality or state of being personal. And that's what we're after: **person-to-person** communication. The word, **personality**, also means the distinction or excellence of personal or social traits, possessing magnetic, personal qualities.

From the start I have asked you **not** to be overly critical of your efforts, to avoid enslavement to your tape recorder, **not** to strive for perfection and to curb the habit of monitoring yourself on headphones—subjecting yourself to watchdog tactics. I sounded these warnings to ward off any possible feelings of inferiority, which could develop as the result of voice-consciousness. Strangely enough, it's the serious-minded aspirant who often turns ultracritical, because he tries too hard to please **himself**. That's what you must offset to stimulate confidence in yourself. Be reasonable in your self-judgment. Have respect for your abilities and talents. Regardless of those "off days," feel satisfied with each session's progress. Let no one discourage you. Refuse to be swayed. And when you deserve it, give yourself a mental pat on the back. Hold yourself in high esteem, but don't lean toward complacency. Seek a happy balance: Feel proud of your accomplishments and pleased with your progress, but keep trying. The more you know, the farther you go. **Balance** is the word.

To achieve a winning personality—on the air and on the street—evaluate your self-confidence. If necessary, take corrective measures. Change your way of thinking. Eliminate the negative and accentuate the positive. **Today** counts! Don't indulge in retrospection. Look to the future and your goal on the top of the broadcast world. You'll find helpful books available on self-confidence, personality analysis and development, and related subject matter. Obviously, a cool-and-calm attitude plus ingratiating manners are clearly evident in the voice with a smile—the identifying mark of a strikingly attractive personality. The active ingredient? A smile.

I make an issue of personality projection because in radiobroadcasting, as differentiated from the sight-sound medium, the "state of being personal" is undeniably essential, and the need for it is greater. In this respect the television announcer with his photogenic qualities, make-up and well-placed lighting works to an advantage over the radio announcer; he is seen. But the radio jock must project his personality via words which smile. The deejay's personality cannot be seen—he must make it **heard.** You may prove this for yourself. Record a commercial with a smile on your **lips,** then repeat the announcement. The second time, put the smile into the way you **speak.** Your tape recorder will tell you when you've succeeded.

To maintain a progress report on his personality-development program, the working jock should keep a watchful eye on those monthly audience-rating percentages as they climb during such periods of the day when he is on the air. Another sure-fire way to meter escalating popularity is to count that fan mail every day.

In the drills below, make the **words** smile. Check with your tape recorder at the end of today's session. Listen for the smile in your voice. Practice well on the bold-face lines for friendliness and sincerity. Smile! Everyone knows how it's done. Relax!

(SMILE) Well, good **morning,** and how are you?

(SMILE) Hello, there, everyone, and **greetings!**

(SMILE) Want to save yourself lots of money? **Of course, you do!**

(SMILE) Get one today! **You'll be glad you did!**

(SMILE) Everyone likes them. **You will, too.**

(SMILE) Ah, man, these stainless blades are great! **Real smooth. Yessir!**

(SMILE) This soup's just downright, good eating. **Delicious, Mmm Mnn!**

Now, apply this technique to the commercial announcements which follow. Start each commercial with a smile on your face and observe the upward inflections on underscored words. When you record these commercials at the end of today's practice session, listen especially for that smile. You can't see a smile on radio, as on TV, so try to hear it in your work. SMILE!

Have you tasted the **new** candy sensation...PLENTY GOOD? Mmmm...it **is** good. Caramel centers, smooth, creamy chocolate outside and plenty of PLENTY GOOD candy flavor in between. PLENTY GOOD is sold wherever good candy is sold, and that means just about every place. Try PLENTY GOOD and **you'll** say...man, that's PLENTY GOOD enough for **me!**

Now, please try it again. This time really have fun with it. Smile **broadly.** Make that chocolate covering sound **smooooth and creeeemy.** If you can't quite feel it, put your imagination to work; mentally taste a **deeelicious,** chocolate candy bar with a **soft, chewy** caramel center, **rich, chocolaty goodness** outside. Now, try it again, then reject your friendly, smiling personality into this one. SMILE!

Going to the beach this weekend? Don't forget a carton of your favorite KOLA. Ice cold, **refreshing**...KOLA does it every time. Yes sir, just about everyone in your crowd drinks KOLA. Pick up a few **extra** cartons, just to be sure you won't run short. Long on **taste** and long on **cooling refreshment**...that's KOLA. Wherever you **go,** wherever you **may be,** there you'll find folks and their favorite soft drink with that **zip...ice cold, refreshing** KOLA. At all supermarkets.

Let your imagination ride high, sound enthusiastic. Use a bright, moving pace. SMILE!

Do **you** mind shaving yourself every morning? Now, that's a silly question, I know, but what I **really** meant to say was, you **can** make shaving a **pleasure...almost,** with **new** KEEN blades. Ah man, they're **really sharp**...KEEN blades can't scrape and scratch your face as do **other** so-called stainless steel blades. No sir! You see, KEEN blades are **unconditionally guaranteed** to give you smooth, **comfortable** shaves..morning after morning, without pull or drag. Know why? Because they're especially **treated** to keep that keen-as-a-sword edge longer..longer..and **longer**. You betcha. Try KEEN blades just once. You'll **never** shave with **ordinary** stainless steel blades **again**. KEEN's the name..on sale from coast to coast.

When we smile we convey pleasure; when we frown we look and sound unhappy. Get a smile into this next commercial. Convince the listener that AROMA cigars are the aristocrat of smokes. SMILE!

If you smoke out of **habit**, you don't **really enjoy** smoking. What to do? Change your brand! How about an AROMA cigar? Yes, switch today to AROMAS for real, **deep-down** smoking **satisfaction**. The tobacco that goes into AROMA cigars is **blended** right...**aged** right. When you smoke AROMAS you get that **mildness and smoothness** you've been **missing** in **other** smokes all along. Perk up your taste **today** with..AROMA cigars. **Mild**...yet **so satisfying**...AROMAS are for **you**. AROMAS...the **aristocrat..of smokes.**

PRACTICE SCHEDULE—12th WEEK

1. **RELAXATION** 5 minutes.

2. **VOCAL DRILLS** 10 minutes.

3. **PRONUNCIATION** 10 minutes.

4. **ENUNCIATION** 10 minutes.

5. **PROJECTION** 10 minutes.

6. **CHARACTERIZATION** 10 minutes.

7. **PERSONALITY** Work well on this important phase to develop believability and sincerity in your work. SMILE as you speak. Make your words SMILE.

8. **READING** 15 minutes.

9. **COMMERCIALS** Apply the technique explained in this week's lesson to the commercials.

10. Reread the lesson a few times.

Lesson 13

The Pause

Judicious use of the pause is the mark of professionalism. Knowing when, how and where to use this attention-getting device gives the seasoned professional that finesse. The newcomer to the profession fears to make even the **slightest** pause; he calls it "dead air." A momentary suspension of your voice should last as long as it takes to snap your fingers, or to tap a pencil on the table. To make a pause unduly long is amateurish. There's a happy medium. However, if you wish to draw **special** attention to, say, a bargain price in a commercial, you may lengthen a pause for a count of two, that is as long as it would take you to snap your fingers twice. When you hear a jock or a newsman rush from sentence to sentence, from news story to news story, ignoring pauses along the way, you may assume that he had little or no training, or improper instruction. Usually, the broadcaster who rushes into, through and out of a commercial is a high-strung individual, anxious to get it over with.

The pause is used to a high degree of effectiveness by the musician, the raconteur and other professionals who perform for the public. Expert in the use of the pause is the politician who eloquently sways his constituents with his rhetorical rantings. There's a rule which will guide you in the proper use of the pause; it has two parts. Remember it well:

1. Place a pause **BEFORE** a word, a phrase, a sentence to create suspense—to command attention for what is to **follow**.

2. Place a pause **AFTER** a word, a phrase, a sentence to accentuate what **has been** said—to allow it to become impressed on the listener's subconscious.

A pause between news stories should be a **must**. Let me show you an example of what I heard one evening recently over a local radio station.

"...in which President Nixon told them everything is being done to alleviate the situation. In Philadelphia where a strike has taken..."

The President did **not** say that "...everything is being done to alleviate the situation in **Philadelphia** where a strike is..." It sounded that way because the man who read the news stories failed to pause momentarily between two stories. He should have read them this way:

"...everything is being done to alleviate the situation (PAUSE) In Philadelphia, where a strike has taken many..."

When doing commercials, place a pause between two adjectives, as explained in an earlier lesson. Place a pause before a telephone number and after it, if you can. If you can't, follow the number with music. Introduce the tune **over** music, not immediately following the telephone number. Here are a few striking illustrations:

WRONG "... and call them now at 6412764. Well, here's Hazel Scott..."

RIGHT "...and call them now. . . at 641 — 27 — 64, that's 641 — 27 — 64. (MUSIC FOR 15 SECONDS, FADE FOR...) Now, here's Hazel Scott...)

WRONG "...Here's an unusual, extraordinary opportunity to get two tubes of toothpaste for the price of one at the un-believably low, low price of only 79 cents. But you must act today!"

This is a well written commercial and on the surface, to the untrained, he would say: "This one I've got to hit with a hard sell!" Why? How would the professional jockey read it?

RIGHT "... Here's an unusual ... **extraordinary** opportunity to get two. . . tubes of toothpaste, for the price of one . . . at the unbelievably low . . . low price of only...79 cents! But you must act...**today!**

Read the last commercial through a few times, record it, then listen to yourself sound like an old pro. You see, it's simply knowing how and when to use a pause. The pause before the word **extraordinary** prepared the listener for the impact of a strong word. The pause after the word **two** accentuated the bargain. The same effect was produced after the first low to make second low sound impressive. (The second low should be voiced as low as possible.) A pause was expressly placed between the word only and the figure 79, again, to create suspense and place importance upon the bargain. And the final pause emphasizes the motivator to act today. Every commercial, when properly written, is composed according to a 4-part formula: the headline or attention-getter, the line which creates interest, the development or body message, and the motivator to create action.

Unless you're the only person who'll read the piece of copy—news, for example, which is read only once then discarded—do not make any pencilled notations on it, such as to denote pauses, inflections etc., to guide you in delivery. But you may wish to mark your copy when you practice on the commercials in the back of the book. Mark it this way:

Here's an unusual,   extraordinary opportunity to get two
    tubes of toothpaste for the price of one   at the unbelievably
low,   low price of only   79 cents! But you must act   today!

Of course, a comma is used by a writer to guide the reader as a separating mark; however, some announcers prefer to still add the virgule (/) so that they won't inadvertently run past the pause. Underscore the words you wish to emphasize or color. But let me hasten to repeat this: never mark up station commercials, promotionals etc., copy which must be read by other staff members. If you do, you'll do it only once, I assure you, because marked-up copy is difficult to read. The markings are extremely distracting for the seasoned broadcaster who is sufficiently experienced to voice a commercial or newscast without jotted guideposts. Furthermore, your markings could be in error and would tend to throw the next fellow way off on his delivery. Incidentally, there's another unwritten rule in broadcast stations in regard to keeping copy clean and in good condition. Marking copy is taboo in professional broadcasting.

So far, we have covered two of the four controllable mechanics of your voice: (1) quality (speaking in a pleasing or unpleasing tone), (2) timing (controlled rate of speed, pauses), (3) pitch (rise and fall of the voice on various levels) and (4) volume (the ability to speak in graded tones of loudness or softness, controlled volume).

Observe the pauses in the following announcements. As a time guide, snap your finger as you pause, or tap a pencil on the table. The faster your pace—the shorter the pause. The slower you speak—the longer the pause, but NEVER make a pause sound like dead air.

Here's a spanking new...a **revolutionary** way to wax your floors in just **half** the time it **used** to take to do the job. Yes, GLOSS is so **easy** to use...so simple to **apply**...and it dries to a hard, lustrous, durable shine...a **tough gloss**...in a matter of minutes. Unbelievable?...Yes, GLOSS is the **unbelievable** floor wax...because GLOSS takes the drudgery out of floor care. Save time...save money...watch your newspaper this week for a money-saving coupon to introduce **new**...GLOSS...the **only** floor wax that's guaranteed...**fully** guaranteed to please you the very first time you use it or your money back. GLOSS...in the bottle and one-gallon can...is now available in all hardware stores and supermarkets. Try...GLOSS...today!

Did you smile while speaking the preceding announcement? Did you lift the bold-face words? Did you emphasize the name of the product? Did you use a medium-hard sell? Were you enthusiastic in your approach? Please try it again.

Here's another:

Are you...wondering if it's bad breath or something that's holding you back from getting that promotion? Well, **don't take chances!** Use MINTSWEET...just to be **sure.** You see...MINTSWEET is **different**...MINTSWEET is **guaranteed**...to kill **millions**... of germs in the mouth...on **contact**...and germs, as you know, are the **cause**...of bad breath. Yes, MINTSWEET gives you **long-lasting** relief...that fresh...**clean** taste just lasts...and lasts...and lasts! Your breath stays **fresh**...because your mouth is clean...MINTSWEET...clean! MINTSWEET...at drug counters...**everywhere!**

Did you characterize the bold words? Did the word **different** sound DIFFERENT? Did the words **clean** and **fresh** sound CLEEEAN and FRESSSH? Did the hyphenated word, **long-lasting** sound LONNNNG-LASSSTING? Did you project on the word, you in the first line? You should have read the line: Are YOU...wondering...The phrase, **don't take chances!** should have sounded like a mild warning. Did the word, **millions** sound like MILLIONS? Lift it! The phrase, **on contact,** is a customer benefit; emphasize it! The word, **cause,** is a strong selling word. Lift it, too. Because the word, MINTSWEET (next to the last line) in a superlative degree modifies the word clean, it must receive a strong inflection.

Are you clipping newspaper and magazine advertising? If not, better start now. You'll work on them beginning with Lesson 18.

PRACTICE SCHEDULE—13th WEEK

1. **RELAXATION** 5 minutes.

2. **VOCAL DRILLS** 10 minutes.

3. **PRONUNCIATION** 10 minutes.

4. **ENUNCIATION** 10 minutes.

5. **PROJECTION** 10 minutes.

6. **CHARACTERIZATION** 10 minutes.

7. **PERSONALITY** Review the previous lesson. 10 minutes.

8. **THE PAUSE** Exercises as explained. 10 minutes.

9. **READING** 15 minutes.

10. **COMMERCIALS** Observe the use and rule of the pause in the commercials. 20 minutes.

11. Reread the lesson. Optional: Alternate pronunciation with enunciation.

Lesson 14

Inflection

Don't shout to attract attention—use inflections. Lesson 13 illustrated the use of the pause and color to effectively emphasize the importance of sales points and customer benefits. Now we'll discuss pitch and volume control, the third and fourth controllable qualities of the voice. They go hand in hand in this technique.

An inflection is a change in pitch or tone of voice, a modulation, a rise-and-fall process applied to such words which we wish to implant in the listener's subconscious mind; inflections tend to highlight important points. There are two types of inflections: the upward inflection and the downward glide. The humming exercises in Lesson 3 are expressly arranged in short upward and downward 5-tone scales to develop flexibility in preparation for this lesson on inflections. An inflection should never exceed a rise or fall of five tones. To overdo inflections, as to overplay color and pauses, makes for an amateurish approach.

As stated above, don't shout to place importance on a word. By gently raising the pitch of the word, you automatically increase the volume **sufficiently** to create the desired effect. We'll discuss the "hard-sell" commercial later. We are now speaking of the conversational, **informal** type of commercial, the style of announcing I personally prefer. Let me illustrate a few lines from a commercial in which upward inflections will highlight five important customer benefits. In printed form, italics or bold face are used to emphasize a word or phrase or sentence. In writing, such as you'll work with in commercial broadcasting, inflections are denoted by underscoring, but here we use bold face type.

AS WRITTEN: SEPTIC mouthwash acts **quickly** to kill millions of germs on **contact** and germs are the **cause** of bad breath.

The copywriter may underline important words to guide you; on the other hand, I have worked with advertising copy which was left entirely to the discretion of a professional announcer and his techniques. Now, let's use inflections, color and pauses to bring the above commercial to life!

AS SPOKEN: SEPTIC mouthwash acts quickly (PAUSE) to kill millions . . . of germs on contact . . . and germs . . . are the cause . . . of bad breath.

Let me remind you again that the pauses as denoted by dots should not sound like **dead air**...they are **momentary**. Tap your pencil to signify a pause. Think of an inflection as a glissando—a gliding action—from tone to tone, upward or downward. The **downward** inflection is mainly used to color such words as **dark, cold, low, miserable**, etc. Example:

Buy one now . . . at this low . . . low price.

The hard-sell type of announcing is fast fading from the scene, and so it should. I know for a fact that listeners and viewers resent the announcer who commands: **"Go to your druggist right now (2 AM) and buy a box!"** I have noted that many hard-sell hawkers lack the training in the finer techniques of the professional, conversational voice. Obviously, that's why they resort to shouting—to sound effective. The hard-sell technique (?) is easily and quickly learned. The pitchman and his "Tell ya wha' I'm gonna do!" routine has become a perennial laugh line, and so it is with the hard-sell announcer who is drawing guffaws in living rooms when he demands that his viewers **immediately** pick up a household product in their supermarket at **midnight**. Like many jazz musicians, they, too, lack control and blast!

To do a hard-sell you simply shout on every key word in the sentence instead of gently lifting only the words you wish to emphasize. Key words in a sentence are those that communicate a complete thought when articles, pronouns and conjunctions are omitted or only slightly intoned. Here are two commercials. The first, as written, the second as it would be voiced by a shouty, hard-sell announcer.

1. SEPTIC mouthwash acts quickly to kill millions of germs on contact and germs are the cause of bad breath.

2. SEPTIC MOUTHWASH ACTS QUICKLY (to) KILL MILLIONS (of) GERMS (on) CONTACT (and) GERMS (are the) CAUSE (of) BAD BREATH!!!

In my opinion, screaming a commercial, shouting at listeners, and using giant type to attract attention is a most insincere form of advertising, akin to the ballyhoo techniques of the circus, side-show barker who yells himself hoarse to attract attention to his dancing girls. Now, this week's commercials.

See the man with the **number-one** buy!...Your CARITE dealer. You bet! CARITE has been America's **favorite** automobile for more than fifty years...and right now, it's America **best**...automobile buy! So, come in **soon**...test-drive a CARITE **yourself.** It's the **best**...and ONLY way to really get to know CARITE as the year's **top** automotive value. Take your choice of models...pick your favorite style while the picking is still good. Next week may be too late. See your friendly...CARITE dealer first chance, but **hurry!**

Dandruff? Then listen! The **finest**...hair care in the world cannot CURE dandruff. Know why? Well, because the problem of unsightly dandruff goes much **deeper** than that...Dandruff problems start at the scalp. That's why DANDINE so **amazingly** goes to work **beneath** the scalp to medicate...to build new tissue...and its tried-and-tested medicated properties have been scientifically tested to **stop** dandruff where it **starts**...deep inside the scalp. DANDINE goes to work **immediately.** You feel that **blessed relief** from a dry,...**itchy** scalp the moment you apply...**clean-smelling** DANDINE. You see, this new DANDINE cleanses, lubricates and **conditions** your scalp...all in **one simple operation.** Your scalp becomes dandruff-free...healthy and vigorous. If dandruff is **your**...problem, don't waste another minute. Go to your favorite drug counter, ask for...DANDINE, in the new plastic, non-spill jar. DANDINE is medicated, yet it's pleasantly scented. Try...DANDINE.

Be very emphatic on this commercial. Lift bold-face words and informally advise the listener. Think of yourself as a dentist.

Why feel **half** safe? Why not use...STAYTITE to be sure...With STAYTITE you avoid **embarrassment and discomfort** when you speak or eat with dentures. When you use...STAYTITE, you feel **sure** of yourself. STAYTITE holds dentures **firmly** in place **all day long.**

STAYTITE is **guaranteed** to keep your dentures from **slipping, sliding** or **loosening** out of place. No old-fashioned **powder** adhesive can do **that**! With STAYTITE you eat the food you **want**...the things you like...steaks, an ear of corn, yes, even an **apple**. STAYTITE is **tasteless** and **harmless** to your precious dentures. Highly endorsed by the American Dental Association, STAYTITE is now available in two sizes. At your druggist...**now**!

This time you're an **insurance counselor**. Again be emphatic; stress the one-premium feature in this insurance policy. Advise the listener.

Have you heard about MUTUAL'S new family policy? If you're a family man, then this policy is for **you**. Here's **complete protection** for **every member of your family**; yes, even for children not yet **born**! MUTUAL'S Family policy is **unique** because you get **maximum** coverage...**full** protection, yet you pay only **one** premium. Your MUTUAL insurance man will gladly explain the many fine features found **only** in this unique family policy. Call him **first chance** you get. He's listed in the yellow pages under...MUTUAL...MUTUAL insurance.

Please carry the techniques learned thus far, inflections, pauses etc., over into the new phase of our work, the development of an authoritative news style.

PRACTICE SCHEDULE—14th WEEK

1. **RELAXATION** 5 minutes.

2. **VOCAL DRILLS** 10 minutes.

3. **PRONUNCIATION** 10 minutes.

4. **ENUNCIATION** 10 minutes.

5. **PROJECTION** 10 minutes.

6. **CHARACTERIZATION** 10 minutes.

7. **READING** 15 minutes.

8. **COMMERCIALS** Employ inflections and other techniques in announcements. 20 minutes.

9. Reread the lesson a few times this week. Are you reading news from press wire copy?

Lesson 15

An Authoritative News Style

The highly paid broadcast journalist uses the aforementioned techniques; he also emulates the raconteur—the professional storyteller. He doesn't merely read news stories. A child can do that. The professional newscaster **tells the news story**. There's the big difference! He knows how to speak with authority, that's why he has a following. To achieve this make-believe sound of authenticity, use your imagination to assume the mental attitude that YOU were **there**; that YOU **saw** it happen; that YOU **are** on the scene; that you **wrote** the story. Regardless of how you conjure it up, your voice will react—you'll **then** tell the story.

Three types of persons handle news material on the air. (1) The unbiased newscaster, who reports the news—**tells** the story. (2) The commentator who expresses his opinions—his own and not necessarily those of the station, the network or sponsor. (3) The analyst, who expertly examines the factors surrounding a news development and passes the results of his studies along to an audience. Each one is a specialist. One knows how to **write and report** a story, the second is qualified to be **opinionated**, the third, because he keeps himself abreast of developments is in a position to study and report why and how an event came to pass and what may be expected to follow suit.

As a disc jockey, report the news, be a **storyteller**, but keep your opinions to yourself—don't editorialize. Too many jocks talk themselves out of jobs. Just recently, a few nationally famous news personalities have been openly accused of being publicly opinionated. In addition to your daily newspaper reading, work for that tone of authority on the exercises which follow. Work diligently on the development of an authoritative news delivery. It's very important.

EXERCISE

Jack Stilwell, reporter on the scene, said **hundreds** of persons perished in the flood...the state's **worst**...disaster!

With its landing gear out of order the giant jetliner crashed on landing. All 129 passengers aboard...burned to death.

The bombing wiped out the entire city. Countless numbers were injured. At last report...500 residents...are still missing.

Twelve hours after the accident the child was still alive. Little Billy never regained consciousness. He died...this afternoon.

The President stated that the Vietnamese situation would probably worsen...before it would improve...according to a late White House report.

The woman's body...badly decomposed...was discovered yesterday. According to police officials...it was a case of suicide.

Make it a daily practice (see practice schedule) to read your newspaper out loud. Read the accounts **precisely**, as if you were telling the news to an imaginary listener sitting opposite you. Make pauses, as explained in a previous lesson. Feel the mood and value of each story. Read at a moderate rate of speed; don't hurry. Develop a professional story-telling style. Remember; YOU were there, YOU saw it happen. Make it sound that way. To help you attain a naturalness in your reading, occasionally read aloud the newspaper columns written by Washington commentators. But always **tell** the story. Test yourself on your tape recorder.

Five-minute and 15-minute news summaries clear the press wires in a newsroom at regular intervals. The 5-minutes summaries are available hourly, while the quarter-hour wrap-ups are sent through six and more times a day. If a station employs a news editor, the DJ will not have to concern himself with the gathering and editing of news. There may be times during your career when you'll be on your own, in which case you'll have to prepare your own 5-minute hourly summary. Proper editing of news in acquired only by experience. I usually suggest to my students to visit their local radio stations and request discarded teletypewriter copy. Do this, too. It's the best and quickest way of which I know to get the "feel" of professional newscasting. Your local station will gladly supply you with all the copy you need for your daily practice.

Here are two of the finest exercises to develop that authoritative tone and delivery. They are the famous **Lincoln's**

Gettysburg Address, and William Tyler Pages's The American's Creed, which was accepted by the House of Representatives, April 3, 1918 on behalf of the American people. Use all commas as breathing places. Make pauses momentary. Speak at a moderate rate of speed. Take your time. Make a news picture of the famous President's speech of November 19, 1863.

Fourscore and seven years ago our fathers brought forth on this continent a new nation, conceived in liberty, and dedicated to the proposition that all men are created equal.

Now we are engaged in a great civil war, testing whether that nation, or any nation so conceived and so dedicated, can long endure. We are met on a great battlefield of that war. We have come to dedicate a portion of that field as a final resting-place for those who here gave their lives that that nation might live. It is altogether fitting and proper that we should do this.

But in a larger sense we cannot dedicate, we cannot consecrate, we cannot hallow this ground. The brave men, living and dead, who struggled here have consecrated it, far above our poor power to add or detract. The world will little note nor long remember what we say here, but it can never forget what they did here. It is for us, the living, rather, to be dedicated here to the unfinished work which they who fought here have thus far so nobly advanced. It is rather for us to be here dedicated to the great task remaining before us—that from these honored dead we take increased devotion to that cause for which they gave the last full measure of devotion; that we here highly resolve that these dead shall not have died in vain; that this nation, under God, shall have a new birth of freedom; and that government of the people, by the people, and for the people, shall not perish from the earth.

Please note all the commas expertly placed in this oration. Pause momentarily at all commas. Speak at a moderate rate of speed. Allow your voice to drop—relaxed—and speak with authority:

I believe in the United States of America as a government of the people, by the people, for the people, whose just powers are derived from the consent of the governed; a democracy in a republic; a sovereign nation of many sovereign states; a perfect union, one and inseparable, established upon those principles of freedom, equality, justice and humanity for which American patriots sacrificed their lives and fortunes. I therefore believe it is my duty to my country to love it, to support its constitution, to obey its laws, to respect its flag, and to defend it against all enemies.

For a compilation of all types of speeches on various subjects, see This Is America, available in a paperback edition. (Pocketbooks, Inc. N.Y.)

Too many disc jockeys consider the weather forecast as of nuisance value. They "kick it around" just to get it over with, and the quicker the better. What they fail to realize is that the broadcasting of meteorological data is a vital public service. Devise ways and means to feature the commonplace. For example, request permission to tape forecasts over the telephone, directly from your nearest U.S. Weather Bureau, then add current temperatures, humidity etc. If your station doesn't program morning and evening weather shows, plan to produce one yourself. Discuss the idea with your program director. Instead of reading press wire service forcasts verbatim, rework the information to reflect your own personality, that is,

1. About the wind and the weather, says the man...
2. Weatherwise, this will be another cold and...
3. Today's weatherword—cold! According to the U.S. ...

Pages 222 and 223 in The Radio Program Ideabook describes a musical weather program. You may use that idea like this:

DEEJAY: Time, 7:44. About things weatherwise—cold!
MUSIC: I'VE GOT MY LOVE TO KEEP ME WARM, UNDER FOR B.G.
DEEJAY: Cold, yes, and windy, too.
TAPE: "Official weather forecast for Smithville and vicinity..."
MUSIC: UP TO COMPLETION
DEEJAY: Present temperature, 74 degrees, humidity 45 percent...

There are dozens of tunes whose titles describe weather conditions: Button Up Your Overcoat, Sunny, April Showers, Winter Wonderland, High On a Windy Hill etc., etc. The general idea is not to become stereotyped. Make your audience expect the unexpected. Think unique!

In the smaller radio station, in the absence of a farm director, the morning man must handle another type of specialized news—farm news. This material is obtainable from numerous sources, including the U.S. Department of Agriculture, your state department of agriculture and from your county agricultural agent. Farm news **must** be localized. Press wire services also transmit farm news summaries, but these must be carefully edited to contain information, both national and local, of interest to your specific agricultural area. Actually, the newcomer should be briefed by the PD as to what type of farm news should be aired; however, many programmers feel a definite disinterest in agriculture, which is a grave mistake.

A morning man wondered why he had few farm families in his audience. It was learned that every morning at 6:15 for almost 10 years he read the N.Y. Stock Market Reports, Dow-Jones averages of the previous day, etc. His PD slept through it all and was unaware that the DJ mistook the log notation, "Market Reports," to indicate stocks and bonds, instead of produce and livestock reports. Another DJ fed his Long Island farm families news about tobacco farming, cotton futures and Chicago livestock quotations, when farmers in his broadcast area produced potatoes, tomatoes, cauliflower, poultry products, etc. That's the way to lose your listenership. Work with your local National Grange, the 4-H Clubs, your county agricultural and extension home economics agents and the others. Arrange brief interviews, or suggest brief, taped talks to be interspersed into your shows. Feed them plenty of weather forecast information, frost and storm warnings, changes in wind direction. That's how to build a solid morning listenership. My advice to you is to contact your county ag agent. Be guided by his advice. It's his job to know about things agricultural. Fig. 15-1 is a typical news release available through county agricultural agencies.

PRACTICE SCHEDULE—15th WEEK

1. **RELAXATION** 5 minutes.

2. **VOCAL DRILLS** 5 minutes.

3. **PRONUNCIATION** 10 minutes.

4. **ENUNCIATION** 10 minutes. (Alternate with pronunciation)

PORK PRICES WILL REMAIN STEADY TO LOW

FOR BROADCAST RELEASE: 11-30-70
19 LINES

(GAINESVILLE, FLA.)---PORK PRICES WILL REMAIN STEADY TO LOW
DURING THE REMAINDER OF THIS YEAR AND THE FIRST HALF OF 1971.
UNIVERSITY OF FLORIDA AGRICULTURAL ECONOMIST DR. KARY MATHIS
TOLD SWINE PRODUCERS THAT ALTHOUGH CONSUMER DEMAND FOR PORK
SHOULD REMAIN FAIRLY STRONG, LARGE SUPPLIES OF BEEF AND
BROILERS WILL KEEP PRICES DOWN. DR. MATHIS SPOKE AT THE
RECENT 15TH ANNUAL SWINE FIELD DAY, HELD AT THE UNIVERSITY
OF FLORIDA. MATHIS SAID IF THE PIG CROP FOR WINTER AND
SPRING IS HELD AT LAST YEAR'S LEVEL, THE PORK PRICES WILL
REMAIN STEADY, BUT IF THERE IS ANY INCREASE IN THE SUPPLY,
PRICES WILL PROBABLY BE THE LOWEST SINCE 1965---GOOD NEWS
FOR CONSUMERS BUT NOT SO GOOD FOR THE PRODUCERS. HE SAID PER
CAPITA CONSUMPTION OF PORK THIS YEAR WILL AVERAGE AROUND 65
POUNDS, UNCHANGED FROM LAST YEAR, BUT FORECASTS AN INCREASE
FOR 1971. HE SAYS THE 1971 SUPPLY OF PORK WILL BE THE LARGEST
SINCE 1952. DR. MATHIS URGED SWINE PRODUCERS TO SUPPORT RESEARCH,
EDUCATION, AND PROMOTION EFFORTS THAT BENEFIT THE SWINE INDUSTRY.
"THE PORK INDUSTRY HAS BEEN NOTORIOUSLY RELUCTANT TO TRY TO SELL
OR PROMOTE ITS PRODUCT," HE SAID.

DWP   -0-

aaace NATIONAL BLUE-RIBBON WINNER
AMERICAN ASSOCIATION OF AGRICULTURAL COLLEGE EDITORS

Fig. 15-1. Typical radio news release made available through county agricultural agencies.

5. **PROJECTION** 10 minutes.

6. **CHARACTERIZATION** 10 minutes.

7. **NEWS** Headline exercises. 10 minutes.

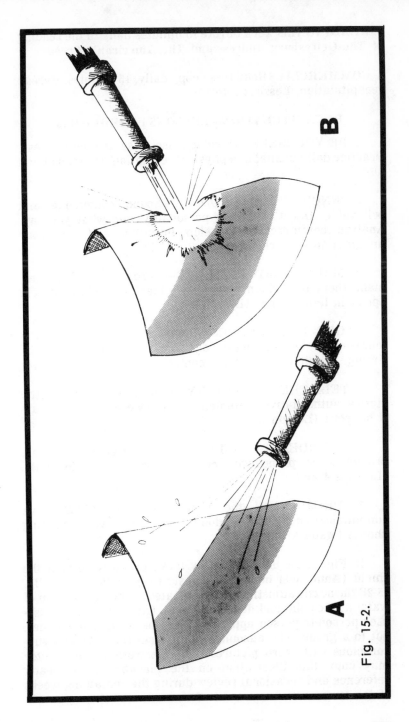

Fig. 15-2.

8. **READING** This week devote 15 minutes daily to the reading of **The Gettysburg Address** and **The American's Creed.**

9. **COMMERCIALS** Read fresh copy daily. 15 minutes. Reread recapitulation, Lessons 1 to 15.

RECAPITULATION—LESSONS 1 THROUGH 15

1. BE YOURSELF—Develop poise, ease and naturalness. Practice daily mental and physical relaxation. (Lessons 1 and 2)

2. KNOW YOUR PRODUCT—Sound convincing and believable. Inject a smiling personality **into** what you say. Analyze commercials. Develop initiative and put your imagination to work. (Lessons 7 and 12)

3. MAKE WORD PICTURES—Words have character, make them live! Shun monotonous black-and-white speech. Speak in living color. (Lesson 9)

4. GET THAT PROFESSIONAL SOUND—Develop the four controllable qualities of your voice: (a) voice quality, (b) timing, (c) pitch, (d) volume control. (Lessons 3, 13 and 14)

5. TELL THE NEWS STORY—Don't read news; tell the stories, authoritatively. Remember, **you** were there; **you** saw it happen! (Lesson 15)

6. BE UNDERSTANDABLE—Make your goal impeccable pronunciation; pronounce it **correctly**, pronounce it **distinctly**. (Lessons 4 and 5)

7. PROJECTION—the basic technique of effective communication. Project, don't introject. Avoid wearing phones to speak to yourself.

In Fig. 15-2A the wide spray lacks pressure to dent the shield. (Announcer **introjects**—speaks to an **audience.**) In Fig. 15-2B the nozzle adjustment concentrates a powerful stream of water at one point and **dents** the shield. (Announcer **projects**—uses person-to-person approach.) He speaks to **one** listener, not to a group. The announcer **impresses** the listener's subconscious with word pictures.) In classwork the instructor may copy this illustration on the blackboard for ready reference and occasional review during the remaining weeks of the term.

Lesson 16

Techniques of the Interviewer

Asking questions to get the right answers seems to be such a simple process—something we do daily, at home and at business—that it hardly seems necessary for an interviewer to employ techniques, and yet he must if he wishes to get more than yes and no answers. I have personally heard a few network interviewers ask guests **ridiculous** questions for which there were no logical answers; their interviewees simply smiled in reply. One fellow, who certainly should have known better, asked a downright **stupid** question, which stamped him as an amateur in the art of conducting effective interviews.

When President Kennedy was assassinated, a network reporter was sent to the home of the late President's sister-in-law in a Washington suburb. He waited on her doorstep until she emerged, obviously in a state of great concern. The TV reporter rushed up to her, microphone in hand, and blurted: "Were you shocked to learn of the assassination of President Kennedy?" Did he expect to get a negative answer? "No"? It requires no reportorial intelligence to ask questions like that or the following ones.

"Did you enjoy your world-wide cruise?" (asked of a movie star)

"Do you expect to win the election?" (asked of V.P. Hubert Humphrey)

You must prepare for an interview, become acquainted with the subject matter, know in advance precisely what leading questions you will ask. Study your questions. Make it impossible for your guest to answer yes or no, unless you want such an answer. The first three questions that follow will get nothing more than yes answers, while the last three are expressly posed to draw out information.

Did you enjoy your trip to Europe?

Do you expect to win the election?

Were you surprised to win first prize?

Tell us about your European trip.

If elected, what do you plan to . . .

How does it feel to win $50,000?

Sometimes a guest "freezes." You must then get her started. Example: If your question is, "How does your club plan to use this campaign money?" (SILENCE) "Will the County Home for the Aged benefit, and how do you expect to share the money"? The general idea is to get a guest started and to keep her talking. That's why an interviewer or a moderator should have some knowledge of the subject matter. I've had to prompt and nudge a number of guests through interviews. Before airtime, put your guest at ease. Bring her a glass of water. Speak for a few minutes about things other than the broadcast. Get her to relax. If you can, say something funny to draw a chuckle. Tell her the interview will sound best if informally conducted. Never ask personalized questions unless you first ask permission. A candid question for which your guest may be wholly unprepared to answer may well cause you and your guest embarrassment. If you're going to ask a question which will require facts and figures, first ask if your guest is prepared to give you such information. Don't put your guest on a spot. You merely ask the questions—she is the featured attraction. You won't make friends and be admired for asking a question which may tend to shame your guest. Actually, you may get yourself uncomfortably involved. Practice interviewing with friends and relatives. It's fun and very instructional.

INTERVIEW SOURCES

Aside from contacting social and church organizations, as previously suggested, for interesting public service interviews to dress up your show, try these:

> American Legion
> Kiwanis International
> The Elks
> The Lions Club
> Boy Scouts of America

Chamber of Commerce
Campfire Girls
Future Homemakers of America
American Cancer Society
The National Grange
Boys Clubs of America
Fraternal Order of the Eagles
American Heart Association
Veterans of Foreign Wars
Salvation Army
Knights of Columbus
Rotary Club
The Loyal Order of the Moose
Knights of Pythias
NAACP
Local Recreation Department
Future Farmers of America
Four-H Clubs
American Red Cross
Girl Scouts of the U.S.A.
United Cerebral Palsy Association
Catholic War Veterans of the U.S.A.
National Society for Retarded Children
Community Chest
League of Women Voters

There are many more local contacts for excellent local and human interest interview material. The **Radio Program Ideabook** (TAB Books, Blue Ridge Summit, Pa.) contains a complete list of national public service organizations with addresses. Also contact:

Sports Fisheries and Wildlife Service
Social Security Office
All recruiting offices
Parent-Teachers Association
Federal Housing Administration
Veterans Administration
School Superintendent
Local ASPCA or animal shelter

Unless you must do a last-minute live interview, make it a point to record your question-and-answer session in advance of airtime. By taping it, you may feel free to edit the tape to fit your allotted program time. If the issue is a controversial one, a speaker may suddenly flare up and sound downright "ornery"; he may even resort to spewing 4-letter words. It doesn't happen often, but there's always the chance that it may. This is another very good reason why interviews should be recorded in advance. I recall two announcers who, when something went wrong with their equipment, expressed themselves in 4-letter words while their mike keys were wide open. About indecent language on the air, the FCC says: "Whoever utters any obscene, indecent or profane language by means of radiocommunication, shall be fined not more than $10,000 or imprisoned for not more than two years or both." And the commission means it!

One time I invited the mayor and a well-known clergyman to the studios for a free-for-all discussion on a controversial issue relative to local government. It was a free-for-all, all right. When the shouting and the unkindly remarks began to fly, I had to signal the control-room engineer to take the program off the air. That was one show I **should** have taped.

Watch your language, even if you're alone in a quiet studio. It's not uncommon for a red warning light to burn out unexpectedly. Never assume that your monitor speaker is turned off; it could well be that your mike is "hot." The Storybook Man of early radio days, used to lull the nation's kiddies to sleep with his bedtime stories. Young old timers may recall his, "Goodnight, boys and girls. Sleep tight." One evening after the customary goodnight business, as usual, the red, on-the-air light went out, indicating that Storybook Man was off the air. The storyteller was in a clowning mood. To make sure that all in the soundproofed control room would hear him, he cupped his hands and shouted: "That'll hold the little 'buzzards' until tomorrow!" But he didn't use the word "buzzards." Panic broke out in the station. "Are you nuts, man? That went on the air, loud and clear," screamed the program director. You see, the red light went out because it burned out. The storyteller's mike was still "hot." Enraged parents from Maine to California bombarded the station with letters of indignation, and so ended the career of The Storybook Man. It wasn't the late Uncle Don who uttered the infamous phrase as some folks suppose. I know. I worked with both entertainers. The Storybook Man personally told me how he had cut short his career with a big mouth and a loose tongue.

There's also the bit about a young announcer with a 50,000-watt, key station, quite a dialectician, who clowned around one morning when he tested his microphone at sign-on. He did a brief impersonation of Adolf Hitler as a test. His test in German dialect went out over the air. The engineer thoughtlessly had flipped his mike switch to the "on-air" position instead of "audition." No harm was done, of course, but suppose the young deejay had uttered something not so funny. It could have been embarrassing.

In the 1950s, a famous Hollywoodian did a daily, half-hour network show. I was on control-room duty the morning his show opened with: "Why in hell don't you guys stop horsing around?" The blast almost bent the needle when the pointer banged into the red. Here's the way the show's producer later explained the faux pas. Because the red studio light wouldn't function, the director had to **point** a go-ahead cue at the vocalist. Still waiting for the red light to go on, as a cue for him to start his theme song, the singer became irked and in- terpreted the director's finger cue as last-minute "horsing around" and bellowed the angry blast. Despite his famous name, the artist's image was damaged, and the network had to drop his show. If it can happen to a professional, why can't it happen when you interview a **layman**? Better tape it.

Would you believe that an old pro with 25 years behind him could unintentionally break the FCC ruling on indecent language? An angry chief engineer brusquely yanked open the control-room door and, in 4-letter words, yelled a critique at a green deejay for riding too high a gain. Before the nervous newcomer could reach for his mike key, a barrage of blasphemy had gone on the air. See how easily it can happen— even to a broadcast veteran who knew all the rules?

Here's an unbelievable but true story. An evening an- nouncer on a good-music FM station felt an uncontrollable urge to experiment—to utter obscenities on the air—just to see what, if anything, would happen. One evening, during a concert program, he calmly faded the music, opened his mike, and defied the FCC ruling on using indecent language, with a 10-word obscene phrase! Uncannily, only **one** of the station's large listenership complained and threatened to report the incident to the FCC, but nothing ever came of the listener's charge. The fact still stands, though, you must be vigilant when you conduct interviews, and as I said earlier, watch what you say, even if it appears that you're alone in a quiet studio. A microphone might be listening!

PRACTICE SCHEDULE—16th WEEK

1. **RELAXATION** 5 minutes.

2. **VOCAL DRILLS** 5 minutes.

3. **PRONUNCIATION** 10 minutes.

4. **ENUNCIATION** 10 minutes. (Alternate with pronunciation)

5. **PROJECTION** 10 minutes.

6. **CHARACTERIZATION** 10 minutes.

7. NEWS Headline review in Lesson 15. 5 minutes.

8. **READING** Review two readings in Lesson 15. 10 minutes.

9. **COMMERCIALS** Read three or four newspaper ads per day. 20 minutes.

10. **INTERVIEWS** This is an important subject. If you can find an interested friend or relative, practice interviewing as per suggestions in this lesson. 20 minutes.

Lesson 17

How To Become An Ad Libber

There are three types of speechmaking: memorized, impromptu, and extemporaneous. The jock who must speak "off the cuff" is an extemporaneous speaker. Rarely does the jock speak verbatim, except when he reads newscasts and commercials. His chatter is definitely ad lib. Basically, you must know your subject in order to ad lib about it. The majority of newcomers, after a year or so on the air, acquire a natural "gift of gab" and become quite adept at this business of ad libbing. Yes, there is a way in which you may hurry the. development of the art.

When a student of mine found it difficult to ad lib, I devised an exercise for him, which, since then, has worked wonders for a number of others who wanted to quickly acquire the ability to speak "on their feet." Check your newspapers, magazines, LP jackets and the yellow pages of your telephone directory for advertisements. Such printed advertising is composed for **reading** purposes. You simply take the information contained in an advertisement and **talk** about it—put the ad into conversational form. There are numerous ways in which you may start such an announcement. The secret to ad libbing, in my opinion, is to think a fraction ahead of your speech. See in your thoughts what it is you **want** to say before you say it. Once you get the knack of this trick, you'll be able to keep talking endlessly. Here are a few illustrations.

AS PRINTED

Ann's Beauty Shop, 1900 Lawford Drive. No appointment needed. Open until 9 P.M.

AS AD LIBBED

Got a date tonight? Then, what are you waiting for? Ann's Beauty Shop is open until 9 tonight, and you don't need an appointment...just drop in for a facial, manicure or hair setting. No waiting, either. There are five operators on duty at

Ann's Beauty Shop, located at 1900 Lawford Drive, in town. Parking? No problem. Plenty of parking in the rear and it's free! (KEEP TALKING)

Speak about Pierre LeSeur, famous French hair stylist now at Ann's, give prices on facials and special weekend prices on settings and manicures. Don't think about **facts**. You are practicing to speak without notes; therefore, speak and **keep** speaking for as long as you can find words. When you run out of things to say, take another ad and work with that one. Try to take different approaches to the same ad:

1. Having a party this week end? Spruce up fast at Ann's...
2. Have you heard? The world-famous Pierre LeSeur's in town at...
3. Need a quick facial? Why wait for an appointment when Ann's...

Read the information on the backside of an LP jacket about the vocalist, the bandleader, etc. Don't read word for word or try to memorize the information, but use it as a **guide**. Ad lib around the background material, and keep talking about the singer, the band, the combo, the artists for as long as you can. Then, take another jacket and do the same. You're an old hand at ad libbing; you ad lib every day, on the street, at home, at business and in school. Apply the same technique to broadcasting.

When ad libbing, it's all too easy to become repetitious and redundant with your wordage. Sure, you don't want to noticeably pause in search of the right word, so you just naturally slip in the first one that comes to mind—one that's easy to recall from memory. But this practice can become habitual, and something must be done about it. It's not at all uncommon for a DJ to resort to pet expressions, outworn adjectives, hoary cliches and those hackneyed phrases. A writer, too, must guard against this practice.

Use the right word to say the right thing. The deejay, especially the apprentice, who must ad lib much of the time wants to keep talking to make a favorable impression, and he may well overuse or misuse a word such as **terrific** when making reference to something spectacular or outstanding. He may talk about the "terrific book" or the "terrific party" or a "terrific song," when actually he means an **absorbing** book or an **enjoyable** party, etc. The chances are he or she doesn't realize that the word **terrific** stems from the noun, **terror**, and means exciting when pertaining to fear. The deejay is a professional public speaker and like all those who work to the public, he leaves himself wide open to criticism—he cannot help it. The word, **funny**, is too frequently used to denote something strange, uncanny or unusual, when **funny** means, joking, merry, amusing. There are deejays who call every musical aggregation a **combo.** We must be specific to be correct. It would be advisable for you to get a copy of **Roget's Thesaurus**; a paperback copy costs under one dollar. Then, in addition to building up your general vocabulary as suggested in Lesson 4, also make a list of the words you overplay. Check your thesaurus for synonyms of these words; run down them once or twice a day until you establish a new memory pattern. You'll soon develop a command of our language in all of its ramifications.

In Lesson 10 we discussed, analogically, the deejay and the slide projector. In a very real sense, the deejay **is** a projector of pictures—mind or word pictures—images of what he sees, reads or visualizes in his imagination. Such images must ring true! Remember, the listener must believe. When you project a word picture of "last night's rain" will your audience "see" a spring shower or violent thunderstorm activity? You must be specific. When you make reference to a "house fire" do you mean the work of an arsonist and his destruction of an historic landmark? By describing the victim of the blaze as "an old lady," will your audience know what you mean the 85-year-old eccentric heiress to a local fortune? And when you chat on about "an old-timer celebrating his 103rd birthday" will your audience recognize the philanthropist who made possible the construction of the local children's hospital and contributes generously to every local charity and fund-raising campaign? Make pictures! Build your listenership by becoming interesting to listen to. Look over the following list of words:

Singer—vocalist, contor, yodeler, stylist, crooner, entertainer

song—tune, melody, selection, offering, aria, number, composition

actor—movie star, entertainer, performer, luminary, Thespian

end—finish, finale, conclusion, closing, epilog, terminal

house—homestead, landmark, bungalow, duplex, shack, lean-to, cabin fire—blaze, conflagration, inferno, flames, holocaust

band—combo, orchestra, strings, ensemble, symphony, quartet

new—unique, fresh, unusual, original, exceptional, unmatched

old—aged, antique, senile, ancient, historic, hoary, feeble, infirm

royal—majestic, sovereign, stately, regal, pomp, imperial, dignity

amazing—astonishing, astounding, striking, flabbergasting

wonderful—striking, stunning, spectacular, fabulous, marvelous, superb

Every DJ wants to tell amusing stories. That's fine, but keep yours short and make them funny. Detailed anecdotes may bore your audience. Check the classified sections of trade journals for the names of publishers who periodically issue lists of one- and two-liners to keep deejays constantly supplied with fresh material. One such deejay service is HOLLYWOOD GAGLETTER, mailed monthly to hundreds of the country's top deejays, TV comics and night-club MCs. For further information about HOLLYWOOD GAGLETTER, write the publisher, Ed Orrin, Boyer Road, Mariposa, California 95338. (See Fig. 17-1.) You may keep a cross-indexed file on such material by typing jokes and other matter on 3 x 5 index cards (one to a card) and file them alphabetically and under subject matter. Keep your chatter clean and aboveboard. Don't talk yourself out of a job and FCC license. See Lesson 16, "The Techniques of the Interviewer," for the FCC ruling on the use of indecent language. Pages 189 and 190 and Chapter 13, "The Art of Ad Libbing" in The Man Behind The Mike, should make interesting reading for you, too.

A New Mexico DJ writes: "I use book-of-knowledge material for ad lib purposes and listeners react very favorably to mystifying questions." I'm not at all surprised. Invite audience participation. Ask listeners to send in unusual news items, or questions and answers about the spectacular. I started quite a trend one time when I read a short poem sent in by a listener. The idea caught on fast. From then on I was

To avoid that rundown feeling —
cross streets carefully.

Definition of a beauty parlor: A
beauty parlor is a place where a woman
gets a faceful of mud and an earful of
dirt. No?

How do you know when you're getting
old? Well, sir, it's when the gleam in
your eye is only the sun hitting your bi-
focals, that's when.

Ever hear the one about the old
fellow who took i'

— 2 —

Remember the time when you could
kiss a girl and taste nothing but the
girl?

Today's definition. What is an
optimist? An optimist is a guy who keeps
his car motor running while he waits for
his wife to show.

Here's good advice! If your wife
wants to learn to drive the family car —
don't stand in her way.

Why is it that the rainy days for
which we save our money, always manage
to come during vacations?

You've reached middle age when
your wife tells you to pull in your
stomach, and you already have.

A mother who can remember her
husbands first kiss, has a daughter
who can't remember her first husband.

Definition of a seed catalogue:
A seed catalogue is a book which shows
you what the seeds you planted would
have looked like if they had ever come
up.

I wear the pants in my family —
under my apron, that is.

He said:
Just set it and forget it — that's
all.

Then there's the bit about the
side-street shop in London with a sign
in the window reading: "We buy junk &
sell antiques."

A little girl and her brother were
observing their parents prepare to go
to a party. Daddy helped Mommy struggle
with the zipper on her dress. Then Mommy
tied daddy's bow tie. When Daddy
fastened Mommy's necklace, the little
boy piped up with, "I wonder whey they
make us dress ourselves?"

A vacation is supposed to put you
in the pink. Instead it puts you in the
red.

Speaking of vacations, it's a
long-awaited rest, but not so for the
pocketbook. Right?

My wife says I'm old-fashioned
because I expect her to help me with
the dishes.

A woman is happy if she has two
things: Furniture to move around and
a husband to move the furniture.

Marriage is like a charity bazaar,
the admission fee is very little, but
it will cost you all you've got to get
out of it.

A young bachelor is like a clock
without a shepherd. An old bachelor
is like a shepherd without a flock.
Hmmmm.

Old gardeners never die — they
just spade away. Well, don't they?

Said the army commander, "Fire
at will!" Asks the recruit, "Where is
he, Sir?"

Now, a thought for the day:
Men say of women what pleases them —
women do with men what pleases them.

Fig. 17-1. Samplings taken from a current issue of
HOLLYWOOD GAG LETTER, a monthly service for
deejays.

flooded with poems. Offer inexpensive premiums, such as ballpoint pens, calendars, memo pads, etc., to your contributors. You may be able to work out a reciprocal deal with your local movie theatre. If they will furnish you with a dozen passes a week as prizes, agree to give the current picture a plug on your show when you award the tickets. If you want to encourage audience participation give this idea a try:

Well, this morning's question comes from Mrs. L.D. of Willston. She asks: How many ribs has a snake? I didn't know the wriggly things had any. That's the question. How many ribs has a snake? I'll check Mrs. L.D.'s letter for the answer, and you think about it out there while Ella Fitzgerald sings...

Audience participation is essential. It makes ad libbing easy and effortless. If you can make it, file away five or six items of interest or gags a day. In a year you may well have a collection of as many as 2,000 choice items. A metal file, which holds at least 1,500 cards will keep your collection clean and fireproof. Start thinking about your collection now. Here are a few helpful titles.

Guinness' Book of World Records (Bantam Books, N. Y.) containing 400 pages of highly informative answers to things spectacular, is an excellent quick-reference book for the deejay. Another thick volume I have in my library is **What's the Answer?** by Fred Garrigus (Books Inc. N. Y.). This is a storehouse of questions and answers to entertain as well as to instruct. **10,000 Answers to Questions** by Frederick J. Haskins (Grosset & Dunlap, N. Y.) may be out of print, but it's a good source of unusual information for libbers. Of course, unrivalled is the world-famous **Book of Knowledge.** If you happen to own the entire 20-volume series, fine! But, for convenience sake, get the paperback condensation, which contains choice material selected from the 20 volumes—the creme de la creme. You may choose from a number of categories: nature, animals, science, plant life, etc. You'll find the answers to most frequently asked questions, on subject matter which will perk up a drowsy audience. Here are a few questions chosen at random:

How big is space?
Is there a hole in the sky?
Do insects have brains?
What's inside the Mexican jumping bean?

Audiences love to get into the act, so plan a contest as I did, using 5-part questions. Following the FCC rules of conducting contests, covered elsewhere in this book, set a deadline, say a month away, or if you wish, make it a regular weekly feature. Have disinterested judges choose the winners, with three out of five to score. In the **Radio Program Ideabook** you'll read how I conducted such a contest with thirty sponsors. Our grand prize, a jackpot of sponsors' products, was valued at $1,000. You may use something similar. This sort of thing gives you a chance to ad lib. There's only one way to become a good ad libber, and that's to find something to ad lib about.

You may want to try a musical game of skill such as I'll cite later. Build up your file. Clip short but unusual items from newspapers and magazines; use them on the air, ad libbed, of course, then suggest contributions to your audience. Your listeners will keep you supplied. Paste these items (with rubber cement to prevent curling) on cards and file them away with your gags. I have a collection of over 7,000 items clipped from yellowed pages of magazines and newspapers from way back when.

Don't overlook the many animal lovers in your audience. Include brief anecdotes about pets. Your listeners will appreciate your thoughtfulness. Announce lost cats and dogs; try to find the owners of strayed animals. I made this a feature on my news program and gained many loyal listener friends. I stopped at nothing: a strayed cow, a screaming monkey swinging from a tree limb, a parakeet that had flown the coop, a frantic collie in the village lake, trying to swim for shore, etc. I used them all. You will earn the eternal gratitude of animal lovers if you take the little effort required to devote a 10-minute portion of your show to "Your Pet and Mine." If you like, invite a local veterinarian for an occasional interview to discuss the feeding and care of pets. Invite the animal owners in your audience to submit questions about animal care and so on. All this will offer you the chance to become an expert ad libber, and it makes good listening, too.

A great way to make friends with the younger listeners in your audience is to encourage them, too, to take active part in your program. Make your show a kind of teenage bulletin board. Request the youngsters to submit gags and things, tidbits about school proms, contests, record hops, etc. Award your contributors with 45s and LPs. Every radio station has duplicates on hand, plus the discards, the discs program directors can't use, such as, rock tunes by unknown artists. When possible dedicate a tune to a faithful listener-contributor, but always credit the source if you want the contributions to continue to come in. It's true, the sweetest music in the world is the sound of a person's name, especially when he or she hears it over the radio.

Of course, as I mentioned in passing, the announcer on the air during mid-morning should prompt the participation of the homemakers listening. Ask them to send in announcements of church socials, card parties, club meetings, fund-raising campaigns and such. Naturally, it is not necessary to credit these items to contributors, but when some special out-of-the-ordinary story or poem is contributed, the sender's name should be mentioned as an expression of your appreciation. The movie ticket award is appropriate with mature listeners as well as with teenagers, but don't become involved by presenting passes to R and X picture shows. If you want to do a quick check on your listenership, start some simple contest and offer movie tickets or LPs as prizes. You'll quickly learn whether or not you have your quota of listeners.

When I first went into the business I was assigned the morning trick on a new station which was in operation for less than a month. I was a "green" announcer, on the air less than a week, and, like all apprentices, I wondered how many people were listening to me. Did I have an audience? The amateur actor can't resist peeking through a hole in the curtain to see how many people are watching his performance. I had to do some "peeking," too. I clipped poems and unusual articles from magazines and read them, as though they had been sent to me. Gradually, as the idea appealed to listeners, I was flooded with contributions. But the concrete proof I was seeking came about a week before the holidays. I ran across a recipe for Christmas cookies and decided to broadcast it. I don't know how it happened, but it did! Instead of 1 **teaspoon** of baking powder, I, inadvertently, read 1 **cup** of baking powder, which would have rocketed my cookies into orbit. Phones began to ring and letters of correction poured in. One listener baked a batch of the goodies and sent them to my home as a Christmas gift. The note inside the box read, "Here are your cookies. I didn't dare use one cup of baking powder as you suggested. You don't know anything about baking, do you? Merry Christmas, Hal!" I, then, knew I had an audience!

In reference to my earlier suggestion to use the information on the backs of LP jackets to guide you in your ad libbing, a listener, in a fan letter to a former student now turned pro DJ, asked him, "Are you reading or ad libbing? You sound readey." It's most unusual for a radio fan to be so frank; nevertheless, she was correct. The DJ sounded readey because he actually **read** the information instead of **ad libbing** around it as I had suggested in the first place. Printing on LP jackets very definitely is intended to be read and not to be spoken, as you'll quickly note in the examples which follow:

AS PRINTED "Almost a decade passed while the songstress suffered severe setbacks, careerwise. She achieved stardom only after..."

AD LIBBED It was rough going for the blonde singer for almost ten years. But she made it to the top only after she...

AS PRINTED "Sparkling, elegant and buoyant, the first waltz was born in 1816 in the inns and beer gardens of Vienna's rural suburbs."

AD LIBBED It was back in 1816 when old Vienna danced its first waltz in the inns and beer gardens of that gay city.

Sometimes an album jacket reveals some unusual information, or some quotation worthy of broadcasting. When it does, by all means read from the jacket, but do as I did—avoid being called "readey." Tell your listeners that you are going to read, like this:

    1. According to this album jacket..."Ella Fitzgerald has now..."
    2. The way Tony Martin says it..."I think the trend of new..."
    3. Let me read a bit of what it says here..."After ten successful..."
    4. Here's how Doris Day feels about her career..."If I had to..."

The periods signify pauses and a momentary pause will denote a quote. There's no need to use the outworn and outdated "...and I quote" or "...end of quote." Simply pause momentarily before you read verbatim and again before ad libbing, for example:

(AD LIBBED) It was back in 1816 when old Vienna danced its first waltz in the inns and beer gardens of that gay city. In that year Thomas Wilson, in one of his writings, described the then unique tune in three-quarter time this way: ...(READING) "The waltz is generally admitted to be a promoter of vigorous health and productive of a hilarity of spirits." ...(AD LIBBING) Promoter of vigorous health? ...Wonder what the man would say about our mod rock tunes?

Speaking of rock tunes, naturally, the mod set would fine little if any interest in the commentary quoted above, but I used it for explanatory reasons.

We have a few more interesting points to discuss related to the art of ad libbing. Sometimes a tired, old quip can be freshened up with a breezy line of dialect. For instance:

AS PRINTED When the maternity nurse showed the new father his set of triplets, he said, "OK, we'll take the **middle** one."

AS AD LIBBED Hear about the Irishman who became the father of triplets? When the maternity nurse held up the three babies for the new father to see, he scratched his head: "Will noo, Oi t'ink we'll tak' the red-headed one."

Dialect quips must be used sparingly and then only by an expert dialectician. Avoid dialects which may cause repercussions: Negro, Yiddish, etc. A Mexican-American group, at the time of this writing, is protesting the Mexican image being created by TV's cartoon character, the long-moustached "bandito" who steals potato chips. In broadcasting we say, "when in doubt—leave out."

Don't become a movie critic or a book reviewer. Deejays used to make interesting chit chat about shows they saw and books they read, but when you consider today's crop of pictures, a majority of them low-calibre productions, why get involved with parental indignation? Leave such information for the newspapers to print. Don't ever discuss, or become opinionated on, a racial issue, a local strike, demonstrations, religious disputes, etc. No matter what your personal feelings, keep them to yourself. When stories appear in press wire copy, read about them, objectively and unbiased. Yours is a music-entertainment show; stay in the middle of the road. Leave news, issues and the like to the discretion of your news editor. More about news in Lesson 18. See also Lesson 15.

PRACTICE SCHEDULE—17th WEEK

1. **RELAXATION** 5 minutes.

2. **VOCAL DRILLS** 5 minutes.

3. **PRONUNCIATION** 10 minutes.

4. **ENUNCIATION** 10 minutes. (Alternate with pronunciation)

5. **PROJECTION** 10 minutes.

6. **CHARACTERIZATION** 10 minutes.

7. **NEWS** Work for authoritative delivery on press wire copy or newspaper. 15 minutes.

8. **COMMERCIALS** Fresh copy daily. 20 minutes.

9. **AD LIBBING** Your success will depend greatly on your ability to ad lib. Practice **indefinitely** on the drills and LP jackets. 20 minutes.

Lesson 18

The Control Room

The control room of a broadcast station is a sanctum sanctorum—the heart of its operation—a maze of mysterious buttons, knobs and switches, meters, patchcords and cables (Fig. 18-1). It is the soundproofed cubicle in which the deejay spins and chats and, in bigtime operations, earns the fabulous salary of the movie star. It's hard work. Literally, there's never a quiet, relaxing moment in any control room when a conscientious deejay is on duty. Telephones must be answered, half-hourly meter readings must be noted, three logs must be kept updated in accordance with FCC rules and regulations, tape recorders must be threaded and reels rewound, records pulled and filed away, news quickly edited and read on-air—for eight hours a day. In most stations he is relieved for a one-hour lunch break, in which case, he works alternately with a newsman, but there are the small operations in which a jock, for the most part of the day, works alone. As I said before, the jock's job is one of complexities, a highly specialized occupation.

There are standard broadcast terms (some call it jargon) and hand signals you should know about. For example, when you can't talk to an announcer in a studio, a simple hand signal from the control room will do it. To point to the clock on the wall will only confuse the announcer; it tells him nothing. But to hold your forefinger up clearly signifies that he has only one minute left to talk. In Fig. 18-2, to get you off to a proper start, you'll find drawings of the popular hand signals used in broadcasting.

From this point, until you begin work on the readings and commercials in back of the book, work daily with the newspaper and magazine clippings which you have collected for practice purposes. Practice on at least four announcements daily. Choose fresh copy each day. Try to quickly analyze and set the mood or character of a commercial. Of course, continue doing 15 minutes of reading from your newspaper daily. Do this indefinitely. The announcements and readings in back of the book are intended for your advanced development.

Fig. 18-1. Modern design in studio-transmitter operation. Notice built-in cartridge machines. In the background are one-kilowatt AM and FM transmitters with the FM frequency monitor. (Courtesy Gates Radio Co.)

127

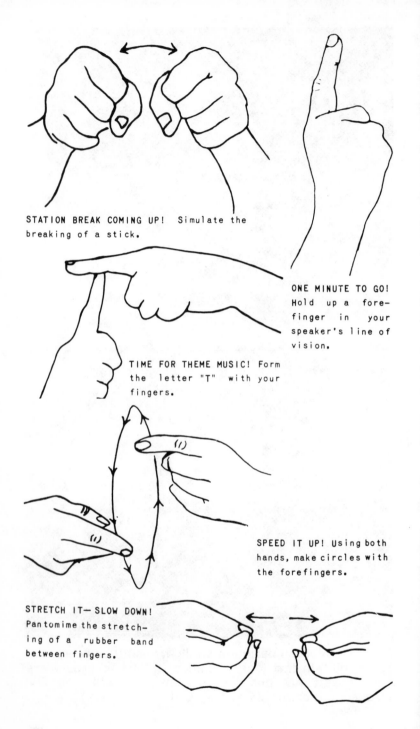

STATION BREAK COMING UP! Simulate the breaking of a stick.

ONE MINUTE TO GO! Hold up a forefinger in your speaker's line of vision.

TIME FOR THEME MUSIC! Form the letter "T" with your fingers.

SPEED IT UP! Using both hands, make circles with the forefingers.

STRETCH IT— SLOW DOWN! Pantomime the stretching of a rubber band between fingers.

128

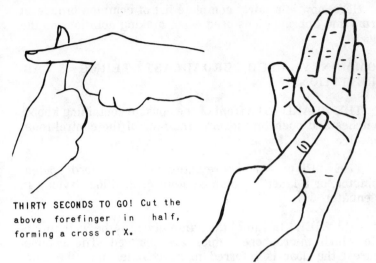

THIRTY SECONDS TO GO! Cut the
above forefinger in half,
forming a cross or X.

SPOT ANNOUNCEMENT COMING UP!

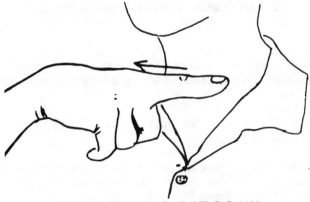

CUT MY MIKE; TAKE IT OFF THE AIR!

TRANSCRIPTION COMING UP! Pantomime the spinning of a record as
when finger cueing a transcription.

GIVE ME THE MIKE! Point to the microphone, then to yourself.

GO AHEAD! Point sharply, as if shooting, at your speaker. Always avoid unnecessary hand movements in a control room. They
may be misunderstood as hand signals.

Fig. 18-2.

Here, now is a fairly complete list of common broadcast terms and abbreviations used when making notations on the logs.

COMMONLY USED BROADCAST TERMS & ABBREVIATIONS

THE BOARD—The front of the console containing knobs, switches and operating levers—the face of the control-room console.

THE "POT"—An abbreviation of the word, potentiometer, or a fader, a volume-output controlling device; an attenuator.

CHANNEL—In radio, the name given to the wall outlets into which microphone cables are plugged. The channel nearest the door is referred to as channel one; the communications cable between studio and control room.

HOT MIKE—An expression denoting an open microphone, sometimes called a "live" mike. The opposite of a "dead" mike.

LOG—An authentic record of performance; a program log, a transmitter log, a production log, a program schedule, etc.

LEVEL—Designating the quantity or volume of sound output—a high or low level.

RIDING GAIN—Broadcast jargon meaning to monitor the volume indicator on the board; to make adjustments in volume output; to observe level.

TICKET—Another broadcast expression meaning an engineer's license: 1st ticket, 2nd ticket, etc.

XMITTER—An abbreviation for transmitter.

TABLES—Turntables.

BREAK—Refers to a station break between programs usually used for station identification; 30-second pause between network programs.

ID—An abbreviation for station identification.

REMOTE—Denotes a place of broadcast away from the studios; out-of-station program.

PATCH—A broadcast term meaning to connect two points: patching two circuits with a patch cord; to temporarily complete a circuit. (Notice the unique, built-in patch panel on the left in Fig. 18-4.)

SPOT—General term for an announcement, especially a commercial message.

THE NEEDLE—The pointer of the volume indicator.

ON THE NOSE—On time; sometimes expressed "on the button."

TRACK—A band on an LP; the recorded portion of a transcription; sometimes referred to as a "cut."

CUT IT—An expression meaning to take a program off the air; cut it short.

COPY—A manuscript prepared for printing or to be broadcast.

ET—Abbreviation of electrical transcription; usually to denote a 16-inch disc recorded at 33-1/3 RPM, as differentiated from an LP or a 45 RPM.

STRETCH—A term denoting a slow-down in the timing of a show; to stretch out a program. (See hand-signals, Fig. 18-2.)

AFFIDAVIT SPOT—A commercial announcement which must be certified as having been performed. (See Lesson 19 for detailed explanation.)

CA—Commercial announcement

SA—Sustaining announcement

PSA—Public service announcement

PROMO—Program promotional

LC—Local broadcast

NT—Network origin

NS—News broadcast

SP—Sports broadcast

PL—Political broadcast

ED—Educational broadcast

AG—Agricultrual broadcast

MS—Music

Also see Fig. 18-11, a commercial program log showing how the above coded abbreviations are used to describe the type of show and nature of the material broadcast.

MICROPHONES

While we're on the subject of the DJ and his control room, let's talk briefly about so-called, "microphone technique." Freely translated this "technique" is purely a matter of using one's common sense when working with today's super-sensitive microphones. Here are a few of my own experiences with various such contraptions.

First of all, if your voice quality, like mine, is heavy and chesty, if the resonance in your voice causes booming, you'll have to avoid working directly to a microphone placed at **chest** level, as when a table mike is used. I am not saying that you should demand any special mike setup—that would be inadvisable and unnecessary. I said you should not work **directly to** such a microphone. If you can, tilt the mike a few inches **backwards** to enable you to speak **over** it. If it won't tilt, turn the instrument slightly to the left or right, so that you may speak to it **diagonally**. If the microphone is suspended from a boom, raise it a few inches over your head (in front of you) and tilt the mike **downward** to allow you to speak **under** it. In a control room you'll work with either a table mike or one suspended from the ceiling or from a boom, or it may be mounted on a kind of gooseneck contrivance. In any case, it will be adjustable to some degree (Fig. 18-3).

Former stage actors, who are especially trained to articulately project their voices to the back of a long auditorium, sometimes encounter mike problems when they get into broadcasting. I came to radio directly from the stage, and

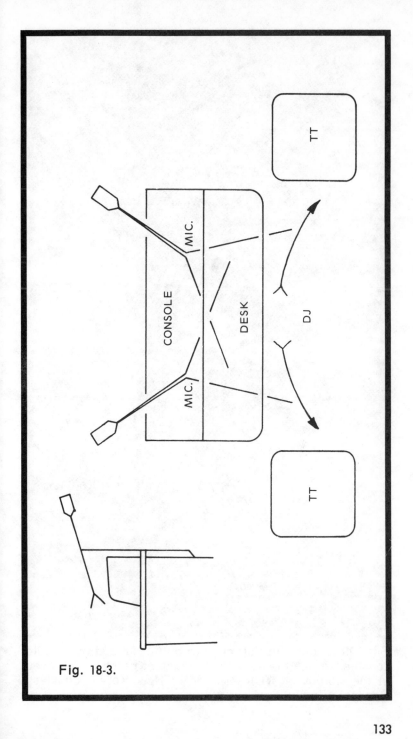

Fig. 18-3.

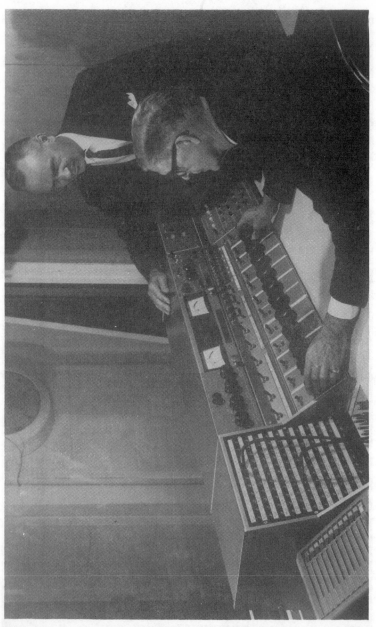

Fig. 18-4. Close-up of custom-built, solid-state, audio console. Notice the built-in, convenient patch panel, used in the studios of WOR-AM-FM in New York. (Courtesy General Electic)

having worked thoroughly on my diction, I was amazed to learn that the plosives in my words "popped." Especially did this occur when I spoke over a velocity mike. A colleague jokingly remarked that the t's at the ends of words sounded like sneezes. Of course, a reasonable speaking distance from a mike must be observed whether you have a light or a heavy voice and regardless of the type of microphone, velocity or dynamic. I used to quickly set my distance like this: With an open hand and fully outstretched fingers, place your thumb to your lips, then move the mike towards you until it makes contact with your small finger. That's it—about 8 to 10 inches—not any nearer for normal speech purposes.

To properly voice a **whispering** type of commercial, work nearer to the mike than you normally would. To avoid blasting

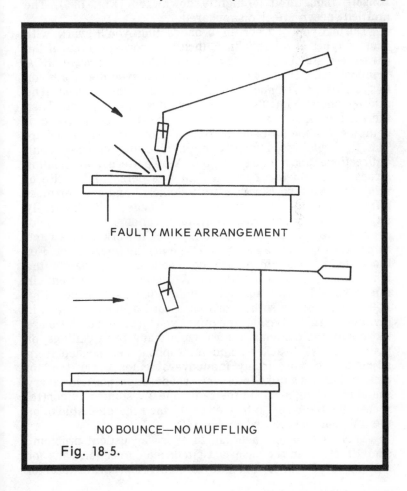

FAULTY MIKE ARRANGEMENT

NO BOUNCE—NO MUFFLING

Fig. 18-5.

on a hard-sell, step back an additional six inches or so. Never work with a microphone in a cozy corner or in a small cubicle, and many so-called control rooms are little more than over-sized telephone booths. Avoid speaking over a mike which is backed up by a ledge, screen, wall, window or equipment. You'll sound muffled—"dead." To broadcast in a long, narrow room will duplicate the effect produced by an "echo cham-ber." We had a control-room problem one time in which the mike, suspended from a boom, was lowered directly in front of announcers at chin level. The deejays had no choice but to direct their voices downward where the vibrations were trapped in a box stacked with commercial copy. The solution was simple. We raised the microphone until it hung over the console, then tilted it slightly downward (Fig. 18-5). The muffled-speech effect disappeared.

During your career in broadcasting you'll work with various types of microphones, including perhaps a few of the old timers still in use today. The established, proven, RCA "ribbon" mike (Fig. 18-6) has faithfully served the profession for 30-plus years, and it is still being manufactured. The microphone in Fig. 18-7 is a modern design table type. Then there's the RCA "capsule" mike, a most versatile piece of equipment when suspended from a boom for group pickup. The "capsule" is instantly adjustable for unidirectional, bidirectional and nondirectional pick-up patterns. Still holding strong here and there in the field is a personal favorite of mine, the Western Electric "salt shaker," and another most efficient microphone is the GE "bird cage" with its easily adjusted pickup patterns, from unidirectional to a cardioid, heart-shaped pattern. Undoubtedly, you'll work with a hand mike (see Fig. 18-8) an essential type for the interviewer. For those roving jobs which demand freedom of the hands, the lapel mike is ideally suited. A newer development in microphone design is the lightweight "tie clasp" model (Fig. 18-9) which may also be worn on a cord around the neck in lavaliere fashion. Besides the mikes you tote around, there are those with table stands, mikes which hang from ceilings, or fasten to desk brackets, and microphones suspended from adjustable booms, freely maneuverable for every kind of pickup. There's a mike for every broadcast purpose, for every sound-recording need; in the radio and TV studios, in control rooms, for the street interviewer, in the recording studio, on the TV sound stage and movie set.

There's a logical solution to every acoustical problem; sometimes, as in the case just cited, the correction calls for nothing more than a mere adjustment. A program director

Fig. 18-6. Old standby RCA "ribbon" velocity microphone, still a favorite piece of equipment after 30-plus years of service to the profession. (Courtesy RCA)

Fig. 18-7. Representative of modern design in table microphones is this RCA Model BK-1A.

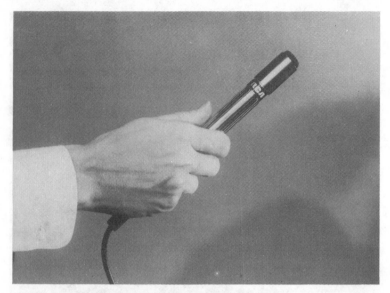

Fig. 18-8. Handy and needed, the RCA BK-16 is a must for the roving reporter, nightclub MC and news interviewer.

Fig. 18-9. Slick trick in microphone design. RCA BK-12A with its tie clasp feature, leaves news correspondent's hands free to hold copy or to move about on the scene to indicate points being discussed or described.

noticed that the voices of his announcers faded every time they swivelled from turntable to turntable to read the song titles on LP labels, or when deejays reached to the left or to the right for recordings, tapes or the production log. Knowing the cause of the off-mike effect, the problem was quickly solved. The single, unidirectional velocity microphone, suspended from the ceiling on an adjustable cable, was replaced by two modern, dynamic mikes with wide pickup patterns. Mounted on brackets above the console and adjusted to the proper angles, the instruments picked up voices over a semicircular area, as illustrated in Fig. 12-10. If you should run into any problems, try simple things first. Your chief engineer is an electronics specialist. He has studied acoustics and microphones. Be guided by his sage advice.

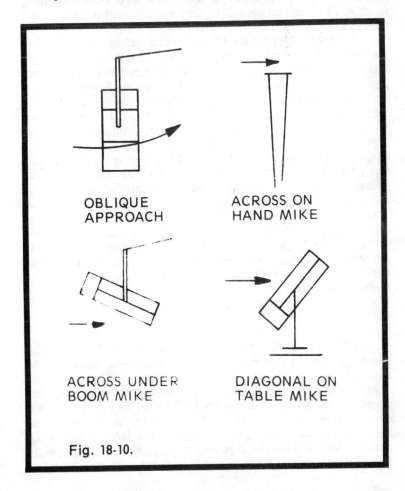

OBLIQUE
APPROACH

ACROSS ON
HAND MIKE

ACROSS UNDER
BOOM MIKE

DIAGONAL ON
TABLE MIKE

Fig. 18-10.

LOGS

Keeping accurate records of the precise times when announcements and programs are broadcast, when station identifications are aired, taking half-hourly transmitter-meter readings and entering them on what are termed "logs" are generally considered necessary nuisances in a control room, but they must be done. The Federal Communications Commission regards such exacting paperwork as highly essential; the FCC may, at any unforeseen time, request a station to submit certain logs for examination, or an FCC inspector may well drop in for an inspection. As you will learn when you study the F.E. Bulletin No. 4 and its accompanying reference material, much emphasis is placed upon accurate log keeping in the FCC examination to secure a commercial radio operator permit.

In a transmitter-studio type of operation, both transmitter and program logs must be kept updated. In a combination AM-FM station, the jock has to keep himself abreast of a program log (or production schedule as it is sometimes called), AM **and** an FM operations logs. On general requirements relating to logs, the FCC says: "The licensee or permittee of each standard broadcast station shall maintain program, operating and maintenance logs. Each log shall be kept by the station's employees having actual knowledge of the facts required...- shall sign the appropriate log when starting duty and when going off duty..." (**Rules and Regulations** Sec. 73.111.) Because of the importance of the subject, I suggest that you read and study Sections 73.111 through 73.119 of the **FCC Rules and Regulations**, found in the Field Engineering Bulletin No. 4 to gain a thorough understanding of the rulings on accurate keeping of broadcast logs. (See Fig. 18-11, a typical radiostation program log and the FCC required code to identify each entry.)

SIGN-OFF

So far we've discussed the general station duties of the morning man. The evening man, the fellow who signs off the station, has a less hectic time of it. In the smaller station he may lock the front door and work in complete privacy for the night. If the station is a network affiliate, he can relax in a comfortable, control-room swivel chair, throw his feet up on the desk and devote the evening to his electronic studies. Of course, there are the deejays who invite friends in for the night for gabfests, bear-and-pretzel parties, etc., but this practice

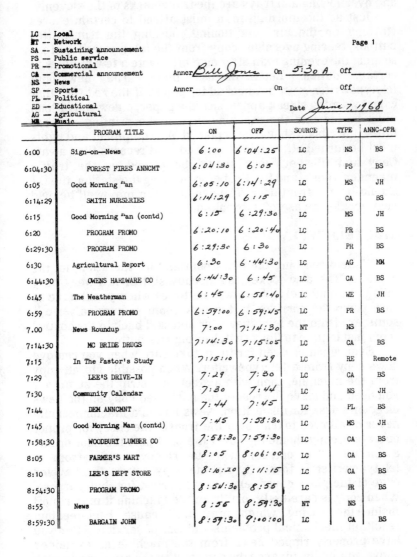

	PROGRAM TITLE	ON	OFF	SOURCE	TYPE	ANNC-OPR
	LC -- Local				Page 1	
	NT -- Network					
	SA -- Sustaining announcement					
	PS -- Public service					
	PR -- Promotional					
	CA -- Commercial announcement	Anncr _Bill Jones_ On _5:30 A_ Off_____				
	NS -- News					
	SP -- Sports	Anncr_____ On _____ Off_____				
	PL -- Political					
	ED -- Educational					
	AG -- Agricultural	Date _June 7, 1968_				
	MR -- Music					

	PROGRAM TITLE	ON	OFF	SOURCE	TYPE	ANNC-OPR
6:00	Sign-on—News	6:00	6:04:25	LC	NS	BS
6:04:30	FOREST FIRES ANNCMT	6:04:30	6:05	LC	PS	BS
6:05	Good Morning Man	6:05:10	6:14:29	LC	MS	JH
6:14:29	SMITH NURSERIES	6:14:29	6:15	LC	CA	BS
6:15	Good Morning Man (contd)	6:15	6:29:30	LC	MS	JH
6:20	PROGRAM PROMO	6:20:10	6:20:40	LC	PR	BS
6:29:30	PROGRAM PROMO	6:29:30	6:30	LC	PR	BS
6:30	Agricultural Report	6:30	6:44:30	LC	AG	MM
6:44:30	OWENS HARDWARE CO	6:44:30	6:45	LC	CA	BS
6:45	The Weatherman	6:45	6:58:40	LC	WE	JH
6:59	PROGRAM PROMO	6:59:00	6:59:45	LC	PR	BS
7:00	News Roundup	7:00	7:14:30	NT	NS	
7:14:30	MC BRIDE DRUGS	7:14:30	7:15:05	LC	CA	BS
7:15	In The Pastor's Study	7:15:10	7:29	LC	RE	Remote
7:29	LEE'S DRIVE-IN	7:29	7:30	LC	CA	BS
7:30	Community Calendar	7:30	7:44	LC	NS	JH
7:44	DEM ANNCMNT	7:44	7:45	LC	PL	BS
7:45	Good Morning Man (contd)	7:45	7:58:30	LC	MS	JH
7:58:30	WOODBURY LUMBER CO	7:58:30	7:59:30	LC	CA	BS
8:05	FARMER'S MART	8:05	8:06:00	LC	CA	BS
8:10	LEE'S DEPT STORE	8:10:20	8:11:15	LC	CA	BS
8:54:30	PROGRAM PROMO	8:54:30	8:55	LC	PR	BS
8:55	News	8:56	8:59:30	NT	NS	
8:59:30	BARGAIN JOHN	8:59:30	9:00:00	LC	CA	BS

Fig. 18-11. Typical radio station program log. Notice the standard code used when making on-air entries.

should be discouraged. Watch out for the FCC inspector! Furthermore, empty beer cans, greasy sandwich wrappings and overflowing ash trays are the trademarks of the slovenly.

Just as the morning man must attend to certain chores (turning on the air conditioning, pushing the transmitter buttons, tearing overnight copy from the teletypewriter etc.), so must the evening man after sign-off devote a few minutes to certain duties. Let's discuss them. The newsroom teletypewriter must be checked for paper. If the red (or other color) warning streak appears on the paper, a new roll or loop must be fed into the machine, and if the printing appears faded, the ribbon should be replaced. All equipment and lights must be turned off, windows latched, and records filed away. Copy and filled-out logs should be placed on the traffic manager's desk, and finally, before leaving the station, the DJ should try the front door. The evening man may well be held answerable in case of a break-in.

THE TELETYPEWRITER

While discussing the newsroom and its operation, let me say this: The disc jockey, as already stated, is a very busy fellow. Undoubtedly, there will be times when you'll have to rush down the corridor to the newsroom to hurriedly rip a summary from the teletypewriter and skid back to the control room just in time to flip a switch or punch a button.

Even when pressed for time, take care when you remove news copy from a teletypewriter. When possible rip **all** copy from the machine, then with a steel rule strip the summary you need and leave the rest of the unwanted copy on the news director's desk for disposition. News left on a machine should never be allowed to trail over the **front** of the case; for proper operation, copy should feed over the **back** onto the floor or into a basket. The correct way to remove copy from a teletypewriter is to neatly rip the copy across the beveled edge of the glass cover, expressly bevelled for that purpose. When copy is carelessly torn from the machine it may rip off inside the casing which may well cause back-feeding, resultant mechanical problems and loss of service. After you have properly ripped news from the machine as explained above, manually advance the copy still on the machine an inch or so to clear the slotted opening. That's the way it should be done, and I happen to know several professionals (who should know better) who simply tear and let the news editor worry about a disabled teletypewriter.

After airing a news summary, the items should be fastened together with a paper clip, initialed and dated, then filed. Perhaps it would be a good idea for you to visit your local radio station. Look over the newsroom and its teletypewriter, then you'll better understand what is being said here. While there, also observe what goes on in the control room.

BULLETINS

When the news director is on duty, as I said earlier, he'll handle all news broadcasts including bulletins. But there will surely be times when you'll work alone, so let's say something about news bulletins and what you should do about using them. Many bulletins clear the press wires, but not all of them are important enough to interrupt a program. Bulletins are harbingers of detailed stories which usually follow in minutes after the bulletin is released. If a news bulletin is interesting but of not too important a nature, the news director may ask you to use it in your show. Don't become dramatic and break in with:

"Here's an important bulletin just handed me..."

In the first place, it may not be that important; furthermore, the procedure is a hackneyed one. Instead, do this: Wait until your music stops, read your commercial, if you have one, then calmly say:

Here's a bulletin from our newsroom. (READ IT) Repeating (IF IT'S WORTHY OF REPEATING)... George Smith will have details of this and other late news stories at 2:55 on the WOOO mid-afternoon news."

Don't be an alarmist! Avoid using the word flash!, or the high-speed wires of Associated Press, etc. If the news is BIG news—interrupt your show, but do it without fanfare. The assassination of the President, a declaration of war in which the United States is involved, or an announcement of a war's end, a momentous decision by the United Nations and so on, rate program interruption to inform the public quickly; it is entitled to receive such information without delay. When you interrupt a show, if you must, fade your music calmly and use the above bulletin format. Better still, if your disc is about to run out, hold the bulletin for another 15 or 20 seconds. Occasionally, a network production supervisor will order a program interrupted for a bulletin of no special significance and most times the bulletin breaks into the program during the climax. By the time the drama is resumed the home audience wonders "who dunnit?" Naturally, this practice irks an audience no end. When the news director opens the control room door and asks you to give him the mike for a bulletin, give it to him at once. If it can wait until the end of a recording, he'll advise you accordingly.

LIBEL & SLANDER

Have you ever thought of how the meanings of words are revealed by their construction? The word, **dirty**, sounds "filthy." The word, **muddy**, sounds "slimy" and so on. Because of their construction, the words, **libel** and **slander** reek with distasteful overtones, and rightly they should. The two ugly words may not mean precisely the same thing, but when they motivate a law suit, both may well prove expensive for the guilty. Correctly, a defamatory remark maliciously **spoken** constitutes slander; when the false report appears in **print** it is termed, **libelous**. But in general, the word, **libel**, is loosely used to denote both types of undesirable actions. Libel insurance is costly. All stations should carry this essential protection. They don't.

One time, as news editor, I found myself uncomfortably close to becoming involved in a libel action. A newspaper carried a story about a local woman accused of licentious conduct. Permitted to broadcast newspaper material, I used that story. The following day a letter from the woman's attorney demanded that I retract the story—or else! And so I did—apologetically. Regardless of the source of your information, YOU, the speaker, may be accused of defamation of character. Again, I say, be careful.

David Dary of NBC news Washington, in his new book, **News Reporting**, writes: "A libelous news story, which has been broadcast, may lead to a civil suit for which damages may be recovered...indictment for criminal libel with a possible fine and imprisonment are not too uncommon." (TAB BOOKS, Blue Ridge Summit, Pa. 17214) Because the deejay must work with news, he, as well as the newsman, should know exactly what he **may** and what he may **not** say on the air. And Dary's book tells all.

Press wire services transmit what is called "advance copy": presidential speeches, significant developments, etc., which is sent over the wire during a slack period of the day or during the night to be held until released. Advance copy usually opens and closes with the warning: HOLD FOR RELEASE. Or, if the time of release if known, the following is plainly typed at the start and again at the end of the transmission:

(GUARD AGAINST PREMATURE USE)

NOT FOR USE UNTIL 7:15 PM EST 6-23)

There's another type of "advance" copy. During major league ballgames inning-by-inning developments clear the wire, noted as "GAME RUNNING." There's also a short hold on this play-by-play printed account of the game. I watched a sports announcer, who couldn't make a major-league game in time, fake a play-by-play description in a studio, using press wire copy of the game. With two tables running sound-effects records, crowds cheering and general ball-park background noises, it sounded great! The wire services must abide by certain rules in their agreements; we must respect their wishes and not jump the gun on them.

PRACTICE SHCEDULE—18th WEEK

NOTE: You are now starting on the consultative section of the book. For all future practice, be sure to include **all** the techniques imparted to you thus far.

1. **RELAXATION** 5 minutes.

2. **VOCAL DRILLS** 5 minutes.

3. **PRONUNCIATION** 10 minutes.

4. **ENUNCIATION** 10 minutes. (Alternate with pronunciation)

5. **PROJECTION** 5 minutes.

6. **CHARACTERIZATION** 5 minutes.

7. **NEWS** Continue to read 15 minutes daily.

8. **COMMERCIALS** Fresh copy daily. 20 minutes.

Because of this section's importance, refer to it often. You must know about, and be well-versed in, station routine.

Lesson 19

Obtaining Your FCC License

To work as a deejay in a transmitter-studio operation, you'll have to show a Third-Class Radiotelephone Operator Permit with **Broadcast Endorsement.** To obtain such a license, a nontechnical, written examination is required. The FCC will send you, without charge, a bulletin which contains all the information—including the answers—to help prepare you for the test. This bulletin, which we'll discuss in a moment, is obtainable from the Superintendent of Documents, U. S. Printing Office, Washington, D. C. 20402. You'll also be sent a complete list of all FCC literature, a few of which I shall mention shortly. The bulletin to which I make reference is The **FCC Field Engineering Bulletin No. 4.** This bulletin is of extreme importance to you. Without it you cannot take your FCC examination, and without a Third-Class Radiotelephone Permit you will not be allowed to work in the control room of a combination transmitter-studio operation.

FCC FIELD ENGINEERING BULLETIN NO. 4

The FCC F.E. Bulletin No. 4 is a special study guide containing reference material for examination for a **Third-**Class Radiotelephone Operator Permit with **broadcast endorsement** for operation of certain broadcast stations. Those stations which may be routinely operated by holders of the above class of operator permit are as follows:

1. AM stations with a power of 10 KW or less and utilizing a non-directional antenna.

2. FM stations with power output of 25 KW or less.

PROVIDED, that a supervisory operator holding a Radiotelephone **First-Class** License is employed on a full-time basis or under contract for part-time work at the station as explained by the FCC Rules and Regulations. The supervisory operator of certain non-commercial educational stations may be the holder of a Second-Class Operator License.

The questions concerned with the 3-part written examination, Elements 1, 2 and 9, are of a multiple-choice answer type in which several possible answers are given and the applicant simply chooses the best answer. F.E. Bulletin No. 4 contains reference material in the form of extracts from radio law and regulations which the applicant may use in formulating answers to most of the examination questions.

Elements 1, 2 and 9 each consist of 20 questions, and 5 percent credit is allowed for each question answered correctly. Each element is graded separately with a score of 75 percent required for passing. The examination may be taken as often as necessary until a passing mark has been obtained. The questions in Bulletin No. 4 show the scope and nature of the examination given applicants. The bulletin is specifically designed to aid the applicant in securing his radiotelephone third class operator permit. Here is a sampling of questions chosen at random from all three elements:

Who keeps the station logs?
Under what conditions may messages be rebroadcast?
What are the grounds for suspension of operator licenses?
Why should an operator use well-known words and phrases?
What precaution should be observed in testing a station on the air?
What stations may be operated by a Third-Class Operator?
When should an operator announce a program as "recorded"?
How often should station identification be made?

Quite obviously, the FCC is primarily concerned with the applicant's knowledge and understanding of its Rules and Regulations on a nontechnical level—proper keeping of logs, accurate reading of meters, etc. Prior to the required examination to qualify as a commercial radio operator, a simple Third-Class Restricted Permit was obtainable by declaration. The only requirement prior to issuance of such a permit was the applicant's proof of citizenship, but then, deejays, newcomers to the industry, committed a variety of violations simply because they were ignorant of the basic Rules and Regulations. In those days, FCC inspectors handed out citations for such infractions as erasures on logs, haphazard transmitter room supervision, etc. Corrections are permissable, of course, but erasures—never! To note a change on a station log, draw a line, in ink, through the error and sign

DIST. NO.	OFFICE LOCATION	EXAMINATION SCHEDULE AT OFFICE
1	BOSTON, MASSACHUSETTS 02109 1600 Custom House India & State Streets Phone: Area Code 617 223-6608	C & A - Thursday and Friday 8:30 AM to 10:30 AM
2	NEW YORK, NEW YORK 10014 748 Federal Building 641 Washington Street Phone: Area Code 212 620-5745	C & A - Tuesday through Friday 9:00 AM to 12:00 Noon
3	PHILADELPHIA, PENNSYLVANIA 19106 1005 U. S. Customhouse 2nd. & Chestnut Streets Phone: Area Code 215 597-4410	P - Monday, Tuesday, and Wednesday 10:00 AM to 2:00 PM T & A - Monday, Tuesday, and Wednesday 9:00 AM to 10:00 AM
4	BALTIMORE, MARYLAND 21202 415 U. S. Customhouse Gay & Lombard streets Phone: Area Code 301 962-2727	P - Monday, Wednesday, and Friday 8:30 AM to 2:00 PM T & A - Monday and Friday 8:30 AM
5	NORFOLK, VIRGINIA 23510 Granby & York Streets 400 Federal Building Phone: Area Code 703 627-7471	P & ANC - Wednesday and Friday 9:00 AM to 2:00 PM T & AC - Thursday 9:00 AM
6	ATLANTA, GEORGIA 30303 2010 Atlanta Merchandise Mart 240 Peachtree Street N. E. Phone: Area Code 404 522-4121	C & A - Tuesday and Friday 8:30 AM
6S	SAVANNAH, GEORGIA 31402 238 Post Office Building York & Bull Streets Phone: Area Code 912 232-7602	P - Monday through Friday BY APPOINTMENT ONLY T & A - 2nd & 4th Tuesday each month BY APPOINTMENT ONLY
7	MIAMI, FLORIDA 33130 919 Federal Building 51 S. W. First Avenue Phone: Area Code 305 350-5541	P - Monday through Friday 9:00 AM T & A - Thursday 9:00 AM
7T	TAMPA, FLORIDA 33602 738 Federal Building 500 Zack Street Phone: Area Code 813 228-7233	C & A - Tuesday through Friday 8:15 AM BY APPOINTMENT ONLY
8	NEW ORLEANS, LOUISIANA 70130 829 Federal Building South 600 South Street Phone: Area Code 504 527-2094	P & ANC - Monday, Tuesday and Wednesday 9:00 AM T & AC - Monday 8:30 AM
8M	MOBILE, ALABAMA 36602 439 U.S. Court House 113 St. Joseph Street Phone: Area Code 205 433-3581	Please call Monday or Tuesday of the same week of exam for appointment C & A - Wednesday BY APPOINTMENT ONLY
9	HOUSTON, TEXAS 77002 5636 Federal Building 515 Rusk Avenue Phone: Area Code 713 226-0611	P - Tuesday, Wednesday, and Thursday 8:00 AM to 12:00 NOON T & A - Tuesday 8:00 A.M. to 9:00 A.M.
9B	BEAUMONT, TEXAS 77701 239 Federal Building 300 Willow Street Phone: Area Code 713 835-3911	P - Tuesday and Thursday BY APPOINTMENT ONLY T & A - Tuesday BY APPOINTMENT ONLY
10	DALLAS, TEXAS 75202 707 Thomas Building 1314 Wood Street Phone: Area Code 214 749-3243	P - Tuesday, Wednesday and Thursday 8:00 AM to 1:00 PM T & A - Tuesday 8:00 AM to 1:00 PM
11	LOS ANGELES, CALIFORNIA 90012 U. S. Courthouse, Room 1758 312 N. Spring St. Phone: Area Code 213 688-3276	P - Tuesday & Thursday 9:00 AM and 1:00 PM T & A - Wednesday 9:00 AM and 1:00 PM
11SD	SAN DIEGO, CALIFORNIA 92101 Fox Theatre Building 1245 Seventh Avenue Phone: Area Code 714 234-6211	C & A - Wednesday BY APPOINTMENT ONLY

DIST. NO.	OFFICE LOCATION	EXAMINATION SCHEDULE AT OFFICE
11SP	SAN PEDRO, CALIFORNIA 90731 300 South Ferry Street Terminal Island Phone: Area Code 213 831-9281	*Examinations are not normally conducted at San Pedro. Contact the FCC office at Los Angeles, California*
12	SAN FRANCISCO, CALIFORNIA 94111 323A Custom House 555 Battery Street Phone: Area Code 415 556-7700	P - Monday and Tuesday - 8:30 AM T - Tuesday - 8:30 AM A - Friday - Extra & Advanced - 8:30 AM General - 9:30 AM
13	PORTLAND, OREGON 97204 314 Multnomah Building 319 S.W. Pine Street Phone: Area Code 503 226-3361	P - Tuesday and Wednesday - 8:45 AM T - Tuesday - 8:45 AM A - Friday - 8:45 AM
14	SEATTLE, WASHINGTON 98104 8012 Federal Office Building 909 First Avenue Phone: Area Code 206 583-7653	P - Tuesday and Wednesday - 8:00 AM to 11:00 AM T & A - Friday - 8:45 AM
15	DENVER, COLORADO 80202 504 New Customhouse 19th St. between California & Stout Sts. Phone: Area Code 303 297-4053	P - Friday and by appointment - 9:00 AM A - 1st & 2nd Thursday - General & Advanced - 8:00 AM, Extra - 9:00 AM T - 1st & 2nd Thursday - 10:00 AM
16	ST. PAUL, MINNESOTA 55101 691 Federal Courts Building and U.S. Courthouse 4th and Robert Street Phone: Area Code 612 228-7819	C - Thursday - 8:45 AM A - Friday - 8:45 AM
17	KANSAS CITY, MISSOURI 64105 1703 Federal Building 601 East 12th St. Phone: Area Code 816 374-5526	C & A - Thursday & Friday 8:30 AM to 11:00 AM
18	CHICAGO, ILLINOIS 60604 1872 U. S. Courthouse & Federal Office Building 219 South Dearborn Street Phone: Area Code 312 353-5388	C - Thursday - 9:00 AM A - Friday - 9:00 AM
19	DETROIT, MICHIGAN 48226 1029 Federal Building Washington Blvd. & LaFayette Street Phone: Area Code 313 226-6077	C - Tuesday and Thursday - 9:00 AM A - Wednesday and Friday - 9:00 AM
20	BUFFALO, NEW YORK 14203 328 Federal Office Building Ellicott & Swan Streets Phone: Area Code 716 842-3216	P - 1st & 3rd Thursday - 9:00 AM to 11:00 AM T & A - 1st & 3rd Friday - 9:00 AM
21	HONOLULU, HAWAII 96808 502 Federal Building P.O. Box 1021 Phone: 546-5640	P - Monday through Friday - 8:00 AM T & A - Tuesday and Wednesday - 8:00 AM and by appointment
22	SAN JUAN, PUERTO RICO 00903 322 Federal Building P.O. Box 2987 Phone: 722-4562	P - Thursday and Friday - 8:30 AM T - Friday - 8:30 AM A - Friday - 9:00 AM
23	ANCHORAGE, ALASKA 99501 54 U.S. Post Office Building 4th Avenue between F & G Streets Phone: Area Code 907 272-1822	C & A - Monday through Friday BY APPOINTMENT ONLY
24	WASHINGTON, D. C. 20554 Room 216 1919 M Street, N.W. Phone: Area Code 202 632-7000	P - Tuesday, Wednesday and Friday 8:30 AM to 3:30 PM T & A - Friday 9:00 AM and 1:00 PM
—	GETTYSBURG, PENNSYLVANIA 17325 P. O. Box 441 Phone: Area Code 717 334-3109	A - 1st & 3rd Tuesday BY APPOINTMENT ONLY (Amateur Exams ONLY are conducted at Gettysburg, Pa.)

Fig. 19-1. FCC field offices and examinations schedule.

your initials alongside the change. Another flagrant violation of FCC rules is the making of entries on logs in **advance** of airtime, or allowing logs to go unattended for any length of time. FCC inspectors make unannounced visits to control rooms, so don't get caught breaking an FCC rule—it could cost you your license!

The Federal Communications Commission has very definite rulings on what **may** and what may **not** be aired, how often station identification should be made, when programs should be announced as "recorded for presentation at this time" and so forth, including the manner in which political matter should be handled for broadcast purposes. Insofar as infractions of FCC Rules and Regulations are concerned, you cannot plead ignorance of radio law. Your commercial operator permit suffices to prove that you **know** the FCC Rules and Regulations, and that you are aware of your obligation to abide by such broadcast laws.

If you feel a continued interest in commercial broadcasting, by all means send for your copy of the **FCC Field Engineering Bulletin No. 4.** Study it carefully; take your time. Follow the instruction it contains, then arrange to take the test when the next examination date comes up in your radio district. The F.E. Bulletin No. 4 explains everything. The address again is: Superintendent of Documents, U.S. Printing Office, Washington, D.C. 20402. Copies of the bulletin cannot be supplied in quantity; however, the government permits its reproduction in whole or in part by anyone interested.

Fig. 19-1 lists locations of the Federal Communications Commission's field offices and a schedule of examinations, dates and times of examinations. By the way, the times shown in the illustration refer to the examination starting times. No examinations are conducted on Sundays or on legal holidays. When a legal holiday falls on a Saturday, Federal offices are closed on the preceding Friday; when a legal holiday falls on a Sunday, Federal offices are closed on the following Monday. Because Federal schedules change without notice, you should contact your nearest field office to verify the examination dates and times as stated in the schedule. Here now is a key to the chart:

C — Commercial examination

A — Amateur examination

P — Radiotelephone examination

T — Radiotelegraph examination

AC — Amateur code exam required

ANC — Amateur code exam not required

After you get your start in commercial broadcasting, you may begin to wonder about electronics. What goes on inside a transmitter? What exactly do meter readings indicate? You'll soon realize, as I did, that you're curiously involved in a mysterious world of electronics, a pulsating phase of sight and sound communication. To increase their earnings, some deejays study in spare time to obtain their first-Class radiotelephone permit, and you may do likewise, but before you buy any books or sign up for a home-study course, ask yourself a few questions. How are (or were) my marks in higher math? Do I have the patience to work out intricate mathematical problems? Am I the scientific or artistic type, or both? Am I mechanically inclined? If frequency modulation, digital techniques and other technical subject matter make interesting discussion, you may safely think about a first-class ticket. However, wait until you are firmly established in the profession.

This industry needs and wants conscientious engineers, all right, and your chances of moving ahead will be far more promising if you can advertise yourself as a deejay-first ticket man. Unlike your complacent colleague who spins and chats, day after day, perfectly satisfied with his earnings as long as he doesn't have to exert himself to learn something new, continue to seek ways and the means to improve your broadcast services. If you're the serious-minded type of fellow, and I'm sure you are, otherwise you wouldn't be reading a book of this type, your experience very possibly will parallel mine, namely the longer your stay in this game, the less you'll seem to know about it, or perhaps I should say, the more you'll want to know about it. It's the guy who stands still who thinks he knows everything there is to know.

There are three ways in which to acquire the necessary knowledge to qualify for a first-class radiotelephone license, via a technical examination. You may study the subject matter by yourself, in which case I suggest that you write to: TAB Books, Blue Ridge Summit, Pa., 17214, for a list of the necessary technical books for home-study purposes, or you may enroll for a home-study course, especially designed for the beginner with no previous knowledge or training in electronics, or if time and money permit, resident instruction in

151

classrooms and workshops is an excellent means. Such courses, incidentally, prepare the student to pass all three examinations, for third-, second-, and first-class permits. Before you think about a first-class license, let me again emphasize that a knowledge of higher math is required. Regardless of how you study for your license, you'll need a copy of the FCC publication, **Guide and Reference Material For Commercial Radio Operator Examinations** (price 75 cents). The fees for filing operator applications are as follows: first class $5; second class $4; third class (with broadcast endorsement) $3, and third class (restricted) $2.

Now, about a radio engineering school. There are many of them. I cannot recommend any one school; there are too many good ones—and a few of which you must be wary. Make inquiries, then investigate carefully. Get ALL the facts—the cost of the complete course. Do NOT put down more than the minimum amount of cash required to get started. Request the names of former students. Write several of them. Ask them questions. Get some advice from engineers at your local radio stations. Choose a school nearest your home. The reason for this must be obvious. Perhaps there's an electronics college in your own town. Send for a copy of **Broadcasting-Telecasting**, 1735 De Sales Street, N. W., Washington D.C. 20036, or **Broadcasting Management-Engineering**, 820 Second Avenue, New York, N. Y. 10017. Enclose 50 cents. Both publications have excellent classified advertising sections. All leading electronics schools advertise in both trade journals. When you have decided on a school—hold everything! See the chief engineer of a local radio station. Tell him of your decision. He may have a better idea. The point I must make here is that there are some schools which feel more of an interest in your money than in your future, so don't be vulnerable! I know, 4-color brochures with their gold-colored covers look impressive. There're supposed to!

As of this writing, the Federal Communications Commission has not established any age limit for those wishing to obtain operator permits and licenses, except that Radiotelegraph First-Class Operator Licenses may not be issued to applicants under 21 years of age. Applicants for examination for an Aircraft Radiotelegraph **Endorsement** must be at least 18 years old, and applicants for a **restricted** Radiotelephone Operator Permit must be at least 14 years of age. The F.E. Bulletin No. 4 also clarifies the matter of age.

Earlier I mentioned certain FCC Rules and Regulations in regard to station identification, political broadcasts, etc. Let's touch briefly on certain types of announcements with which you must become familiar. According to FCC law, station identification may be a simple: **WOOX, Detroit, Michigan.** Sometimes a station slogan is added, but unless you're instructed otherwise, station identification should consist of call letters and location. Of course, frequency may be mentioned. When an FM station duplicates AM programming a two-in-one identification is in order:

This is WOOX AM and FM, Detroit.

Or you may elaborate:

This is WOOX AM and FM in Detroit, Michigan. 940 on AM dials, 101.5 on your FM receiver. Four o'clock. Stay tuned for the news.

Another important type of announcement is called a disclaimer, which precedes and follows political broadcasts. A disclaimer is a public denial or renunciation demanded by the FCC to stipulate that political opinions aired are not editorial views of the station. A disclaimer may be a brief: **The following is a paid political announcement,** or **The time for the following program was paid for by the Columbia Democratic Club,** or **The views expressed by the speaker are not necessarily the opinions of this station or its management.**

When a regularly scheduled program is canceled in favor of a special feature, the substitution is called a pre-emption. When a show is pre-empted, a courtesy announcement should precede and follow the special presentation.

(BEFORE) The program, Three Faces East, usually heard at this time will not be heard (seen) this afternoon so that we may bring you the special Christmas program which follows.

(AFTER) The program, Three Faces East, was not presented this afternoon because of the special Christmas show. It may be heard at its usual time next Wednesday afternoon at three o'clock.

While on the subject of station identification, let's discuss sign-on and sign-off. Some stations make their sign-on and sign-off brief, others sneak in plugs for their program and news policies. In reference to sign-on and sign-off requirements, the FCC simply requests complete identification, which, of course, includes location of the station's transmitter. To familiarize the reader with what is meant by sign-on and sign-off, here are a few sample forms of such station identification.

SIGN-ON

(NATIONAL ANTHEM) Good morning, this is (ANNCR). At this time, radio station WOOX in Norton, New York, begins its broadcast activities for today. WOOX, owned and operated by Great Northern Communications Corporation, transmits on an assigned frequency of 940 kilocycles with a power of 1,000 watts as authorized by the Federal Communications Commission. Our studios and offices are in the Hotel Norton, our transmitter is located on Beacon Hill, in Norton, New York. WOOX is on the air daily from 6 AM until 12 midnight. (INTO NEWS)

SIGN-OFF

(FINAL NEWSCAST) At this time, WOOX leaves the air until tomorrow morning at six. WOOX, owned and operated by the Great Northern Communications Corporation, transmits on an assigned frequency of 940 kilocycles with a power of 1,000 watts as authorized by the Federal Communications Commission. Our studios and offices are in the Hotel Norton, our transmitter is located on Beacon Hill, in Norton, New York. WOOX is on the air daily from 6 AM until 12 midnight. Until tomorrow morning at six, this is (ANNCR) saying good night. (NATIONAL ANTHEM)

Some stations insist upon standard station breaks; that is, the station may include a slogan in its identification, such as: This is WMMN, your friendly voice of service, CBS in Fairmont, West Virginia. When with that station some years ago, all new announcers were briefed and instructed to include the phrase, "your friendly voice of service." If your station allows you to seek originality, compose one or two original styles in station identification. Here are a few examples; you may wish to use them for practice purposes.

1. Serving the tri-state area, you're tuned to WBBB, in Boston. Time 7 o'clock.

2. Those in the know say it's so. Hear the best over WKKK, Springfield.

3. On the air around the clock, you're listening to KLLL, San Francisco.

4. This is powerful Channel 7, WZZZ in Gainesville, Florida. 9 o'clock.

5. For news and music, stay tuned to 1270 on your dial, KXXX, Los Angeles.

6. Stay tuned now for "Three's a Crowd" over WLWL, Greensboro, at 980.

7. It's Christmas Seal time...WCCC, Brookville, Connecticut.

8. Hear Fordham versus Army over KMNN, Anniston, Alabama. Time now 6 o'clock.

Program promotionals are quite effective when hitch-hiked to station breaks. For example:

9. WILL, New Kensington, New York. The news follows. At 7 o'clock, "Bachelor Father."

10. Stay tuned now for the Bill Reed show over KOOO, Bloomington, New Mexico.

11. One thousand dollars will be awarded to the lucky listener! Be sure to stay tuned to WKKK, Corona, Virginia for the program..."What's the word?"

The Radio Program Ideabook deals in detail and illustrations with the subject of station identification, promotion etc. Incidentally, you may be interested in knowing how stations illustrate for prospective advertisers the area covered by their signals. Fig. 19-2 is an artist's drawing of a typical coverage map.

Are you following through on my suggestion in Lesson 16 to practice on standard AP or UPI teletypewriter copy? If you haven't gotten around to it yet, please do so now. You should become thoroughly familiar with press wire service summaries. A weekly visit to your radio station for discarded news summaries, sports features and other copy will keep you well supplied. Also keep reading fresh newspaper and magazine advertising daily. Can you quickly interpret a piece of advertising copy? By this time you should.

Earlier in this lesson I mentioned special announcements: disclaimers, courtesy, promotionals, etc. There's another type of announcement with which you should familiarize yourself.

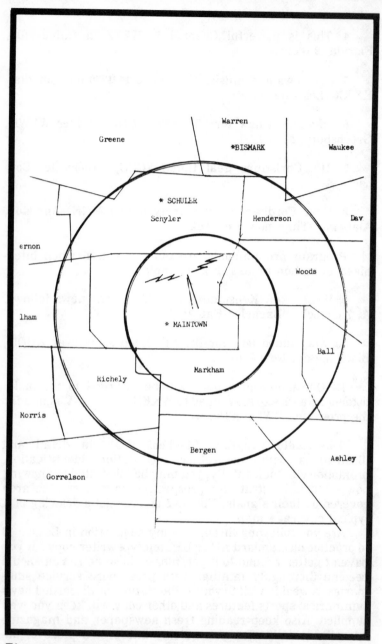

Fig. 19-2. Artist's drawing of typical broadcast area map. Area (inside circle) represents the station's primary broadcast area. Outer circle denotes the perimeter of the secondary area.

Time	Program	Type			
9:59:30	March of Dimes	PSA	9:57:30	9:57:55	C.A.
10:00	GEORGE MONROE SHOW	PTC	10:00	10:30	C.J.
10:14	* McBride Drug Company	CA	10:15:10	10:16:5	C.J.
10:18	* Wood Jewelers	CA	10:17:55	10:18:55	C.J.
10:29:00	Program Promo	PR	10:29	10:30	C.J.
10:30 10:30 C.J. 10:31 10:34:30 10:35:30 C.A	Red Cross	PSA			C.J.
	NEWS (Moore Lumber Products Co.)	NC	10:30	10:34:30	C.J.
	GEORGE MONROE SHOW CONTD	PTC	10:34:30	10:59:00	C.J.

Fig. 19-3.

It's called the "affidavit spot," and here's what it means. National advertisers place business with radio stations through their advertising agencies, and such business is contracted for in a very detailed manner. The exact broadcast times of programs and commercials are carefully noted in the agreement, and each month when the station bills the agency, a list of such broadcast times, duly notarized, must accompany the statement as proof of performance. Hence, this type of commercial is termed an "affidavit" spot. The sworn statement is an affidavit of performance. This must be done. National business is big business, when one considers a national gross advertising billing of close to $5 billion as reported by 10 of the largest advertising agencies handling radio and television accounts. Is it any wonder that they must insist upon a monthly proof of performance?

Most deejays are unacquainted with affidavit spots. Because the station must swear to a proof of performance, affidavit commercials should NEVER be moved without consulting the person in charge of traffic. In fact, no commercials should be moved without an okay from traffic. I know that some sponsors listen religiously to their commercials. If their ad is scheduled to be aired at, say, 2:35, and the deejay takes the liberty of announcing it at 2:45, the sponsor may well assume that his spot was missed. Initials on the log denote proof of performance, but this may not satisfy an advertiser who insists upon personally hearing his broadcast. Earlier, I touched on the FCC approved manner in which corrections should be made. Let me repeat: Even if you must move a promo or a public service announcement (noncommercial), check with traffic, then make the deletion or correction. Draw a line in ink through the entire entry, then at the end of the deletion or correction sign your initials, as shown in Fig. 19-3. For illustrative purposes, let's say that the deejay discovered an error on the log. The local news should have been scheduled for 10:30; therefore, the public service Red Cross spot had to be deleted. He made the deletion and initialed it. It must be remembered that the deejay on duty is wholly responsible for what goes on the air and one never knows who may be listening.

In a newscast one time I came across a short quote credited to a news magazine. Instead of crediting the publication with the quotation, apparently a passage in an exclusive interview, I passed over it lightly. The next day I received a brief letter from the publication's editorial offices in a large city miles away requesting that credit should be given when so stated in the press wire copy. Obviously, a local spotter was listening and reported the matter to the news magazine. Stick to the facts, stay with your log. Never delete or make ANY changes on the program log without first securing permission to do so. Think of your log as your bible and follow it to a T.

PRACTICE SCHEDULE—19th WEEK

1. **RELAXATION** 5 minutes.

2. **VOCAL DRILLS** 5 minutes.

3. **PRONUNCIATION** 10 minutes.

4. **ENUNCIATION** 10 minutes. (Alternate with pronunciation)

5. **PROJECTION** 5 minutes.

6. **CHARACTERIZATION** 5 minutes.

7. **NEWS** 15 minutes.

8. **COMMERCIALS** Fresh copy daily. Are you using inflections, pauses and coloring? 20 minutes.

9. Reread these important lessons occasionally. Now is the time to make a comparison with your original recording 19 weeks ago. Listen for improvement. Check on technical weak spots.

Lesson 20

Getting Started

During the 1920s and the early 30s, before schools of radio technique, college courses in communication and educational radio became available, getting started in this business of broadcasting was comparatively easy. I remember well how school teachers, actors, singers, salesmen—anyone with what was then called "a gift of gab"—were freely accepted as staff announcers and were taught the mechanics in an infantile but rapidly advancing industry; the blind led the blind, as it were, in a then unique and fascinating world of mysterious communication. The situation is quite the reverse now. The industry has matured; today's qualifications and professional standards are high. But a fabulous career is promised the talented and trained. There are various ways to acquire that professional nonchalance, the seasoning which comes with experience and subsequent self-confidence.

Executives in most of today's busy broadcast stations cannot take the time to teach newcomers the intricacies of broadcasting; the modern commercial outlet, it must be remembered, is not a "school." Managers cannot allow amateurs to toy with costly and sensitive electronic equipment, nor will they permit the neophyte to experiment at the expense of their hard-earned listenership ratings. Of course, there is the small-time radio station operator at the grass roots level who will gladly offer a "green" deejay, with some specialized technical instruction, on-the-job training in a commercial environment in exchange for a modest salary, usually the minimum allowed by law. Operating costs are kept at a low level, and the "green" deejay gets paid while he gains that much-needed experience.

I am not insinuating that all small-station managers who accept inexperienced personnel are mercenary characters, but there are shrewd operators who, to save themselves money, will hasten to engage the services of a mike-happy youngster. There are a number of unscrupulous managers in this business who will feel no qualms whatsoever about taking brazen advantage of an over-zealous beginner, the newcomer who is willing to "shake" on any deal in order to get that first break. The fledgling should guard against the tactics of those who hunt for bargains in talented flesh. The ambitious neophyte, if he is observant, will quickly "catch on" and will garner enough experience to strike out for a progressive station in a larger market which can offer him standard hours, fringe benefits and a salary commensurate with his ability to produce broadcast services.

It is a fact that many small stations under excellent management are forced to hire "green" personnel. In some cases, stunted revenue, as the result of limited market conditions, cannot stand the drain of professional salary requirements which may well run high these days. Also, as is popularly the case, minor markets simply do not hold any appeal for the deejay with an eye to the future, the broadcaster with a built-in, goal-searching mechanism; he is aiming for the bigtime in metropolitan areas. You may get your start in your own hometown radio station, but don't jump the gun. Better to get some practical experience behind you before you apply for work in a commercial radio station.

There are a number of ways to become acclimated to working to the public. The high schooler may participate in school forums, join dramatic groups or work as a public address announcer when his school stages sports and other public events. He may spin discs at record hops, act as his school's news reporter, or as moderator on a current-events quiz show featuring girl-and-boy teams, or school versus school. The Radio Program Ideabook contains a list of high school radio programs. Ask to see the book at your public library. The student who plays a musical instrument should join a band or organize a combo of his own. A parent should address PTA, church and club meetings, also present occasional talks at fraternal, civic and service-club luncheons. Offer to act as master of ceremonies for your club's upcoming show and dance. If you sing, plan a short recital during your club's monthly social hour, or arrange to sing at Sunday church services. As I said before, it's a woman's world, too.

Here's a highly effective means of breaking in. Every town has a discount department store or a farmer's market which employs an announcer, male or female, who sounds off on the buys of the hour. The work isn't easy. Sometimes you may have to speak from scrawled notes or ad lib from newspaper clippings, or hurriedly compose your own copy. Seldom will you work with typewritten announcements. Announcers usually work three days a week, on Thursdays and Fridays from approximately 6 PM to closing, about 10 PM, and on Saturday from 4 PM until closing. The rate of pay is generally based upon the minimum hourly wage rate as stipulated by law. Rough as this sort of work may be, two or three months will suffice to get you started writing those letters of application. That has been the experience of a number of my students, now with major stations in larger cities.

If you're a college student or of precollege age, by all means plan to work behind the mike in a commercial operation near your campus. It's the most pleasant and certainly a highly profitable way to put your higher education on a self-paying basis. Skyrocketing college costs force students to take part-time work. A 22-year-old Ohio State University senior, for instance, attends morning classes, works in a bank afternoons and tends bar at night. Dates? He hasn't time for that sort of thing. What spare time he does have must be devoted to his studies. It's rough. But it must be done. A bank loan pays his tuition. The college student-worker is no newcomer to the American educational scene.

During a 5-year period, from 1965 to 1969, the number of full-time college students who had to work to support themselves and their higher education grew by an amazing 64 percent to almost 2.1 million students! As every college student will agree, the costs of food, rooms, books, clothes and what not have risen sharply and continue to climb upward. Some college men and women must seek employment because of the difficulty in obtaining low-interest loans to finance their learning, and, in many cases, financial conditions in the home dictate that the student must sustain himself in college or forego a coveted college degree. College job-opportunity bulletin boards used to overflow with help-wanted ads. Not so today. And summer employment for college students is virtually nil. Now, do you understand why I say if you have broadcast talent—and not every student is fortunate to be so gifted—investigate broadcasting as the ideal way to compensate for your financial shortcomings.

There's a publication entitled, "Need a Lift?" This year's issue is a 128-page handbook which offers invaluable information on subjects such as scholarships, fellowships, loans to finance one's college education, the outlook on part-time employment for the college student and much more. It also lists the various sources of educational assistance. Let me stress here and now that "Need a Lift?" is an excellent handbook for ambitious young people who want authoritative information. "Need a Lift?" is published annually by The American Legion and costs only 50 cents per copy. Order yours directly from The American Legion, Dept. S, Box 1055, Indianapolis, Ind. 46206.

AMATEUR RADIO

This lesson would be incomplete without mentioning another exceptionally effective way to acclimatize yourself to actual broadcast conditions; namely, to operate your own home radio station. There are two ways to do this. You may, at a nominal cost and virtually without mechanical knowledge, establish your own ham station, a constructive, educational and fascinating hobby, in your garage, basement, play room or in a corner of your bedroom. Modern transmitting equipment takes up little space on a table or small desk (Fig. 20-1). In regard to FCC rules and regulations governing licenses and the proper operation of an amateur radio station, write to: Superintendent of Documents, U. S. Printing Office, Washington, D. C. 20420. Request information on amateur radio station operation. Incidentally, there's an excellent book available entitled, **Ham Radio Incentive Licensing Guide** by Bert Simon (TAB Books, Blue Ridge Summit, Pa.).

Completely assembled amateur equipment, ready-to-go, is available at large electronic supply houses. Prices vary considerably, depending upon power and type of equipment. For a catalog of prices and models write: **Lafayette Radio and Electronics, 111 Jericho Turnpike, Syosett, New York.** This mail-order house has dealerships in many large cities. There might be one in your town. Another nationwide supplier of electronic equipment with stores in many large cities (781 stores to date) is **Allied Radio Shack** stores. This company also has a mail-order department. To secure the name and address of the nearest Radio Shack, or to receive a catalogue or information on some special piece of equipment, write: **Allied Radio Shack** 2617 West 7th Street, Fort Worth, Texas. 76107.

"CARRIER CURRENT" STATIONS

Growing rapidly in popularity in this age of instant communications is "carrier current" radio, chiefly utilized by a number of campus broadcast stations. Because carrier radio does not require air waves to carry its signals, licensing by the FCC is not required. A mini-station uses a local network of conductors. It sends its signals along power lines for a distance commensurate with the power output of the mini-station's transmitter. Boosters are used when extended coverage is required. This type of radio offers the aspirant to

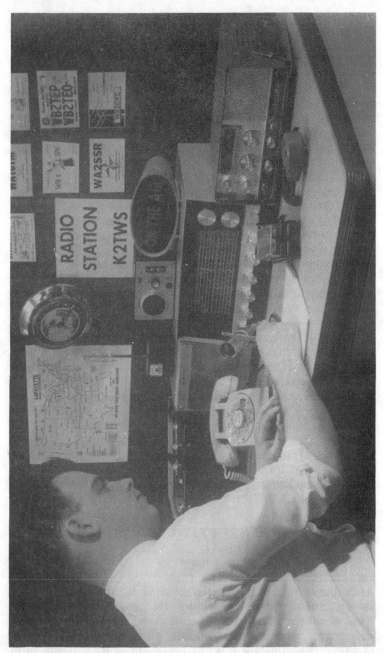

Fig. 20-1. A well-equipped amateur station. (Courtesy Lafayette Radio-Electronics)

164

broadcasting a most interesting, educational and low-cost means of gaining experience behind the mike. A small transmitter, microphone and perhaps a record player on a table in a corner of your bedroom, den or play room equips your personal mini-radio station. A small-town movie theatre manager operated carrier radio in his office. He later went on the staff of a commercial station as an announcer-operator well acclimated to working behind the mike. If carrier current radio sounds interesting, investigate for yourself. Write Lafayette Radio & Electronics for their catalogue. Also consult with your local light and power company on their views and check the FCC for late rulings, if any, on this mode of communications. On a local level, carrier radio may well prove to be a powerful medium. One thing is certain: carrier output radio makes for a highly fascinating hobby with unlimited public service possibilities. Campus Radio Station WRHS in Robbinsville, N.C., mentioned earlier, is a carrier current operation. It also maintains a booster in a lumber yard at the edge of town to increase its range.

Will your transmitter require an FCC license? No. A low-power transmitter, such as you would use to operate a current carrier system, says the FCC (OCE Bulletin No. 12), does not need an FCC license. "The band 540 to 1600 kHz (kilocycles) allocated for licensed broadcast stations may be used by a carrier current system without a license on the condition that: (1) no harmful interference is caused to licensed operations in your area, and (2) the technical and other requirements of part 15 (detailed in the above bulletin) are met." As you can see, the requirements are not stringent, simply common sense rulings by the FCC. Of course, before you consider any further interest in current carrier radio, send for the bulletin mentioned above. It tells all you must know about such a broadcast system. Also ask for OCE Bulletin No. 11 which deals specifically with nonlicensed transmitting equipment, with which you should become familiar.

Here, in part, is what the FCC says about current carrier radio: "In this type of operation the output of a low-power transmitter is coupled into the power distribution system, or some other network of conductors, which carries radio frequency energy along to any receiver that is connected to it or is in close proximity of the system." Of course, it must be realized that the responsibility of assuring that radiation from a carrier current system does not exceed the FCC permissible field strength and does not cause interference to authorized commercial broadcast services, lies entirely with the owner and operator of such a carrier current station. This is important! OCE Bulletin No. 12 says, "The amount of radiation can only be determined through the use of a standard field-strength meter operated by an engineer experienced in this work."

Although carrier output radio may be of intense interest to you, avoid hasty action. Before you purchase equipment or begin installation, establish first that the services of a competent radio engineer are available in your area to determine the electromagnetic energy radiation. Specifically, the FCC states: "The maximum radiation from any part of the system (power lines or other conductors) shall not exceed 15 microvolts per meter at any distance greater than 290 feet from the system's conductors." Furthermore, the Commission explains that "even a fraction of a watt of power may easily produce a radiated field strength in excess of the allowable limit."

A carrier current system is regulated by Section 15.7 (page 2, OCE Bulletin No. 12) of the FCC Rules and Regulations: **General Requirements for Restricted Radiation Devices.** OCE Bulletins 11 and 12 are obtainable from the Office of the Chief Engineer, Federal Communications Commission, Washington, D. C. 20554. Again I suggest that you seek the advice and assistance of the chief engineer of your local radio station on the matter of carrier current radio.

Now, let me tell you the success story about a student of mine—at the time a senior high schooler—and a few friends with kindred interests, who established their own, honest-to-goodness radio station, played top-40 and jazz tunes, read local news stories and announced public service messages etc. Actually, there isn't anything unusual about running a broadcast station (there are over 6,000 of them on the air today), but Radio Station WXK in Providence, Rhode Island—that was different! You see, when those ambitious and talented, precollege-age broadcasters pooled their resources and abilities to construct and to successfully operate their own radio station, with all the familiar paraphernalia that makes radiobroadcasting the intensely interesting and fascinating profession it is—that is an admirable accomplishment to be sure, a refreshing achievement far removed from today's pot and pills.

The six enterprising, youthful operators, with long-range plans for professional broadcasting were on the ball with their thinking. Maybe it was tough for a 17-year-old to be accepted in commercial broadcasting for experience sake, but that hindrance didn't stop them from gaining that essential background, first-hand, on-the-air experience. "Why not start

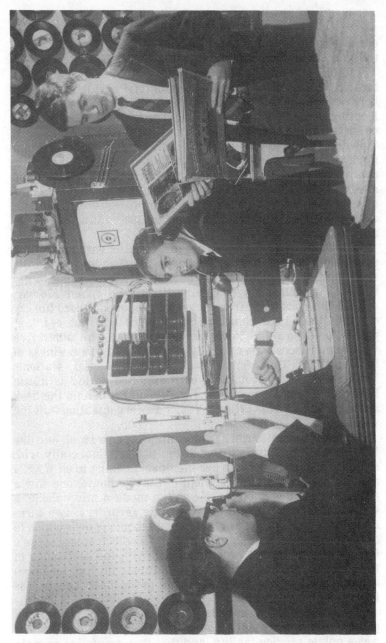

Fig. 20-2. Program Director Stephen Molnar at the WXK controls with two of his associates, Dave Fields and Paul Moverman. (Providence Journal-Bulletin photo)

our own radio station," they reasoned. And so they **did**. Let me tell you about their unique venture.

Radio station WXK's transmitter-studio operation was located in a quiet, residential section of Providence. Neighbors never complained about an unsightly 150-foot steel tower looming precariously in their backyards, because there was no skyscraping antenna to gripe about—that is, the WXK "tower" rose only 10 feet into the air! The Federal Communications Commission permitted the "peanut whistle" to operate as a nonlicensed facility, provided, that WXK radiated a signal over a broadcast area covering not more than a one-mile radius of Providence. The nonprofit enterprise broadcasted with an authorized power of 100 milliwatts on an assigned frequency of 1170 kHz.

This amazing, miniature broadcast outlet with its bigtime overtones was on the air Saturdays and Sundays, when its staff was not attending high school classes. According to my student, the station's program director, Stephen Molnar, selected his rock tunes from a carefully indexed record library of more than 1,000 choice LPs. "We tried to put out that professional sound," Steve smiled proudly. The other five "board members" were equally serious about this business of broadcasting. One fellow took charge of the station's "newsroom," while another youth assumed duties as music librarian. The older member of the group sat behind the desk in the station's "front office." Yes, it was organization—all the way!

It takes money to run a radio station, even a small one like WXK, so all six boys supported the project financially with monthly dues of fifty cents per member. Looking in on WXK's modern studios, in the basement of Steve's home, one saw a professionally designed console with a modern microphone, a well-constructed transmitter, two tape recorders, two turntables, a few desks, typewriters and a telephone over which to accept local news stories. Regarding the electronics, Steve's father, a professional radio engineer, with the assistance of two of the operators, constructed much of the technical equipment (Fig. 20-2). Three of the group held Third-Class Radiotelephone Permits.

Yes, these fellows had a very definite programming policy; they were keenly aware that their broadcast station was a public service facility, and that they wanted to operate precisely as do light and power and telephone companies—in the public interest. WXK broadcasts such vital messages as hurricane and other storm warnings, emergency calls for special blood types, hazardous road conditions, and similar announcements of impending danger.

I asked Steve and his friends how they felt about today's commercial broadcasting. All six were in agreement that the modern deejay talked too much and that today's radio programs offer a wide margin for improvement. All six radio "executives" are now very close to professional broadcasting; a few already have shows of their own on local stations. Steve is now on the WPRO staff in Providence. Whether you plan to have broadcasting help you pay your way through college, or if you wish to stay behind the mike for a long-range career, give serious thought to gaining that essential experience, in a farmer's market, discount center, or perhaps you feel an interest in ham radio. No matter how you gain your experience, emulate the six young men in the story. Prepare yourself now for the greater things that will surely come into your life! As a professional coach, I can safely tell you that broadcasting—both media—is big business and to succeed in this branch of show business you must think BIG! Isn't that exactly what the lads who ran WXK in Providence did? You, too, can think big in the career of your choice. So, let's get started!

PRACTICE SCHEDULE—20th THROUGH 25th WEEK

Note: Here is a basic 1-hour practice schedule for the remainder of the course and thereafter as needed.

1. **RELAXATION** 5 minutes.

2. **VOCAL DRILLS** 5 minutes.

3. **PRONUNCIATION** 5 minutes.

4. **ENUNCIATION** 5 minutes.

5. **PROJECTION** 5 minutes.

6. **CHARACTERIZATION** 5 minutes.

7. **NEWS** 10 minutes.

8. **AD LIBBING** 10 minutes.

9. **COMMERCIALS** 10 minutes.

You should now be sufficiently developed to adhere to a 60-minute schedule. If, when recording your work, you notice a technical weakness, simply increase study time accordingly. Occasionally, review the recapitulation, Lessons 1 to 15, and the recapitulation which you will find at the end of Lesson 25 (Lessons 16 to 25).

Lesson 21

Effective Business Letters

Whether you answer an advertisement or solicit a number of stations in search of a job, you'll have to write a few, simple and brief business letters. To expect professional consideration, they'll have to have that professional appearance. Here, now, are several important pointers on the subject.

Type—don't write—your letters on white letter-size paper. Clean the keys, use a dark, black ribbon. Do not use company stationery unless the letterhead is your own. Never 'X' out errors, avoid erasures. Use correction paper for clean corrections. Shun strikeovers. If you can't type a neat, well-positioned letter, have someone who can do it for you. Take the "Dear Sir" approach only when you must; otherwise, make it, "Dear Mr. Smith," and finally, use a No. 10 long envelope. Do things the professional way.

Make letters brief. Leave details for your resume; that's what it's for. If a station needs you, a manager will ask for more information. If your services are not needed, even a 10-page letter won't change a manager's mind. Never state your salary requirement in your first letter; let the employer broach the subject in due time. Unless you're specifically requested to state your salary requirements, leave the matter of remuneration "open" for the interview.

Three steps must be taken to get a job (1) The exposure (advertisement or inquiry by letter), (2) presentation (resume, photo, audition, etc.), (3) the interview (your first meeting with the "boss"). Each step must lead to the next; the "boss" must want to know more about you. It's an old show business tactic. "Always leave them applauding for more!" say the pros.

Make your initial inquiry brief:

Mr. George Smith Gen. Mgr.
KXXX Radio
Post Office Box 543
Central City, Wis.

Dear Mr. Smith:

I am interested in locating in Central City. At present I am morning man with KXOW in Vernon, South Dakota. By chance do you have an opening for a morning man? I can also sell on my own time.

Sincerely yours,

(YOUR NAME)

Mr. Smith may ask you to send him a presentation, or he may advise you that KXXX is fully staffed at the present time. When you do send an employer a presentation, clip the following covering letter to your printed material. Using the same opening as above, make the body of the letter read:

Thank you for your letter of June 18, 1969, requesting a resume and audition of my work. If you have other questions, please write me about them. Thank you.

Sincerely yours,

(YOUR NAME)

When you answer an advertisement, again, attach a brief covering letter:

Advertiser
Box 655
BROADCASTING
Washington, D. C.

Dear Sir:

In reference to your advertisement (BROADCASTING, July 6, 1969) for a morning man, may I ask you to please consider the attached presentation. Please note that I hold a first ticket and am capable of doing maintenance.

Sincerely yours

(YOUR NAME)

If you want to try the solicitation campaign method to get started, here's how it's done. (I don't recommend it; too many of them fail.) One hundred copies of a professionally styled resume are printed (not carbon copies or mimeograph reproduction). These resumes, as schools of broadcasting do, may contain a photograph of the applicant. Or a separate picture may be sent along with the resume. Also included in the solicitation campaign presentation should be a brief covering letter. The main reason I dislike the solicitation method is because all material must be **printed** and "scattered," with tongue in cheek, like casting a baited line in a quiet lake hoping that a lone fish will nibble. As a program manager I never formed much of an opinion of the sender of a soliciation presentation. In my opinion, only the man who finds it difficult to get a job will resort to this practice; the professional broadcaster follows his flight plan and contacts specific stations as set down in his plan. This is also soliciting, but of a very different kind.

Let me warn you about the unethical practices of some "academies" of broadcasting. A student of such a "school" showed me a copy of his resume which was prepared and printed by the school. Composition was most amateurish, and it contained a glaring display of bad taste, sheer stupidity and brazen effrontery: An entire paragraph in the student's resume was devoted to advertising the **school**, yet the youngster was charged the unbelievable sum of $18 for only 100 copies! A print shop advertises 100 copies, by offset printing, of camera-ready matter on 8½ x 11-inch stock for only $2.75! And the youth had already spent almost $1,500 on a course of instruction!

Besides being the beginner's way of getting that desperately needed start in the business, if only eight or ten resumes are required, mass-printed copies of your resume with photo insets may prove costly, even wasteful. After you get your first job, you may find yourself with a stack of outdated resumes. That is why I suggest that you custom-type resumes as you need them. However, if typing a neat piece of copy is a chore, of if time doesn't permit it, use photocopies. Ideally suited to approach a half-dozen or so station managers, or to answer ads in trade journals, this instant-print method is exceptionally economical, 15 to 20 cents per copy. If the copying machine is properly adjusted, you won't be able to distinguish the original from the duplicate, and it is just as good looking as offset printing. Incidentally, a large 8 by 10 glossy is not necessary. I much prefer to see an informal snapshot of an applicant attached to his resume. You'll find copying and duplicating services listed in the yellow pages of your telephone directory. If you plan to contact only a few stations, or to run an ad, or to answer classifieds, save your money and use the photocopy method. Test the machine to see if it turns out dark reproductions. Photocopies of your original resume with snapshots attached is in good professional taste.

To conduct a solicitation campaign—a **mass** mailing—have copies of your resume **printed**. Never mail out carbon, mimeo or ditto copies. To submit carbons of resumes, references and other informational material, reeks of amateurism. Don't do it! When making a **mass** mailing, it will save you money to have a photo printed directly **on** the resume. A small cut runs about $3 to $5 at the top, but the snapshot should **not** be pasted in place on your camera-ready copy. Attach it to the typed resume with a paper clip. Of course, you must leave white space in the left or upper right-hand corner for the picture. With offset printing, as differentiated from letter press, your original is **photographed**; therefore, keep your copy clean, make several test copies before typing out the final draft. Make sure you work with clean type, a new ribbon and try to avoid errors. In case of an error, **don't erase.** Type the word correctly on a separate piece of paper, then cut it to size, and carefully paste it over the mistake. Use rubber cement, **not** white paste. When typing your resume, use even strokes for good photographic reproduction. An electric typewriter will produce perfect results for offset printing. If you have further questions, consult your printer. See the professional resume synopsis in Lesson 24.

As for a mailing list, a copy of a current **Broadcasting** yearbook will furnish you with the call letters and addresses of all AM, FM and TV stations in the nation. The choice is yours. See the appendix for a directory of trade publications.

Lesson 22

Classified Ads

Advertising must attract inquiries, sell products and services, draw customers into the advertiser's place of business. Classified ads, too, must pull! But it must be done honestly without misrepresentation. In Lesson 21, we examined the three steps, and we covered the writing phase of Step 1, exposure. Notice in Letter 1 the applicant offered a two-in-one deal as a "hook" to get a reply—he offered to sell on his own time. In Letter 3 the writer informed the employer that besides being an announcer, he held a first ticket and knew how to service equipment, an extremely fine "bargain." When you can, offer an employer an inducement—a reason to prefer YOU.

Classified ads do not have to be wordy to be effective. They may be short, but not too short. Pronouns, conjunctions, articles should be omitted, but facts must be there to prompt replies—to make your ad pull. You must make a word picture, as it were. Here are are a few examples. Notice their brevity yet effectiveness:

1. MORNING MAN. Excellent educational background. Third class permit. Will go anywhere. Box   (PUBLICATION)

2. COMBO MAN. First ticket. 12 years. East only. Willing to do maintenance. Box   (PUBLICATION)

3. ANNOUNCER-WRITER. Well schooled both phases. Experienced. Northwest only. Available now. Box (PUBLICATION)

In Ad 1 the applicant is willing to go anywhere. In Ad 2 he has a first ticket, 12 years experience and can do maintenance, and in Ad 3 the applicant announces and writes and is available immediately. Be careful how you word it!

Three leading trade publications carry classified advertising sections:

Broadcasting-Telecasting, 1735 DeSales St., N.W., Washington, D. C. 20036 Publishes weekly. Issues a yearbook.

Broadcast Management-Engineering. Broadband Information Services, Inc., 200 Madison Ave., New York, N.Y. 10016. Publishes monthly. Carries classified advertising section. Issues yearbook.

Billboard, 165 West 46 Street, New York, N. Y. 10036

Broadcasting-Telecasting is available by subscription or may be ordered singly from the publisher at 50 cents a copy. This magazine has a general broadcast readership. Its classified section is widely read and is an excellent and preferred medium for the beginner. Billboard, undoubtedly, is a must for the modern DJ. It contains lists of top tunes of the month, top-40 releases, background on performers, etc., a thesaurus of information for his chatter on the air. This magazine is available on many newsstands in the larger metropolitan cities. BM-E may print an occasional article on production and salesmanship, but for the most part this is a very fine publication of primary interest to management and engineers. If you hold a First-Class Radiotelephone License, BM-E's classified section will reach the eyes of general managers and their chief engineers. Insofar as advertising rates are concerned, a postcard to the publishers will bring you their current word rate. The other two major trade papers are available by subscription and in the theatrical districts of large cities on newsstands. They do not carry classified advertising. They are:

Variety, 154 West 46 Street, New York, N. Y. 10036

Radio-TV Daily, 1501 Broadway, New York, N. Y. 10036 (mainly of interest to general and commercial managers)

For the beginner, I suggest a 6-month subscription to Broadcasting-Telecasting and the purchase of an occasional issue of Billboard.

Are you following through on your daily practice? Keep plugging away, day after day, and pay no attention to those "off" days. It's like dropping a dime in a piggy bank every morning—it adds up in time. Stick with it! Very soon you'll reach the readings and commercials in the back of the book to put the polish on your performance—that finesse. Did you send for the FCC FE Bulletin No. 4? If you haven't yet done so, do it today while you think about it. It may take two weeks before you receive it, and it will take time to study the questions and answers and other interesting information. Also, sometime soon, check on the location of the FCC field office nearest you and that office's examination dates. Government schedules change without notice, so before you go to take your examination, do a preliminary check.

Lesson 23

Your Professional Presentation

You're now ready to prepare your presentation: Step 2. There are five parts to a presentation, each one a working part to orient you toward Step 3, that important interview. (1) the outer envelope, (2) your covering letter, (3) your resume (see next lesson), (4) your photograph, (5) your audition tape (Fig. 20-1).

The outer envelope should be a new 10 x 13 kraft carrier; the return envelope, a 9 x 12, stamped and addressed carrier. Addresses on both should be neatly (with a dark ribbon) typewritten. If you wish, type the addresses on labels. Never fold anything. Place a piece of pad backing in the outer or inner envelope to prevent bending or crushing in transit. An impression of the man inside the envelope will be established and retained from the moment your new "boss" glances at the name of the sender in the upper left-hand corner; he'll "see" you—favorably or otherwise—in the appearance of your outer envelope. Clip—don't staple—the material together in this order: covering letter, photo, resume. Your name and address should be noted on each piece, including the carton in which you place your tape. Identify yourself at the start and finish of your audition. To prevent misplacement among dozens of other tapes on a program director's desk, seal the carton with a piece of cellophane tape. Make your audition material brief. You may be rewound before you get to your best work. Use a fresh reel, 4- or 5-inch is best. On the carton mark the speed at which the tape was recorded. You should sound your best; use only a professional quality hi-fi tape. If you have an 8 x 10 glossy photo, use it, but a snapshot will do as well. See further directions in the next lesson. A professional looking presentation will receive professional consideration, and who knows, perhaps an interview.

Relative to your audition tape, keep it interesting to listen to. Broadcast station executives are busy people. A help-wanted ad in one of the trade journals usually produces an avalanche of replies; the program director's desk may be swamped with tapes and envelopes. As a former program director myself, I always preferred the short, concise audition, the tape which I could hear in its entirety without having to rewind the applicant's efforts. So, save yourself work and save the program director's time by making your audition brief, and that also goes for an air check. (The matter of preparing an air check is thoroughly discussed in **The Man Behind The Mike.**) For your audition material, choose a few announcements from this book. Pick a conversational and a medium-hard sell. From press wire copy, about four short news stories will do. Open your audition with an introduction. Make it simple. No news format is necessary. Say: "This is John Smith auditioning." Pause briefly, then read your news, followed by the two commercials. If you wish to add a reading or some commentary, do, but keep it **short.** When through, again identify yourself: "John Smith speaking. Thank you for listening." The identification on the tape is **important.** All tapes look alike and the PD may have to audition 20 and more of them. There could be a mix-up. When I used to listen to an applicant's work, it didn't take me more than a few minutes to rate his audition. My advice is, make it effective—make it brief!

Should you assume a professional name? I suppose you've thought about an air name. There seems to be some mistaken notion among graduates of theatrical academies and schools of broadcasting that the neophyte **must** adopt a fresh, new name when entering show business; that it's the **professional** thing to do. If your legal name is hard to remember, difficult to pronounce or problematic to spell, consider a change, or more advisedly, simplify or abbreviate your present name. Consider well the possible legal entanglement involving your pseudonym and your legal name. In some states you may work under as many names as you choose, provided that such changes of names are not made with ulterior motives in mind; in other states you must seek court approval and legalization of your adopted name. If you possibly can, work under your own name. The act of assuming a professional name does NOT, in the least, reflect professionalism. So, think about it carefully.

One top-name vocalist has an extremely simple legal name, Gerry Dorsey. He achieved success only after he took the classical moniker of the German composer, Englebert Humperdinck, as his professional name. Another equally popular entertainment, Herbert Khaury, achieved stardom and riches when he simply called himself Tiny Tim. If you can, try to retain your own first and middle names. For example, if your legal name is Henry James Zobolovkowitz, call yourself,

Henry James. It's common practice: Ray Anthony, Bill Henry, George David—they're all good names. Check on unbiased opinions to weigh the pros and cons. Consider the tremendous success stories of the Cronkites, the Linkletters, the Kaltenborns, the Sevareids and the others with unusual names. They're doing okay for themselves. Aren't they?

Now, let me pass along some advice based upon my personal experience. Keep the record straight! If you decide to operate under an assumed name, purchase government savings bonds, insurance, automobiles, and arrange to receive your payroll check under your legal— full legal name. Of course, your Social Security account will be properly credited under both your legal and your professional names, but you must notify your local Social Security office accordingly. Use your own good judgment. Don't change your name unless it is absolutely necessary!

Lesson 24

How To Write a Resume

A carefully prepared resume may well prompt an interested employer to grant you a hearing. Your summation should present an influential, yet truthful, outline of you and your services: a fact sheet, listing your talents, abilities, education, specialized training, references, personal data, experiences, etc. Be aboveboard with statements to effect a true evaluation of your resume.

If you lack experience, say so, in passing. If you feel a continued interest to want to expand into other phases, sales, programming, etc., mention it, but don't elaborate. You see, managers seek employees who are ambitious. Don't "color" your resume with promises, unless you know from experience that you can deliver the goods; if you can't, your acceptance may be short-lived.

Don't commit yourself to a personal meeting before you consider well three factors: (1) the distance involved, (2) transportation costs (3) the time-consuming element. Connections are sometimes made on the strength of an attractive presentation alone. Few stations pay transportation and moving expenses. Seldom will a manager volunteer to defray the high cost of traveling.

Think carefully about references; they must be above reproach. The name of a fellow announcer—a peer—won't do. Superiors, yes. Because educators deal in theory with amateurs, their certifications are not freely recognized as sources of professional references, but as character references, yes!

Of course, as a beginner, you're not expected to show a commercial employment record, but do list any part-time employment, for example, in your local radio station, in a newspaper office, in a discount center as PA announcer, etc. Your first contact very possibly will be established, not via a presentation, but by way of a direct approach on a local level. Fig. 24-1 is a typical simple resume.

But, hold everything! Before you drop that important presentation into the mail box, ask yourself the following questions:

RESUME SYNOPSIS OF   Charles Arden III   ADDRESS   456 Smythe Blvd.
                                                          Silver Springs, Va.
                                                          23987

                                               TELEPHONE Area Code 305-721-6565

JOB OBJECTIVE   Morning DJ with parttime sales possibility on own time.

EMPLOYMENT   1963-present WRRR Warren, Penna. Morning announcer, some
RECORD   selling.

                 1960-1963 Writer for Jones and Donahue, advertising agency,
                 Chestertown, Penna. Parttime announcing for WCTC, as evening DJ.

                 1956-1962 WDLA Walton, New York as DJ Also did some play-by-play
                 baseball.

EDUCATION   General grammar and high school education in Sommerset, Pa.
                 Graduate of New York School of Broadcasting (two years) also
                 RCA Institutes home-study course to obtain my three radiotelephone
                 licenses.   Attended adult education classes in Sommerset High
                 School to study writing and elementary journalism. Two years
                 college (Liberal Arts course) H and H University, Claire, N.J.

OTHER   Conducted a school reporter program over my local radio station
EXPERIENCES   for 1½ years, and participated in a school forum series over
                 the same station as moderator. Also worked Saturday in the station,
                 in its music library.

PERSONAL   Born in Sommerset, Pa., June 2, 1933. Height: 6-1 Weight: 178,
                 Married, two children, Military status: Deferred. Salary open.

REFERENCES   Robert L. Moss, Gen. Mgr. WCTC, P.O. Box 897 Chestertown, Penna.
                 Mrs. William Fawley, director, Jones and Donahue, Metro Building,
                    Chestertown, Penna.
                 George Adams, President, Great Northern Radio Corporation, Buffalo,
                 New York.

OTHER   I am working at the present time, however, Mr. Smith, general
INFORMATION   manager of WRRR, Warren, Penna., knows of this application and
                 has agreed to a short notice of one week. I have also secured
                 Mr. Smith's permission to take time off for a personal meeting.
                 Please note that would like to do some parttime sales on my own
                 time. It may be that I will find it advisable to, some day, devote
                 fulltime to radio advertising sales. Have done very well in that
                 phase with WRRR.

Fig. 24-1.

1. Does my presentation make a good initial appearance?

2. Is the covering letter brief, neatly typed and written in good business form?

3. Is the photograph an informal, recent likeness?

4. Is my taped audition in good condition as a top professional would submit?

5. Will I be able to guarantee "quality control" in my work?

Robert L. Jones
679 State Street
Brooklyn, New york
11772

Mr. Jack Smith Gen. M
WXXX Radio
9800 Palmer Avenue
Middleboro, Penna.

Dear Mr. Smith:

Thank you for your recer
to send you further info
ground and experience.

Attached is the informati
ing a brief aircheck of my
city. If you feel a conti
services I will be happy t
meeting.

Sincerely,

Robert L. Jones

Mr. Jack Smith Gen. Mgr.
WXXX Radio
9800 Palmer Avenue
Middleboro, Pa.
16547

EDUCAT.
BACKGRO

OTHER
EXPERIEN

es in college, edited schoo
months with local Little 7
l with RCA institutes for n

T 169 HEIGHT 5' 10" M

PERSONAL

Warren, Penna.

REFERENCES

ctor, Jones and Donahu

of Pennsylvania, Pitts
consultant 678 Medford Avenue, F

OTHER
INFORMATION

present employer understands my problem in leaving my
has agreed that I may accept another position on short no
like to offer at least a one-week notice period
I can arrange for an interview within a one hundred mil
Westport.

Some applicants mail their resume with photograph separated fro
audition. I have always suggested that your resume, photograph, with c
and audition tape makes a more-effective impression when mailed as a c
tation in a neatly-addressed envelope. When a presentation is mailed i
there is always the chance that the tape may arrive a week or so afte
your presentation causing confusion as to which tape belongs to whic
your entire presentation intact for immediate attention as explained

Unless you definitely plan a solicitation campaign, do not have
Immediately after you get the job your resume become
send out carbon copie

Fig. 24-2.

6. Did I project personally in my audition?

7. Is my resume neatly type? Will it make a professional impression?

8. Does my employment record make me sound like a floater?

9. Is my presentation directed to the man who does the hiring?

10. Is there something I should not have said in my presentation?

11. Should I or shouldn't I have mentioned salary requirement in my resume?

12. Am I making this move in accordance with my "flight plan," or will this job, if I get it, take me farther from my goal?

At this point, the newcomer is leading up to Step 3, the personal meeting. He must examine the five parts of his presentation and make corrections if needed. If a presentation makes an overall favorable impression, the chances are that you'll be granted an interview.

Lesson 25

The Interview

This is the third and final step leading to that job. It should be handled properly and with care. What you say and what you do during a personal meeting with a prospective employer may be instrumental in getting you the job, or cause the opportunity to slip from your grasp. I have interviewed many applicants for work in broadcasting. Let me give you the picture from my side of the desk.

In the first place, if you are the timid type and are inclined to feel uncomfortable in the presence of strangers, consider the possibility that the man you're about to meet may also feel ill at ease when faced by you. Frankly, I don't believe you should feel concerned about your timidity. Try to put your new "boss" at ease with a friendly smile and a sincere greeting and you'll forget all about your own feeling of inferiority. The famous British essayist, G. K. Chesterton, hit it on the head when he said, "The real great man is the man who makes every man feel great." That's the general idea.

Obviously, you won't feel comfortable unless you observe a few commonsense rules of proper conduct, appearance and politeness—common consideration for the man who may be your new employer. To allow the "boss" to twiddle his thumbs while he patiently waits for you to "show" is unforgivable. The old chestnut, "Sorry I'm late," won't help to ease his first unfavorable impression of you. So, make it a point to be on time for your appointment. Be in the outer office when your name is called. The initial impression—when you appear in the doorway of the front office—will count! Wear a neatly-pressed business suit, tie and collar, of course. Avoid sports attire unless sportswear in business is acceptable in your area. It must go without saying that the informality of the mod set has its place, in dress, mannerisms and grooming, but that place is not in the general manager's office.

Make it, "yes sir" and "no sir." Avoid the colloquial "yeah." A young applicant for a job once asked an employer why he wasn't chosen for the job, and why his friend was given the preference. The employer said, "I hired your friend because his shoes were shined, because he was polite and gentlemanly, because he wore a neat suit with collar and tie, because he cared enough to make a good impression. His business-like attitude put him on the payroll." Think about that before you go for your interview. Leave that leather jacket at home. Of course, your talent, ability and training will bear tremendous weight, but why overshadow your assets appearancewise?

I now direct these remarks to both the male and female applicant. Without affectation of any kind, strive to make as good an impression as possible. An employer may frown upon the habit of smoking, or he may be allergic to smoke of any kind; he may be asthmatic. Because you have no way of knowing this, refrain from smoking. Don't request permission to smoke. It's embarrassing to be told, "Please don't smoke." It happened to me one time. Accept a cigarette if you wish. Let me make another important suggestion, and important it is: If your appointment is set for the afternoon, abstain from having beer or a cocktail with your lunch. Telltale beverages hang on and may well eclipse your favorable features. Why take a chance?

Because this business of broadcasting is a woman's world, too, now let me address the talented girl with aspirations to a career in this profession. It's well known that employment agencies which place women, exclusively, issue instruction pamphlets to new applicants who register with them. Say the agencies: "Wear a simple business dress. Avoid mannish attire. Go easy on make-up, sparingly on jewelry." To that I say, Amen! Now, I realize that the girl applicant wishes to appear attractive, but she may overdo those embellishments which, when used tastefully and with discretion, may enhance her appearance and personality. Let me ease your thinking on this matter. An employer highly desires neatness, friendliness, good manners and the other positive attributes which you should cultivate, but style-conscious ornamentations and exotic fragrances will make little, if any impression on a personnel manager. Actually, dangling earrings, dazzling rhinestones and whiffs of potent perfume may tend to distract the interviewer. What's more, it's YOU who should get exclusive attention—not your embellishments. You may relax in the thought that refinement and good taste are quickly recognized—no gilting is necessary.

Certain pertinent matters should be discussed during an interview, once it has been established that you're hired. Your exact duties should be clearly stated. The station's increment structure should be clarified. What the station expects of you and what you may expect in return must be made known. Sick leaves, vacations and other benefits are best taken up during the interview; whatever the stipulations, they should be clarified then and there. Griping and dissatisfaction result when an employee learns, after a few months on the job, that he must work legal holidays, or that he will not be granted a vacation until after a full year of employment, etc. Of course, there may be some "horse trading" on the matter of salary.

If the station is unionized, as are those operations in the larger cities, the man behind the desk will advise you accordingly and tell you the base scale and union increment structure. If the operation is a non-union station, the matter of earnings will come up for discussion with the usual question, "What salary do you expect?" Don't answer that! Let the employer play the first card by suggesting that he, because of his first hand knowledge of the station and what the market will allow, should name a figure. From then on it will be up to you to bargain, accept or reject the offer.

If the interviewer, whether he is the general manager or a department head, has a sound understanding of business administrative practices, he'll leave no loose ends. The trained executive will proceed to clarify a number of points: exactly what the station expects of you and your services, the number of hours to be worked and periods of the day as set down in your working schedule, your "off" days, etc. He'll also explain his operation's management—employee policy in regards to talent fees, overtime, vacations, fringe benefits, periodic increases in salary and other related points. When you shake hands on the deal you'll have the complete picture, and that's the way an interview should be handled.

Because of the importance of this section—to effect a successful interview—seriously consider the results of a survey conducted early in 1970 revealing the opinions of 150 personnel managers and other hiring officials. The questions, "How tolerant have American Businessmen become about the mod job applicant wearing a miniskirt, sideburns, moustache or beard?" and, "Shall it be off-beat clothes or conservative, traditional attire in today's business world?" Mark well what I am about to report:

Almost 80 percent of the 150 executives queried emphatically stated they would refuse employment to the applicant sporting a beard! About 90 percent of the personnel managers admitted they would reject the male applicant wearing should-length hair. However, most of them said they had no objection to long sideburns and felt no prejudice toward a flowing handle-bar moustache. Now, relative to the female applicant, just about 60 percent of the executives questioned said they probably would turn down girls appearing for interviews in miniskirts, but then, 45 percent said they had no objection to girls flitting around an office attired in miniskirts. About see-through blouses, that was something else. They stood almost unanimously on that one: "Definitely, no!" What about the Afro hairstyle for black job applicants? Almost half those surveyed agreed that such a coiffure was acceptable but on the female employee only, while 41 percent found the Afro hairstyle okay for the male black jobseeker. Well, there they are the facts as the result of a person-to-person survey conducted by the American Society for Personnel Administration and the Bureau of National Affairs Inc. Be guided accordingly.

So much for managerial opinions—pro and con—on the unconventional clothes and customs of today's youth. What are the views of the moderns? Why do they do what they do, dress the way they dress? Recently a group of young persons was queried about the wherefores of sideburns and moustaches, jeans and boots, medallions, headbands and other diverse adornments. The survey was revealing. John Bregenzer, assistant professor of anthropology at the University of Dayton, Ohio, who conducted the 200 or so interviews, discovered that there's a good reason behind way-out clothes and shoulder-length hair," they're trying, through their hair and clothes, to define themselves; to seek out people who agree or are friendly with them and to avoid those who are not." Mr. Bregenzer further learned that we may well go astray in our thinking if "you try to judge a student's politics and attitudes on the basis of his clothes and coiffure."

Mr. Bregenzer's findings sound logical, of course, but as I have stressed repeatedly, let's face it: The beginner needs a start in a competitive, highly reputable profession which demands top qualifications of him, favorable, professional and personal references, certification of an excellent general education and specialized training. Because of such stringent standards, in good broadcast circles, the nonconformist should not attempt to force a precedent; rather he should make every effort to create a favorable, initial impression—to be freely welcomed by a mature industry governed by a collective 50 years of rules and regulations. The important point here is that it's very possible, especially in a small-town market, the locale of his apprenticeship, that the neophyte may have to deal with a manager of the old school who abides religiously by staid customs. I have repeatedly advised students to get the "Lay of the land" before applying for work, to visit their local radio stations, to get acquainted with its staff and pointedly ask questions of off-duty deejays. The inquiring newcomer will quickly learn all he needs to know about the station's standards—high or low, rigid or flexible—and about its policy, lenient or outmoded. Knowing this, the new broadcaster may then be guided accordingly in his approach.

Professor Bregenzer points out: "When cultures and animals lose their diversity and become overly the same, it may not be too long when they will become extinct." Who wishes to argue the point with a professor of environmental and social relations and cultures? Anyway, there you have the two-sided picture, the pros and cons on a modern-day issue—mod clothes and customs. Perhaps it would be well for us all to remember that while this may be a changing world, the process of updating customs and accepting new departures is a painfully slow one.

Now, something of special interest to the graduating high schooler who wishes to cut short his education in favor of going commercial. The Government has issued its newest edition of "The Job Guide For Young Workers," a publication which dwells on a variety of job opportunities for the ambitious. I haven't read this new pamphlet, but it seems to me it should contain valuable information for those who look to radiobroadcasting for a profitable career. It costs $1.50. If you plan on furthering yourself educationally, the Government booklet, "How the Office of Education Assists College Students and Colleges" should prove helpful; cost 65 cents. Both printings are available from the Superintendent of Documents, U.S. Printing Office, Washington, D. C. 20402.

To round out this lesson on how to get your first job, a final but important thought: It's common practice for an anxious job applicant to actually talk himself out of an opportunity. Wishing to make a good impression, the overzealous unintentionally "colors" his background. This is unnecessary. The job applicant should let his resume act as a silent salesman—the purpose of such a factsheet. When you're called in for a personal meeting, you may assume that the station **needs** your services, that you're **wanted** and that the chances are in your favor; you may well be hired if, in your resume, you gave the "boss" a few good reasons to say yes. When you face your prospective employer, trust in his good judgment and take the "reversed tack." Let me explain.

The world renowned French psychotherapist, Emile Coué, early in the century, expounded a famous theory, undoubtedly proved as the most significant and far-reaching discovering in psychotherpeutics. Coué's **Law of Reversed**

Effort has long since been accepted by many practitioners the world over and recognized as freely practicable. According to M. Coué's way of thinking, the greater the effort, the harder we try to accept a theory or principle, or to accomplish something, as when we pressure ourselves into trying to recall a telephone number, a name or an address—the greater becomes the implication that that particular task is too difficult to accomplish, or to believe, or to accept, whichever the case may be. In reference to trying to remember dates and names, we actually set up a mental block, explains Coué, arresting the activity of our subconscious mind which remembers all. When we relax and permit our subconscious mind to freely function, the desired information is released promptly. For our purposes, let us say that the more we try to talk ourselves into a job, the stronger grows the resistance. How can you make the **Law of Reversed Effort** work for you— to help get you your first job? Simple!

First, don't appear or feel overanxious during your interview. Don't resort to mere talk to sell yourself. Prepare an effective resume, then let that instrument, like a personal manager, speak in your behalf. Do you get the picture? Think of your interview as a get-acquainted session to establish a mutual understanding of facts and figures. Harness those Is— don't let them run rampant. Soft-pedal talk—be a good listener. Answer questions freely and don't elaborate on replies. Make the "boss" feel important—address him by name. Respect the employer's keen sense of values; let **him** recognize a good talent buy. Don't try to influence his thinking; hiring you should be **his** idea, not **yours**. Do that, and good things will happen. Apropos of this subject and its importance relative to getting your start in this glamorous business, may I strongly suggest that you read and study Dale Carnegie's book, "How To Win Friends and Influence People." It has started millions of men and women on successful careers. Why not you?

RECAPITULATION—LESSONS 16 THROUGH 25

1. **Don't become a floater.** Work with a well-formulated "flight plan." Make every job count! Stay on your job until a better one comes along. Make changes for betterment, not because of boredom. Employers are not interested in how **many** jobs you have held, but they **are** interested in how **long** you were kept on each job.

2. **Forget school—leave theory in the classroom.** Broadcasting demands experience; don't talk school. Managers aren't interested in what you learned in the classroom. It's what you can do for them in a practical way that counts!

3. **Guard against becoming a perfectionist.** Perfectionists develop inferiority complexes because they try too hard to achieve perfection. It cannot be done. Do the best you can—that's enough. Relax!

4. **Don't jump the gun.** Get all the general educational background and specialized training you can **before** you get into full-time professional broadcasting. A broadcast station is not a school of radio technique. Working broadcasters rarely find the time for a self-improvement program. Get yours—now!

5. **Know yourself.** Are you the artistic type? Do you lean towards the scientific? Check on the four As: Aspiration, Attitude, Aptitude, Action. If mathematics is your weak subject, better forget about electronics. Don't insist upon doing what **you want** to do; follow through on the work for which you are best suited. Get an aptitude test. Ask for objective opinions.

6. **Succeed with a mental blue print.** Think of your "flight plan" as being a goal-searching missle. Consult your plan regularly to make sure it will keep you on the beam, to "steer" you towards your goal without detours and other time-consuming errors. Know where you want to go, why you want to go there, exactly what you want to do when you get to your goal and how you plan to accomplish the feat in the shortest time without floating about from place to place. Make every move count! Make every change a step upward toward the top of the heap. Change jobs only if betterment is indicated, not simply because you're bored with the routine.

7. **Set your sights for the proper niche.** Consider carefully the four As mentioned in the introduction. **ASPIRATION:** Do you ardently desire self-expression in this medium? Do you genuinely long for a career in broadcasting as your life's work? Or is it shallow fancy? Make sure! **ATTITUDE:** I have expressly been frank and blunt in presenting the **negative** side of broadcasting as a career to enable you to think of work behind the mike as just that—**work**—and to enable you to view your career in the light of reality. From what I have stated in

this book, do you truly think you can retain the proper mental attitude toward broadcasting for many years—a lifetime of activity? Again, you must be sure! **APTITUDE**: You owe it to yourself and your success in this keenly competitive profession to learn if you have "it," the basic qualifications, the natural leanings, the inborn talents, the patience to develop them, the time and inclination to carry through, the financial backing to gain the essential general educational and specialized backgrounds. All this has a direct bearing on aptitude. And you must be sure! **ACTION**: Are you made of the kind of stuff that drives you forward, up, and away? Do you generally follow through on ideas and plans? It will take perseverance to succeed in this industry. Do you have that much needed stick-to-it-iveness? Can you keep plugging along when the going gets rough? Are you able to exercise gumption? Can you take the initiative when required? Do you have the spunk to fight for what you want? As Henry Ward Beecher put it: Victories that are easy are cheap. Those only are worth having which come as the result of hard fighting.

If you want to be sure about the four important A's which have now come into your life, remove the glamour, applause, fan mail, adoration, the spotlight of popularity and fabulous earning potential, and think of your occupation as a disc jockey as **WORK**—a career in which you'll succeed financially and otherwise if you can stick with it, come what may. Please review the basic techniques as given in the preceding 25 lessons. Be patient, persevere and observe daily application as I have suggested. I must say it again: You'll have those "off days"; we all have them, and they pass away, too. Follow through on what I have told you in this book and you may well find this fascinating business of broadcasting a richly rewarding experience as well as a pleasant and profitable occupation.

Radio Sales & the DJ

At first glance, the subject matter—radiosalesmanship—may seem irrelevant to the general topic of this book: the disc jockey and his career. Some DJs try part-time radio sales to augment their salaries, but fail; therefore, I felt it necessary to touch briefly on radio sales and how the jock can succeed as a part-time sales representative. The knowledge and understanding of salesmanship, as it applies to selling the intangible product (an advertising IDEA) may well solve the young broadcaster's financial problems during his early days in the business.

Depending upon your financial resources, you may or may not find it difficult to live comfortably on a modest salary in an inflationary environment. If you haven't tried it, let me assure you that living away from home is costly. In some grass-roots markets it's possible that the minimum hourly rate of pay prevails, while some small stations offer newcomers workable base salaries. Supplied with advance cash when you leave home, you may not feel the pinch for a while. But after the newness of it all wears off, you may become bored with the routine, restive to increase your earnings, and, as is not uncommon with newcomers, you may decide to move on to greener pastures. That's usually mistake number one in the career of a deejay, and too many neophytes make the error of searching for the "perfect" job in broadcasting; they never find it because there's no Utopia in this or in any other field. After several job changes in a few years' time, the deejay becomes classified as "a floater." This he must avoid. And he can avoid it.

Small-station experience is priceless! In my opinion, the fledgling with so much to learn about broadcasting should remain in his initial small market for an appreciable time. He must absorb the fundamentals of broadcasting—garner that precious grass-roots background which he may never again experience as he makes his way up and away. I fondly recall my early seasoning of trial and error in the control room of a small-town radio station (at only $100 a month!) before I really became airborne. Escalation in this business is rapid; it's difficult to recapture what has gone before. If you missed the basics, you missed them.

How not to become a floater? Remain put in your first job for a year or so, longer if the work is pleasant and if you feel there's still more to be learned about basic broadcasting. While you soak up knowledge and build a solid foundation for your career, set up your "flight plan" so that when the proper time comes you'll feel confident and capable to make a progressive, worthwhile move toward personal prestige in a more populous, thriving market on the staff of a more powerful, perhaps a network-affiliate operation. That's doing it the right way—the professional way.

Despite a nominal salary, you can stay with it. The answer is to sell radio advertising on your own time! I did for a while, and through personal contact with advertisers learned a lot about the commercial phase of the business. Having met me in person, they wanted their ads to be heard on my show; my services became of more value to the station and the commission checks bolstered my income. A number of smaller stations welcome enterprising deejays who broach radio sales as a side line. Larger operations usually frown on the practice; they maintain a full sales staff. And, of course, that's as it should be. Incidentally, the deejay on a metropolitan station works on a guaranteed salary plus talent fees paid to him for special assignments. In metropolitan areas, salaries are usually geared to the cost of living in the specific city; hence, part-time sales by deejays in larger areas are rare, indeed. However, in the small market, selling radio advertising is a great way to ease up on financial pressure, but you must know how it's done. It must be remembered that as a radio advertising sales representative you are the seller of the intangible, an unseen product, a departure from hawking can openers and other household gadgets and peddling nylons.

When you approach a station manager with a money-making (for him) proposition, such as selling radio advertising on your own time, he'll grin all over and virtually throw you a sales brochure and a pad of contract forms. A quick "wish-you-well" handshake will send you into the market place with a stack of hard-to-sell accounts to crack. But don't become discouraged. You can crack them.

Observe protocol. Before you speak to the general manager about selling, check with the commercial manager about your plans to sell radio advertising on your own time. If he's unsure as to station policy regarding part-time selling by staff announcers, he'll refer you to the front office. Sometimes department heads resent it when a staff member goes directly to the top man up front. Furthermore, a commercial manager may have some excellent advice for you, and he may be instrumental in getting you started on sales. So, see him first.

Commission percentages paid to deejay-salesmen vary. I have a student who was offered, but refused, 5 percent. Another accepted 10 percent and two deejays, former students, are selling on their own time for 15 percent. Horsetrading tactics may be necessary. An ambitious deejay who is willing to devote his spare time to increase station revenue, in all fairness, should be shown the same remunerative consideration extended to full-time sales personnel. For your information, salesmen receive commissions on the total amount of the contract, for as long as the account remains active. However, commissions are not collectable until the advertiser pays his bill. In stations I know, salesmen are held answerable for the collection of monies due the station.

Before you extend credit to a new account, or even approach a would-be client, it would be well to check with your local credit bureau. You'll find it relatively easy to sell a bill of goods to a deadbeat; he has little and perhaps no intention of paying his radio or newspaper advertising bills. Cross the delinquent prospect off your list before you give of your time and talent sans commissions.

I know of a number of deejays who tried their hands at radio sales and failed. A week or two, perhaps three weeks of knocking on doors and that ended their career in radiosalesmanship. They failed because neither they nor the manager, who tossed them into the field, most times into a remote sales territory, realized that salesmanship—any type of salesmanship—is a science, and as such, the seller must take the scientific approach. Advertising agencies know this. Top, trained sales representatives will tell you: Don't try to sell something—give the customer a reason to buy, and he will.

What does the advertiser buy? Not time, of course, no more than he buys space in a publication. The merchant is interested in an advertising IDEA—a gimmick, a scheme, the powerful brainchild of an ideaman, which may bring customers into his store and hence make his advertising dollar pay rich dividends. The tingle of his cash register is proof of performance. In radio or TV advertising, the station's broadcast facilities are utilized to promote a cleverly composed piece of copy. In a newspaper the client sees a professionally planned layout, elaborately illustrated with a line drawing or photograph to graphically expose the product or service and a well-composed attention-getting headline with a subsequent power-packed commercial message. Don't try to sell your prospect commercial announcements, 5-minute newscasts, or a segment in a deejay show without an IDEA behind the program or announcement. The salesmen before you took the wrong tack, and that's precisely why you're stuck with a stack of so-called hard-to-sell prospects. Don't be a "time" salesman—become an IDEA man! Armed with a money-making, advertising idea—something you worked out exclusively for a client-to-be—you may feel fairly confident that your prospect will listen to your proposition. The important point to be remembered for successful radiosalesmanship is: Know your PRODUCT—know your PROSPECT, and you'll all make money.

Before we get into a few actual advertising ideas and how they motivated sales, let me say that this treatise merely scratches the surface insofar as radio salesmanship is concerned. The interested reader will learn much from a new book, **How To Sell Radio Advertising,** by Si Willing, which clearly covers the radio-sales picture at the grass-roots level, precisely the information and guidance you need as a beginner, and it offers the seasoned radio salesman the sage advice of an old hand at this business of broadcast sales. For a galaxy of tried and tested advertising and programming ideas, again I refer the deejay to my book, **Radio Program Ideabook.** Both volumes are published by TAB Books, Blue Ridge Summit, Pa. 17214.

Problem 1

The prospect operated a jewelry store. His complaint: "Times are bad. Business is slow. Money is tight. Who can afford to buy a new watch? So, why advertise?

Anticipating his plaintive reply, I came through with a prepared idea: "If you can't sell new watches, why not go after watch repair business?" I then ad libbed the first line of a commercial: "Watches tell time—when they run, and who hasn't a l-a-z-y timepiece around the house..." He bought the idea!

Problem 2

A feedstore owner was steadfast: "The way your station handled my business, no more radio advertising for me!"

While he ranted on, I spotted a placard tacked up on the wall of his barnlike establishment: "Baby Chick Week April 7-13." Hand-printed underneath were the words, "Drawing for 100 baby chicks on April 10. Get your lucky coupon today." I asked the elderly merchant if he would care to do a public service interview with me to publicize National Baby Chick Week. He accepted eagerly. A matter of hours after I aired the interview during my Saturday morning show, the man called me on the phone. Seems his friends heard him on the air and complimented him on the broadcast. We had him on the air with six 5-minute segments in my show starting the following Monday morning. A brief 3-minute public service interview did it. An idea paid off!

Problem 3

Another former advertiser who claimed no results from his advertising dollar was the operator of a Sleep Shop. His commercial was spotted at mid-morning.

No wonder he failed to bring customers into his place of business. Listeners are wide awake at 10:00 in the morning and very definitely not interested in ways and means of inducing sound and restful sleep. We suggested that he sponsor our "dead air" and place his commercial at exactly 12:00 midnight, just before our official sign-off. His copy opened: "Now, the period of silence which follows until we return to the air at 6:00 in the morning is brought to you by THE SLEEP SHOP, etc." We had him back on the air.

Problem 4

Our salesmen tried and failed to sell radio advertising to a hardware store owner. I suggested that his advertising message should be set up in the form of a service to his listeners. He listened attentively.

Sample copy was drawn up. Each piece opened with the line: "Now, today's handyman hint brought to you by ACME HARDWARE:..." Following the handyman hint, the commercial dealt with a product or products related to the handyman hint. For example, when the hint explained the proper way to clean paint brushes, the commercial sold brushes and paint-brush cleaners, etc. Books of handyman hints are available in bookstores. Household hints may be used for such accounts as house-furnishing establishments, department stores, sewing centers, etc. Sponsors like custom-planned advertising ideas which serve dual purposes.

Problem 5

A paint store owner sponsored a 5-minute segment of a 15-minute noontime news program. He could well afford to contract for the entire period.

Because he wanted a daily change of copy, we suggested that he, personally, announce his own messages. He agreed. In one week he requested to contract for all three 5-minute segments. He enjoyed "playing radio station" and the longer an advertiser is permitted to "play radio station," the more often will he renew.

Problem 6

The MacRae Company was a building supply firm which wouldn't hear of radio advertising. They ran newspaper advertising and couldn't be convinced of the effectiveness of broadcast advertising.

For this account-to-be we invented a character we called, "Sandy," who was one of our staff men who did an excellent Scotch dialect. An audition tape of "Sandy MacRae, the thrrrifty Scotsman" doing a commercial did it! MacRae thought the idea was "terrific" and gave it a try.

Problem 7

An Italian record shop operator agreed that "radio advertising could very effectively sell albums for me, if you had Italian listeners, which you don't."

He was right. So we built a special show to attract an Italian audience, which we tagged "Momento Musicale." Delighted, he furnished us with the records and his daughter served as hostess for the unique program. To make the idea pay off for us in revenue, a pizza parlor, spaghetti house, and an Italian grocery store completed the multiple sponsorship. Our arrangement with the record shop owner was a reciprocal deal.

There was also the skating rink operator who sponsored "THE TEENTIMERS," a boy and girl team who, with their music and chatter, attracted young customers to his establishment. A ship-to-shore radio dealer was highly pleased with his "FISHING NEWS" program (tides, weather, etc.). And we also gained a satisfied client who ran a used car lot. In a 5-minute newscast, instead of a wordy message (everyone knows what a car lot looks like) we ran a "daily special" and described the car as completely as possible in 150 words. And there were others.

In each of the preceding instances, an **idea** motivated the prospect to buy radio advertising or induced the advertiser to renew his contract. As a deejay-salesman, work on **one** prospect at a time; hitting the market en masse will get you nowhere. Preparing an effective sales presentation is time-consuming work. You must have the right answers when you approach a prospect. First things, first, remember.

From your list of leads, choose a prospect who sells a product or offers a service with which you're somewhat familiar. That will make it easier for you to come up with ideas. Next, check on his credit rating. Your station bookkeeper may already have such information. Acquaint yourself with his operation. If he runs a restaurant, have dinner there a few times before you approach him commercially. If the prospect owns a service station, make his acquaintance by becoming a customer, and so on.

To prepare a sales presentation, secure the following information: What product does the advertiser sell, or what service does the prospect offer? Type of customers: age and sex group? Why did the advertiser cancel or refuse to renew his contract? If his former business was mishandled, in what way? Why did other salesmen fail to gain his confidence? The periods of the day when the former advertising was scheduled? Nature of advertising: spots, news, program segments, other? If figures are available, study the audience rating during the period of his advertising. Most times you'll quickly spot the reason for the cancellation or the merchant's refusal to advertise over the air, as we did in the case of the Sleep Shop owner whose announcements were scheduled at the wrong time of day.

After you analyze all the answers, you must come up with an exclusive advertising idea which will act as a "counterirritant." Do you follow? Whatever you offer the prospect—spots, news, music segments, sports, weather shows—consider well the time of day to best capture the advertiser's potential customers. Only when you have an effective and complete presentation prepared, should you visit the prospect. Don't hesitate to listen carefully to his ideas; he may come up with a winner! Also bear in mind: The harder the sell, the stiffer the buyer's resistance, so don't sell; give the prospect a reason to buy, and that reason should be an IDEA. Be careful! Don't scare him off with talk about a long-term contract. Gain his confidence. Offer the advertiser a 13-week trial agreement. You may also allow him to cancel at any time by inserting the letters TF in the contract, which means **til forbid by the sponsor**. After you have signed your client to an agreement, regardless of the length of time of contract, work for a renewal. "Service" is the keyword here.

Contract renewals are virtually impossible to secure unless accounts are properly serviced; therefore, service your clients regularly. Personally call on the advertiser once a week if only to say hello and to show your personalized interest in his business and radio advertising results. Keep your finger on the pulse by seeing to it that his copy is changed or revised in accordance with the sponsor's wishes. If weekly servicing sounds like too much work—forget radio sales. A program director complained bitterly that an advertiser refused to renew his contract simply because he, the PD, failed to service the account. The program director's excuse, "Who has time to service accounts? I have a program department to run!" Programming is a full-time job, I know. He should have left radio sales to those who understand the science of salesmanship.

Don't wait until an advertiser cancels. If, during your weekly visits, you notice a waning interest in radio advertising or suspect even the slightest doubt in the mind of the client as to the effectiveness of his radio advertising, start working on some new angle, a unique idea, perhaps an entirely different approach on the air. Before you allow an advertiser to cancel, suggest a test to prove that he is reaching potential customers. Giveaways of inexpensive premiums, such as memo pads, calendars, ballpoint pens, etc., may prompt the advertiser to continue his broadcast activities. A department store hinted to me that it had been thinking about changing radio stations when its contract expired. Immediately we spoke about making a test. During the days of World War II, anything made of metal was scarce; therefore, when the store's manager suggested a few dozen 20-gallon trash receptacles which they had stashed away in the warehouse, we agreed on a test. Mention of the metal containers was withheld from newspaper advertising that week and the cans were kept under the counter. Two days after we advertised the trash cans on the air, the advertising manager called me on the phone to say that they could have sold 100 cans! The store gladly renewed. So, if you want to keep increasing your earnings as a jock, you must prevent cancellations and encourage renewals. It's up to yo. Only a satisfied advertiser will sign up the second time.

A final point before concluding this section: copywriting. You are personally answerable for your client's commercial messages. It's a part of your job to see to it that the advertiser's messages are written according to his instruction and that they are properly formulated to produce results. After the copywriter has finished with your commercials, if they appear well-written, conversational and composed according to formula, ask your client for his approval. If any changes are made, the revised copy should be neatly retyped. Check the copy again before it goes on the air. Remember, as a radioadvertising salesman you are actually a liaison man between the station and its clients; therefore, yours is a 2-way responsibility.

Some stations go so far as to insist that salesmen write their own copy. That's fine—if they are familiar with the finer points of writing commercials. I have never asked a station scribe to write copy for my accounts; I much preferred to do my own. If copywriting is of interest to you, Chapter 14 "Try Copywriting" in The Man Behind The Mike will help you. To be effective and motivating, commercials must follow a formula: (1) the headline: to attract attention; (2) the message: to create and sustain interest; (3) the motivator: to induce action. Another fine book on the subject is William A. Peck's, The Anatomy of Local Radio-TV Copy. (TAB Books, Blue Ridge Summit, Pa. 17214) This volume treats the subject from A to Z on a local level.

In summation, let me say that selling radio advertising during your free time, after a hectic 8-hour session behind the mike, may prove challenging; yet in my estimation, radiosalesmanship is the ideal way to augment your earnings as a DJ while you trek your way through the hills and valleys of your apprenticeship.

Broadcasting —
A Woman's World

I often wonder why more female talent doesn't find its way into broadcasting. The profession abounds in rare opportunities for today's talented Miss. This big, wide and wonderful world of sight and sound offers the woman of talent an inspiring and exciting life's work of fun and profit, plus financial independence—a career far more promising, to my way of thinking, than some of those pursued by other career women.

From first-hand observation as a broadcast careerist and coach, I can safely attest that many of today's talented youngsters appear well equipped with level-headed attitudes and natural aptitudes to approach the public, to sit behind a mike, to look pretty for the TV camera or to munch on potato chips and sip cokes under the hot lights of Hollywood's TV-commercial studios, or to knock out sales-producing advertising copy, or even deftly spin LPs and chat merrily en rapport with radio fans like a girl disc jockey should. Could YOU be one of the thousands of talented young women who dreams about a glamorous career in show business with a built-in, goal-seeking mechanism geared for a soft landing on the top of the broadcast heap?

Broadcasting is a multifaceted combine of arts and sciences; it welcomes young thinkers and those who dare to think big, and that may include you. Yes, the business needs newcomers with versatility and perseverance to seek that proper niche which may well bring the aspirant a soul-satisfying life's work—fame and financial happiness.

As I see it, today's career woman, from worker on up to executive, handles herself expertly well. In our commercial environment we find the girl taxi chauffeur, the female cop, the woman real estate broker, and to be sure, the lady school-bus driver, who has repeatedly proved herself most reliable and resourceful and quite capable of safely maneuvering a cumbersome vehicle with nary a scraped fender through narrow, congested streets and on heavily trafficked highways. And there's the modern homemaker—busy as she is—who knows how to paint a house, how to make minor plumbing and electrical repairs in the home and how to quickly change a tire, to mention only a few of her extra-curricular activities. In suburbia it's not at all unusual to observe an ambitious housewife handling the garden tractor just as easily as she wheels the baby buggy.

At the time of this writing, a 22-year-old coed was graduated with honors from the University of Florida, Department of Building Construction, the first woman so acclaimed for her unique achievement. I'll bet the lady, if she had to, could lean against a riveter or man a pneumatic drill, straddle the seat of a bulldozer or operate a crane, even help to string a lacy, steel network across a river. The point is this: If women can assume unusual responsibilities, and they **can** and **do** the unique, why isn't more female talent channeled into our profession? I am of the firm opinion that many a talented Miss is wasting her precious youth monotonously pounding a typewriter, or perhaps marking time behind a dime-store counter, or checking out groceries in a supermarket—a boring and dull routine for a creative mind, wouldn't you say?

Ask the average junior Miss about her plans for the future. The chances are she'll answer: "I want to be a secretary." Not another secretary? Why not try to discover your capabilities other than the development of dexterity at the keyboard? What else can you do? Sing? Act? Write? Play music? Maybe you'll fit into the broadcast picture after all. Evaluate yourself! Solicit unbiased opinions from your class instructors. The question is: **What can the real YOU do?**

Broadcasting needs and wants writers and actors, dancers and choreographers, reporters and commentators, announcers and deejays, etc. Before you settle for a humdrum, so-so livelihood, think about radio or television for an exciting career. What has all this to do with becoming a girl deejay? Simply this: You cannot expect to start at the top; you must gain the basics, learn the business from the bottom up, and that radio station "just around the corner" from you in your hometown is about the best jumping-off place I can think of.

Women have more than proved their expertness in the area of professional broadcasting. The industry proudly recognizes its top-notch female directors, highly creative groups, programmers, personnel managers, directors, talent buyers and many others of the gentler sex who work quietly and unobserved behind the scenes. We have a few women station managers, too, who admirably hold their own with enviable audience ratings in multiple-station markets alongside their male competitors. Surely, the lady commentator at the UN, the interviewer and the weather gals are no longer strangers to the TV tube. And what about the girls' voices one hears on radio stations? As I said, broadcasting is big business for those who dare to think big. Do you?

Do you like to act or model? Perhaps that's your peculiar talent. Casting agencies are always on the alert for new faces and vibrant personalities. They must keep a constant supply of fresh talent flowing into the hoppers of Hollywood's production mills where they grind out most of television's screen gems. What else do they do there? They produce those exceptionally profitable and entertaining TV commercials. Does that appeal to you? It may be your forte.

Earlier, we touched on TV-commercial making and how photogenic persons, oldsters and youngsters, even housewives who so naturally shout the praises of a "new and amazing washday miracle" act, sing and look pretty for the glass eye of the little black box, and how some of the folks you watch munching on potato chips or crunching a chocolate candy bar earn a "starving" $125 for an 8-hour-day's work; off-camera work pays a "measly" AFTRA scale of only $90 a day. Do you think that munching on potato chips, sipping a bottle of pop or crunching on a chocolate candy bar AND getting paid for it sounds like fun? Maybe so, but, sorry, it's a tough nut to crack. Look at it like this: To be paid $125 for a day's work on-camera, you've got to be good! You're expected to reek of professionalism. Retakes at that rate of pay, must be few; producers have their strict budgets. You see, talent, alone, won't suffice. It's specialized training and experience you must acquire. Others have done it. Why can't you?

Educationally speaking, I repeat, consider a liberal arts background if you can possibly afford it. Your success in this profession is not contingent upon a college degree. These days, a rank attained by scholastic achievement is not so freely accepted as proof of performance. A high school diploma is highly desirable ("essential" is the better word). Specialized training as acquired in the privacy of your own room via a correspondence course, or in the classroom of a school of broadcast techniques, (choose your school with extreme care) will help immeasurably to quickly establish yourself in commercial broadcasting. The industry has matured. Management frowns upon raw talent; it seeks developed, trained talent.

Remember, it isn't what we want to do for a living that really counts; rather, we should incessantly search for a specific phase in a vast field like broadcasting for work for which we are best suited. We must also ask ourselves if we are, psychologically and physically, equipped to stay with a certain activity week after week, year after year, for a long time.

Already mentioned are the various Madison Avenue enterprises which service our profession with scripts, transcriptions, news releases, press wire services, advertising clients, audience and frequency measurement services, etc. There may come a time when you'll want to spread your wings, and, undoubtedly, you'll think about advertising agencies, public relations firms, script-writing services and a few others. But, for the moment, forget about Madison Avenue. You see, these satellite enterprises, while they pay exceptionally attractive salary figures (perhaps the best in the business), must insist upon engaging only the creme de la creme in creative minds, artistry and craftsmanship. Ad agencies employ 75,000-plus persons.

Insofar as getting started is concerned, the same information passed along earlier in the book applies here; namely, to look around for some seasoning after you complete your specialized training. And again I suggest doing public address announcing in your local discount department store where the bargains of the hour are blared over loudspeakers every 10 minutes. Of course, if your high school or college maintains a campus broadcast station, you're in good hands and lucky to get "on-the-job" training along with your instruction. Following your period of "hardening-off," as it were, you'll be ready, willing and able to try for your first commercial broadcast job.

Now, let me tell you how a few girls got their starts. When one of my girl students completed her seventh lesson, she took it upon herself to approach the program director of her local radio station. When she told him how well she was doing with me, the PD, a family friend, agreed to give her a "break." She was hired as summer-replacement deejay. She did exceptionally well, so much so, that she had an afternoon, hour-long show of her own that fall. When I last heard from her, the girl was majoring in journalism and was headed for a radio-news career. She'll make it, too!

As program manager, way back when, I announced the innauguration of a new mid-afternoon program entitled, "For Women Only" to feature a girl announcer. The manager thought I had flipped: "What, a show with a **female** disc jockey? That won't work!" Could we attract advertisers to such a show? I had to find out and was determined to give the idea a try. After a few weeks of coaching and a short period of on-air supervision, our gal deejay built up quite a following with interesting guests, such as pediatricians, home economists, nutritionists, child psychologists and other program highlights. It wasn't long before we had a waiting list of advertisers. And they said it wouldn't work.

Knowing the "right people" can be highly beneficial in any line of work; in show business, these very important persons may be extremely instrumental in making recommendations, securing promotions, throwing commercial assignments (paying attractive talent fees) your way, etc. Undoubtedly, you'll meet those "right people" on the way up. I did. And they'll gladly give you that much needed boost. But the degree of your success, aside from help from your influential contacts, basically, will depend upon YOU. You must have something "on the ball"; those very important persons will be intensely interested in something **worthwhile** to promote.

Preparation is the word! Prepare yourself for the day when it will happen, when that big challenge (some call it a "break") will sneak up behind you and gently tap you on the shoulder. That's the way opportunities present themselves—unannounced—and you must be ready for them. Ask any pro. If you feel any doubts as to a woman's place in this fascinating world of broadcasting, consider the success stories of two Madison Avenue career women, Mary Wells and Jacqueline Brandwynne, rated as the two most successful business women in the United States in the advertising field. The ladies own and operate their own highly profitable advertising agency on New York's famed Madison Avenue. Yes, glamorous broadcasting is a woman's world, too!

In conclusion, I say, look to the applause, the lights and the popularity of the movie star—it's all for you! Don't envy the TV actress who earns up to $60 an hour or the successful writer, or producer, or choreographer, or director, or the others who loll securely in the financial security broadcasting offers the talented female. They could be YOUR opportunities, too. But, whether you choose to work for stardom and international fame, or prefer to stay put in broadcasting in your hometown, the success factor is the same: Keep your eye on your goal, whether that goal lies across the nation or across the street.

How To Build Your Popularity

It's easy to build your popularity! Improve the sound of your station to increase its audience rating! Let me quote briefly from **The Radio Program Ideabook**, Chapter 2, which deals with audience rating! "Is there a single factor which keeps a broadcast station in the number-one spot (and the disc jockey, too) year after year with an unfaltering audience rating? Yes, definitely! The intriguing factor...escapes one so easily because of its utter simplicity...the top-rated radio station provides its audience with a REASON to LISTEN!"

It's that simple and YOU can do it! If you want to quickly establish a following, give your audience a REASON to tune you in. Whether you're a deejay in a top-40 operation, or spin discs in the control room of a middle-of-the-road station, conduct a once-weekly feature program in stereo sound, or work an all-night trick out in the hills dishing out country and western sounds, the success factor is the same: give your listeners a REASON to tune your way and they will! The same success factor, despite economic changes, cements the thriving publication in first place with an enviable, guaranteed circulation. Its competing periodicals, like outwinded stragglers in a foot race, exhaust themselves and fall by the wayside. The monthly periodicals which boast of three-million-plus readers give their subscribers REASONS to read their printed pages. And top-rated TV stations, too, remain firmly situated in their broadcast areas because their programmers know the secret: Give viewers a good REASON to watch.

Unless you're with a key network station, consider well the audience-building power of human interest, **local** interest features. Brief interviews with members of social, religious and fraternal, as well as service clubs, will produce wonders. It's the quickest way of which I know to attract perhaps hundreds of new listeners at a time with a brief 3-minute question-and-answer session. Share your spotlight with local people who make the local news stories—the human interest angle which listeners love. For example:

1. The teenager who rescued a homeless dog from drowning in the village lake.

2. The oldtimer, at 100, who has very interesting things to say about life in your town, then and now.

3. The serviceman home on leave with his first-hand account of life in foreign lands, etc.

Of course, your choice of music, and what you say and how you say it, will either build your popularity or cut it down to size. Speaking of music, program directors in many smaller stations prepare music sheets for their announcers; however, morning men and those deejays who conduct special shows pick their own tunes, and the choice must be right. Need I mention that popularity and prestige go hand in hand? Incidentally, news concerning the men in the armed services, has proved to be an exceptionally welcome radio-program feature. On pages 200 through 206 in **The Radio Program Ideabook**, you'll find a format for a show entitled, "What Your Serviceman is Doing!" Also listed on those pages are the addresses of informational sources where you may obtain news from men in all branches of the services, taped interviews recorded in the battle areas of the world, transcribed features about the armed forces, etc.

I used to watch local newspapers for human-interest interview ideas. For example, when I read about a plan to solicit funds for the construction of a much-needed new hospital, I contacted the campaign chairman and arranged to make a series of 3-minute interviews, which I used during my shows from time to time. When I learned about the razing of an old, famous landmark to clear the way for an ultramodern apartment building, I smelled a human interest angle. Keep an eye on your local newspapers daily. Try to include at least one 3-minute interview during each hour show.

An important word with which you should become familiar is promotion. Promote your show. It's simple. Ask evening announcers to give your morning show (or the other way around) a plug. Request permission from your copywriter or program director to record a few promotions. Make them brief, like this:

Hi! This is Johnny Jones. I host an early-morning show starting at six. The news, weather, fishing news, tides, and of course, wake-up music make up "Rise 'n Shine." See you in the morning!

And in your own show, reciprocate by plugging your colleagues' programs. Also, every day promote the interviews to be aired on your future programs. Ask the persons whom you interview to do some newspaper publicity on their upcoming broadcasts and to announce the program to their club's membership. You must blow your own horn, but do it gracefully. Encourage others to give you a boost. There's a new publication, **Radio Promotion Handbook**, written by William A. Peck (TAB Books, Blue Ridge Summit, Penna.) This volume reveals ways and means to quickly develop better audience ratings. It's an exceptionally informative 256-page book. Every newcomer should own a copy.

Consider the following truism well: Don't choose music for your program simply because YOU like the vocalist or the combo. Don't speak on subject matter of interest to YOU, unless your choice parallels the likes and tastes of your audience. Because the choice of musical selections also has a bearing on timing, I shall leave this subject matter for further discussion in the section, **The Art of Timing**. See also **A Guide to Good Timing**. As you can now understand, the accumulated effect of good music, interesting features, clean production, friendly chatter, used sparingly, and good taste in showmanship spells the word R-E-A-S-O-N—a **reason** for listeners to tune you in regularly.

Regarding program promotionals, use tape cartridges. Because they are convenient to use (no threading necessary) your colleagues won't mind occasionally slipping one into a player to plug your show. A DJ friend uses cartridges to record his opening and closing musical themes, special station identification messages and program promos. He tells me they're perfect for the purpose. Get recording artists to promote your program, too. Here's how. Write to recording companies. Explain that you feature so and so during your afternoon or morning program. Request a few station identification messages to be recorded for you by the singing star. Specify the name of the artist and furnish the typed out copy. These brief messages will make quite an impression on your audience when your listeners hear: "This is Frank Sinatra. Have you heard Bill Smith's wake-up show over WOOO, in Claremont? Listen tomorrow morning!" Naturally, the vocalist does it to sell his albums, yet at the same time he gives you a pat on the back.

There are still other ways to up your audience rating. You may want to publish a monthly radio newsletter, conduct a radio column in your local newspaper, or start your own fan club. A former student, now a professional DJ with WQRS in

Detroit, has come up with a powerful audience builder. Andy Stoffa has tried them all, ballpoint pens to bumper stickers, but this promotion, he says, is the best yet! He calls his latest audience-promotion gimmick, the "Big Band Era Quiz." The novel musical contest poses a series of 18 questions for the young oldtimers in his audience who still remember the sounnds of the big ones: Glenn Miller, Ozzie Nelson, the famous Dorseys, et al. The imagination produces wonders! Speaking of the big bands, there were almost 300 of them. If this subject matter is of interest to you, there's a priceless volume available on the big-name bands and their music-makers under the title, **The Big Bands**, published by the MacMillan Company, New York. $9.95. This excellent reference book for the deejay who features this type of music contains interesting biographical data on band leaders past and present and makes reference to most of the popular big bands of another era.

Contests make great audience stimulators. I have used them successfully, but there are rules and regulations to abide by—FCC rulings and postal regulations—and there's the matter of professional ethics and good broadcast practices to consider. Here's the way the National Association of Broadcasters feels about conducting contests:

"Contests should be conducted with fairness to all entrants, and shall comply with all pertinent federal, state and local laws and regulations. All contest details, including rules, eligibility requirements, opening and termination dates, shall be clearly and completely announced or easily accessible to the listening public. Winners' names shall be released as soon as possible after the close of the contest...."

On the subject of premiums and prizes offered to winners, the NAB Radio Code of Good Practices reads:

"...There shall be no misleading descriptions or comparisons of any premiums or gifts which will distort or enlarge their value in the minds of the listeners."

This simply means tell it like it is without coloring. For example:

DON'T SAY

A beautiful **gold** ballpoint pen.
A handsome **leather** memo book.
Send for this **priceless volume**.
Valuable collection of famous recipes.

DO SAY

A beautiful gold-colored ballpoint pen.
A handsome leatherette memo book.
Send for this valuable booklet.
Helpful pamphlet of famous recipes.

If you want to come out of a contest unscathed by criticism and free of any distasteful involvements, legal or otherwise, stay with the rules all the way.

Production Practices

After successfully completing the final step in the process of getting your start in the business, you are now ready to work out an apprenticeship in a commercial broadcast operation. Now your thoughts should turn to production—**good** production practices, that is. There's a right and a wrong way to run a control room; you cannot depend, nor should you rely, on your colleagues to teach you more than general station routine. Control-room operational duties include: accurate reading of meters, the precise entries of such readings on the transmitter log and carefully recording times and other necessary data on the program log, the authorized manner in which station identification should be given, plus other control-room routine in keeping with FCC Rules and Regulations.

You'll recall that a deejay in a transmitter-studio operation is held strictly answerable for any infractions of FCC rulings and there are many of them. The deejay is also personally responsible for any faux pas, productionwise: wowing in LPs, missing commercials, running over on his program, joining the network after a show has started, etc. Putting this in another way, slovenly production in the progressive, quality broadcast station simply will not be tolerated. Let's discuss some of the major production practices, good and bad.

As with any serious undertaking, easy-to-listen-to production demands ample preparation—planning and forethought. Broadcasting is a trying, split-second business; you must constantly be conscious of the time element. That ticking contraption on the control-room wall challenges the harried deejay to a daily game of "Beat The Clock." It's fleeting sweep-second hand, hourly, dares the announcer to beat the time beep—if he can. That's the way it is. Of course, LPs and announcements may be thrown on the air in carefree fashion without giving production a second thought, but then, any beginner can do that; it's the "technique" of the amateur. It happens all the time in some small-time stations, but such pseudo production simply transmits as a slobberly sound.

There's no short cut to professionalism. Good taste, artistry and originality, plus hard work are needed to put out a **good** sound.

Consistency in quality broadcast production, from sign-on to sign-off, day after day, may well be likened to what is known as "quality control" as practiced, for example, in the food and drug industries. To uphold an enviable reputation for high-standard merchandise, and to retain those priceless ingredients—purity and potency—in his products, a manufacturer conducts periodic quality-control tests; the series of digits on the label of a pharmaceutical product (its control number) symbolizes quality. Laxity in broadcast production as well as in the manufacture of tangible goods cannot help but result in mediocre, second-rate products. To succeed in this profession of arts and sciences, with its preponderance of multitalented contenders for the honors, I urge you to put the emphasis on **quality**—first!

Improve the sound of your station with good production! Regardless of artistry, ingenuity and ability, the lack of forethought will ruin any production. I expressly make a point of this because the newcomer to broadcasting over-enthusiastically will rush headlong on the air only to run into production problems. It happened to me. Distasteful production will ultimately chase your listenership scurrying to another frequency for more pleasing and easier listening. It isn't only the newcomer who offends with inferior broadcast fare. Disinterest and complacency overtook a bored broadcast veteran with whom I once worked. I used to watch him let programs "just happen." He was a professional, all right, but despite his seniority and experience, I knew better than to emulate him and his easier way of getting things done.

A lack of preparation is evidenced, for instance, when LPs are allowed to spin on-air before a turntable gains momentum. "Wowing," as it's called in broadcast jargon, results. Too much theme music at the start and a monotonous grind of musical fill at the close of shows, unmistakably spell amateurism. "Sorry we're late, gotta run," is the trade mark of the inexperienced. Silent spots ("dead air") are giveaways that the DJ is at a loss of something to say or can't find an LP to spin—perhaps not even in the control room. Rattling-paper noise over a "hot" mike openly reveals that the unprepared jock is frantically clawing his way through a stack of commercials in search of that elusive piece of copy he failed to have in readiness. Despite meticulous preparation, one of the above bugaboos may occasionally occur. Broadcasting is an unpredictable business, and no one is infallible; we must allow a reasonable margin for error, but when blunders become common practice and become aurally annoying, they also become inexcusable. Recently, a television station twice in a matter of minutes flashed a "transmission difficulty" slide on the screen during a trouble-free program. Its video engineer occasionally permits illumination to fluctuate from virtual darkness to glaring brilliance. It's a common practice for sound levels to drop, then suddenly rise to ear-deafening proportions. On a few occasions, commercial slides appeared inverted. When such things happen frequently, we must assume that inexperienced apprentices are at the controls or that slovenly people are at work. What else?

I urge you to develop good broadcast habits right from the start. Get to the station ahead of time. Check your log—in advance—for new programs, new commercials, changes in schedule, etc. Have your musical selections set up in playing order at least a quarter of an hour in advance of airtime. Cue in your theme music before you go on duty in the control room. Avoid that last-minute telephone call which might take but a moment; remember the clock on the wall. Your program director may be an excellent business administrator, yet he may be in the habit of issuing verbal orders. The professional PD, to inform you of any new shows, schedule changes, etc., will place memo messages in your assignment box. If the man in charge of your program department, your immediate superior, insists on shouting orders down the corridor, make it a practice to ask questions when you report for duty. You may be held responsible for not making inquiries. Play it safe!

Any factor which tends to distract you, divert your attention from your equipment and routine, should be strongly but diplomatically discouraged. Visitors, without being aware of it, may throw your entire show out of line by engaging you in conversation about your "fascinating work." Off-duty staff members, sometimes, are the worst offenders. With nothing much else to do to while away their time, they may hang around the control room to chat and distract you. As I said, diplomacy is the keyword here. Politely ask them to leave. No one should be permitted to loiter in the control room, not even a program director or station manager. Personal telephone calls should be forbidden while you're on duty, in the control room or elsewhere. Unless a call is directly concerned with a program, such as a quiz show, the telephone operator should be instructed to never refer phone calls to you while you're at the controls. I can assure you from my personal experience in control room operation that distraction in any form will reflect unfavorably upon production.

Encourage concentration by discouraging distraction! Do it firmly yet pleasantly. Avoid being typed as a perfectionist or a grouch or a prima donna. I had an occasion to ask a general manager to leave the control room when I noticed that his trifling conversation caused me to miss a meter reading. He wasn't offended; in fact, he apologized and left promptly. I recall an announcer who took an uninvited guest by the arm and directed him out of the control room. The "guest" happened to be the corporation president, who later nominated the young man for the position of program director. "I like his spunk!" he remarked. The deejay who told off the corporation's top executive got the job! But your best bet is to take the tactful approach.

A poorly maintained control room—equipment in need of servicing—is definitely a contributing factor to sloppy production. Noisy switches and dirt-laden faders, off-speed tape equipment, wowing turntables, weak amplifying tubes, damaged microphone cables are a few of the destructive nuisances with which a disc jockey must contend. Even a studio clock which chirps annoyingly instead of beeping like a good clock should, or a flickering fluorescent tube, or a squeaky swivel chair surely won't make things any easier for the pressurized jock in his cubicle. I've put up with them all over the years. When you get into commercial broadcasting, resolve not to wait for a colleague to report mechanical trouble. Do it yourself. Just as faulty copy should be brought to the attention of the copywriter, and damaged recordings referred to the program director or music librarian, engineering trouble should be noted, in writing, and the report should be left on the chief engineer's desk for action. To fail to notify your chief about some mechanical problem may again become your bug-a-boo the next time around. Even seasoned broadcasters, jocks with years in the profession, cannot produce top-notch programs if they must fight turntables, recorders, switches and buttons, chirping clocks and squeaking swivel chairs.

In all fairness let me emphasize that equipment malfunction shouldn't always be blamed on engineers. Any technician worth his ticket highly desires and is proud, indeed, that his station puts out a clear, loud, good sound. How can a chief engineer be held answerable for equipment failure when deejays take the "who cares?" attitude? And there are DJs who simply don't give a hoot. True, some engineers are very lax when it comes to maintenance; they wait until a station must leave the air to replace a weak tube. But laxity, happily, is not the rule. Engineers, as I have known them, are con-

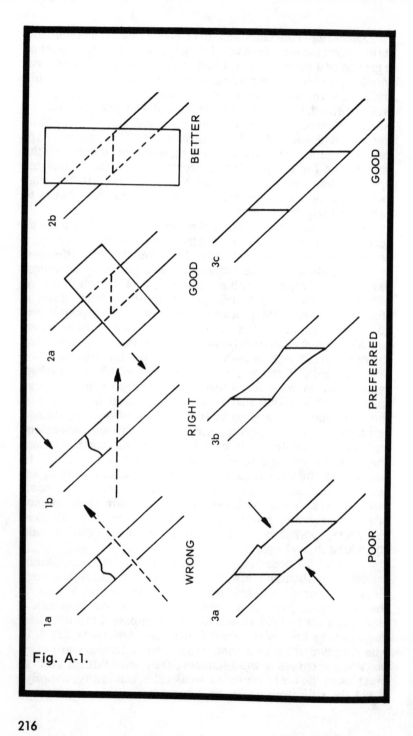

Fig. A-1.

scientious fellows who will gladly work around the clock to keep their stations on the air.

When an LP develops a cutover or a scratch, it's replaced. Not so with tapes. Despite signs of wear, brittleness, flaking and breakage, the deejay, in most stations, must tolerate the condition; he is forced to work with worn out reels and make repairs when needed. Even among seasoned professionals there are those who do not know how to make a strong, lasting splice. True, there are splicing gadgets, but frankly, I have become quite adept at patching tapes without the assistance of such a contraption. Follow the simple directions given in Fig. A-1 and you, too, will become expert at splicing tapes as it should be done. Use a piece of cardboard as a worktable. Overlap the two broken ends, then with a sharp razor blade make a clean, diagonal cut across the tape (illustration 1b) or if you must, bring the two breaks flush. As indicated by arrows in the illustration, hold the tapes firmly in place with the small and forefingers of the left hand. Gently blow away loose tape. Press a short length of ½-inch splicing tape—not ordinary cellophane tape—diagonally over the cut (illustration 2b). With a razor blade trim off the excess splicing tape, either flush or slightly indented (illustrations 3b and 3c). Never leave splicing tape protruding from the sides (illustration 3a). The exposed adhesive may cause drag when the tape passes over the playback head. When ordinary cellophane tape is used for splicing purposes, the adhesive, especially during warm weather, may adhere to playback heads, and eventually spread to other tapes. To keep the ends of tapes flat and secure during splicing, I wet the emulsion sides of the ends, then press them into place on my working surface. They stay put long enough to complete cutting, splicing and trimming. Try it.

Those who prefer to splice with a mechanical aid will find an inexpensive gadget to do the job available wherever tape recorders are sold. The device cuts broken ends of tapes

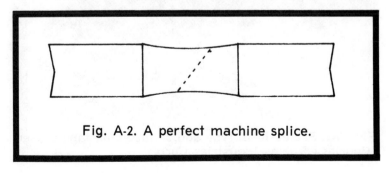

Fig. A-2. A perfect machine splice.

Fig. A-3. Handy magnetic tape splicer. These devices are available for ¼-, ½-, and 1-inch wide stock. (Courtesy Robins Industries, Inc.)

Fig. A-4. Professional type audio-video bulk tape eraser. (Courtesy Robins Industries Corp.)

218

obliquely at the proper angle; it trims off excess splicing tape concavely from the sides of the repair to prevent the adhesive from contacting the recording and playback heads of your equipment. According to the manufacturer, the gadget makes perfect splices in seconds (Fig. A-2). The operation is quite simple. No razor blade and ruler are required for clean, straight cutting and trimming. Guides hold the tape in a straight line; a sliding knob has both a cutter and trimmer (Fig. A-3). The deejays who would rather make repairs freehand deftly work with a pair of scissors and they're quite good at it. Try both ways. Regardless of which method you choose, there's no shortcut to making a clean, break-resistant splice. A hastily repaired tape may well invite trouble. Even the most professional splice cannot guarantee against breakage where the splice ends. I used to test all my splices by giving the tape a quick, snappy tug. After a few practice splices you'll be ready and able to make a split-second patch when production demands an emergency repair.

While on the subject of tape-recording accessories, I consider a bulk demagnetizer as essential equipment in the control room (Fig. A-4). Since such a device is missing in many radio stations, operators must rely upon the wiping head of their recorders and trust that on playback all will sound well.

A tape eraser is inexpensive. It can handle tape up to 1-inch wide and reels 7 inches in diameter. To completely demagnetize a tape takes only seconds. Background noise levels on tapes are reduced from 50 to 90 decibels below the saturation minimum. Operation is simple. The unit plugs into any 115-volt outlet. The reel of tape is dropped onto the spindle, the current turned on, then using the fingers, the reel is slowly rotated for about 10 seconds. Flip the reel and repeat the rotating process, and that's it—a clean, noise-free tape, entirely demagnetized for safe recording. Make it a rule never to record a program or a commercial on any tape (unless it's brand-new) before erasing it completely on a bulk demagnetizer. It makes good sense to spend a quick 10 seconds "wiping" a tape before recording, just to be sure.

Some deejays find it difficult to offer the ultimate in good production because they must work with inadequate equipment. There are still many broadcast stations which operate with only two turntables and one tape recorder. If you should run into a problem station in which you must operate with limited equipment, there isn't much you can do about it. The same may be said if you must function with a limited number of LPs. Again, diplomacy might work, but hold off requesting additional equipment until you feel you belong where you are. As a newcomer, do the best with what you have by inserting originality and personality into your shows.

Untidiness takes its toll in reduced efficiency and enthusiasm. Haphazard installation of equipment clearly reflects a disorganized attitude; it creates the impression that management doesn't give a hoot, just as long as the station is on the air and is making money. Carelessness with used coffee and soft-drink containers, sandwich wrappings, cigarette butts and overflowing ash trays should be tolerated. Clean up that control room without appearing to be the immaculate one. Who knows, you may start some serious thinking on the part of management to enforce a few reasonably strict rules regarding control room operation.

Stagnant programs, hackneyed introductions and closings, stale program formats are powerful audience chasers. The newness of it all will wear off soon, and when it does, rather than work with an ill-concealed lack of enthusiasm, approach your program director with a suggestion and request permission to ad lib or to write out your own intro and closing copy. Very possibly he'll appreciate your thoughtfulness and ambition to personalize programs. You may also want to write out your own news introductions and closings. (See **The Man Behind The Mike** Chapter 12, "News Reporting.") Discuss program ideas, your own ideas, with the program director. He'll welcome fresh sounds.

Handle playback heads as you would precious gems. Extremely sensitive, a stylus will quickly go out of adjustment if only slightly jarred or dropped. Even when in a hurry to get a tune on the air, the process calls for a steady hand and s-l-o-w motion.

Avoid backtracking. To backtrack means to place the pickup on the disc and manually spin an LP until music starts, then to back up the recording to the playing position. This practice damages the fine microgrooves. Don't do it. I always advise students to count the number of dead turns, then to allow the disc to run in again just short of where the music begins. For future playings, make a note of the number of dead turns on the label, alongside the title of the selection.

Modern turntables gain momentum almost immediately, while older models get off to a sluggish start. Most jocks disregard the slow or fast-starting table by using this method: Five or ten seconds prior to music, they place a finger against the edge of the LP to hold it in playing position while they start the table spinning. Then, when music is indicated, they open the fader and release the disc, in that order, for a clean, tight segue. Of course, extreme care must be taken not to jar the stylus while holding the LP in the playing position.

Another good production practice concerns tape cartridges. As with LPs and reel-to-reel tapes, cartridges should be handled with extreme care. Because the tape is enclosed in what appears to be a sturdy plastic case, some deejays unintentionally give cartridges rough treatment. Working hurriedly they may, for example, throw a cartridge across the room into a box. Sometimes they miss and the delicate cartridge hits the floor. Cartridges are fragile. Plastic cracks easily. Careless handling quickly jars finely adjusted mechanisms. The malfunctioning of tape cartridges may often be blamed on mishandling. It takes only a few moments to do a quick check on a cartridge before putting it on the air. The wire bar may be out of place; the head opening may have been tampered with, etc. The chief engineer will advise you on this. Unless you're expertly familiar with the mechanics of tape cartridges, ask an experienced colleague to open the case and make adjustments. There are now publications available which deal exclusively with the handling and repair of tape cartridges. I suggest you check your book dealer on this.

Now, a final word about good production practices—riding gain. Riding gain means to keep your eye on the pointer of the volume indicator and to make adjustment so as to avoid overloading or a low-level input, as illustrated in Fig. A-5. Riding too high a level causes distortion; too low an input

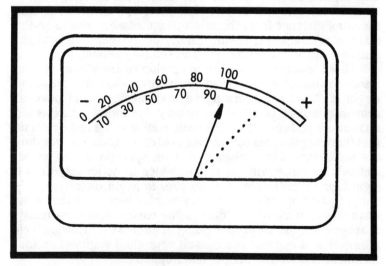

Fig. A-5. Voice should peak at 100. Music at minus 80. Dotted line denotes overloading.

results in a weak signal in the station's secondary broadcast area. Erratic levels, surges and frequent fading may definitely be termed slovenly operation; it reflects amateurism. One hears it all the time: The commercial on the tail of a quiet, dramatic sequence, which rockets itself into the living room, the dialogue which suddenly fades into nothingness, the brassy crescendo of a big band and its dynamics, the DJ's voice which "sneaks in" on the air, the hard-sell "artist" who rides himself at too high a level just to be sure his cacaphony will be heard. And all too frequently a television drama's dialogue is blatantly washed out by "background" music. Careless sound engineering, poor production. Listenable levels, making smooth segues from voice to music, from music to voice, from local to network programming, calls for professional gain riding.

Prolonged usage steadily and gradually weakens amplification tubes; hence, you cannot set a level and forget it for more than a day. You should take a moment, daily, before going on the air, for a voice level to preset your fader for the day. This may quickly be done by flipping your mike switch in the audition position, then, while you adjust your fader, sharply speak a series of MAH! MAH! MAH! MAH! etc., until the volume-indicator "needle" repeatedly kicks 100 or slightly under. You're then set to go on the air with a flip of the switch. This is referred to as "presetting" a level. When taking a voice level, be sure to test in your full voice and at precisely the speaking distance from the microphone as when you're on the air. Occasional overpeaking cannot be avoided and a slight flutter of the pointer into the red will cause no distortion.

There is some difference in opinion on the riding of gain insofar as music is concerned. With music you can't set it and forget it. Most engineers agree that music should peak at around minus-80 to allow for brassy dynamics. Unexpected forzandoes will send the VU needle well into the red. It's true that there are devices to compensate for overloading, but they are not designed to replace a vigilant operator at the board. Actually, a surge will cause the device to noticeably drop a signal for several seconds. You see, to avoid distortion, this unique piece of equipment compensates most efficiently for gradual overloading; the man in the control room, basically, is answerable for the proper riding of gain. As for music levels at minus-80, I suggest you consult your chief engineer on that technical matter for his personal opinion.

In larger stations, announcers may work in a number of studios during their broadcast day. The may be asked for voice levels as many as a half-dozen times during their sessions. This is done by reading a piece of copy or news until you get the okay sign from the control room. Keep your eye on the VU meter, your ear on the monitor, your fingers on the fader. Do this, and you'll make a genuinely worthwhile contribution to good production practices.

The Art of Timing

Yes, timing is an art! Timing is perhaps the most important word in show business. A television director may ask a performer to allow two seconds before speaking a line, or to pause momentarily before reacting with a smile or a frown or some other facial gesture. The pause here (see Lesson 13) is employed to give naturalness and believability to the actor's performance. The comic's joke, minus expert timing, falls flat. The politician is well aware that the momentary pause is a powerful attention-getting device and uses it frequently in his campaign speeches. Few disc jockeys realize the effectiveness of the pause—the importance of timing, so they just spin and chat.

Timing is the art or practice of regulating the tempo, mood or pace of a musical or dramatic performance or an action, to heighten the effectiveness of the sequence. The ski jumper, boxer, golf pro, billiard champ and others who participate in contests know that winning at sports depends, to a great extent, upon their sense of split-second timing.

When a DJ talks too much, his timing is off. When he opens his show with a dragg, insteady of a bright tune, he's off time. When he plays two slow or two fast numbers in succession, timing is poor. A dragged-out opening theme and the drone of monotonous fill at the close of a show constitutes poor timing. When the jock rattles off announcements and news at breakneck speed, or makes undue pauses while glancing at the clock, timing is off. When a morning man, as some early jocks do, yawns and ho hums, believing that his sleepiness colors an early-morning show, his timing is at its worst. A show must never stand still. It must move ahead steadily at an easy-going pace with an ebb-and-flow rhythm to sustain listener interest. There's no substitute for timing.

I recall a play we did in summer stock. It was a good story with a unique plot and the script was loaded with excellent laugh lines. Regardless of a professional cast, during each evening's performance we could feel audience interest wane at the close of act two. We simply couldn't put a finger on the precise lines or stage business which caused the timing to go off. It would seem that when a drama critic shrugs his shoulders during a first nighter, he is unable to say for sure just why he doesn't particularly care for a play. Yet the same play after a few changes in the dialogue and a rehearsal or two may well enjoy an all-time, long-run theatrical success. Timing is a very important word in show business!

Top performers, like Jack Carter, Myron Cohen, Alan King, Sam Levenson and the other professional raconteurs, have one thing in common; they are past masters of the art of timing. Notice how they speak at exactly the right pace to fit their characters and to keep the audience attentive. Notice how they observe those important momentary pauses to get guffaws and even hand and facial gestures are synchronized with speech to create effectiveness. Shouldn't this technique of expert timing be yours, too?

The DJ with a definite flair for radioshowmanship will give serious consideration to his choice of music, whether it is top-40, C and W, middle-of-the-road or otherwise, to create a rhythmic flow in his show. The wise jock should never overtalk himself—talk himself out of an audience. Ask radio listeners and you'll learn the jocks who babble on endlessly don't attract listeners; they bore an audience. Seldom will a listener take the liberty of candidly telling a jock that he simply talks too much and to ease up on his chatter. By the same token if a jock insists upon talking about matters of specialized interest, rather than of a general interest, he may well lose listeners without being aware of the loss of audience. Showmanship counts! It's the tastes of your listeners you must consider, not your personal likes.

The majority of jocks never run down a timing on their shows. They simply pull a stack of discs and keep spinning and chatting and reading commercials until their 5- or 6-hour session runs out. There isn't anything wrong with that, because it would seem needless to total the overall timings of a few dozen LPs and a handful of commercials. But there are jocks who conduct 1- or 2-hour programs, and for their benefit we should discuss how to time a production for a fast start, clean close and tight, overall presentation. In any case, as a working professional, you should be able to time a show as it is done in bigtime circles. So few deejays know, for example, how to "backtime," or how to close a program without having to fade a theme, or how to take a leisurely pace and easy-to-listen-to style knowing that a program will run out without rushing and cutting because it's properly timed.

First, let's talk about getting your theme music off the air in its entirety without amateurishly fading it at the close of the program. For simplicity, let's assume that your theme music runs exactly 2 minutes and 30 seconds, and that you must be off the air for a station break at precisely 11:59:30. Obviously, to run the theme out to completion it must start running at 11:57:00. If you want to give your show that professional sound, do this: At sometime during the program, cue up your theme disc or tape on an auxiliary table or recorder. When 11:57 rolls around, start the table or machine spinning with the fader closed. You'll be set to cross fade from your last tune to the theme while you sign off the show and your program will end at precisely 11:59:30 on the nose! Make sure your last tune is an instrumental for easy fading to your theme.

Your opening theme should never be allowed to run on endlessly as so many jocks are in the habit of doing while they make themselves comfortable, or set up their shows, or search for their commercial copy, or, believe it or not, decide to make a quick telephone call. Do this, and you'll soon hear from your program director. Again, preparation is the word. Have your first tune on top of the stack of recordings, or if possible, have it cued in before you go on duty. Pull all the copy to be read during your trick. Check carefully that copy is lined up in accordance with your production schedule. The general idea is: be set for a bright, attention-getting introduction to your show with a well-timed opening theme. Start talking after about 20 or 25 seconds of theme, and make your opening remarks brief. Get on with the show proper! Make it move with a bright tune with a beat, not a draggy vocal. Get on fast—that's good show business!

To prefectly time, say, a half- or one-hour show is a simple procedure. I have already explained how to neatly close out a program as it is practiced by virtually all major producers. To arrive at an overall total of running time, check the labels of the discs you plan using for the time of each band. List such times in a column, add one minute for each of the commercial in the show, add 20 seconds of chatter for each disc and finally, include 45 seconds for opening and 45 seconds for closing. Let's suppose your total runs 30:20, and you must be off the air at 29:30. This means you're 50 seconds over, doesn't it? You may, if your final tune is an instrumental, fade it at 11:58:45, then start your sign-off talk while you cross-fade into the theme. It's that simple! If you're way over, say by two minutes, you may delete one tune, but always let the final selection be an instrumental. As I said, to speak over a vocal, as you'd have to do if your final LP is **not** an instrumental, sounds bad.

Sometimes a show runs out **short**. Should your total running time add up to only 28:05 instead of 29:30—40 seconds early, don't s-t-r-e-t-c-h your closing theme to fill, but read a 40-second program resume from your production schedule. If you have a public service announcement handy, read that for 40 seconds, or give some local fund-raising campaign a 40-second plug, then while you fill with talk, fade your theme underneath for background, and bring it up full to completion on the nose at 11:59:30. Don't become discouraged if you fail to time out the first or second try. Practice will do it.

A Guide to Good Timing

Get your show on quickly—move it along—get off fast. Avoid lengthy opening and closing theme music.

Make your first tune a bright one with a beat—not a draggy ballad. The final tune should be a moving instrumental in case you must fade.

Balance your show. Intersperse instrumentals with vocals. Work with two or more musical groups. For relief, feature a novelty or two: Hawaiian, marimba, piano, etc.

To create rhythm, vary mood, tempo and pace from tune to tune. Surprise your audience with the unexpected. Keep your show in motion—don't bog down.

Don't talk too much or too long. No jock was ever criticized for being non-talkative. The loquacious one soon bores. Speak at a moderate rate of speed.

Choose your subject matter with discretion. Avoid controversial discussions, such as racial issues. Never become opinionated—don't editorialize. Speak on subject matter of general interest. Be guided by the likes and dislikes of your listenership. To treat this phase of your work lightly may damage your popularity.

The pause is a powerful, attention-getting device. Use it freely, but make it a pause—not dead air.

Never tell your audience you're late—you must rush. That's amateurism. As a professional you should make adjustments in your timing as you proceed—subtly speed up or slow down—delete a tune or add a public service announcement along the way. Listeners aren't, in the least, interested in your production problems. Never pad with meaningless music to fill time. Do a resume instead.

To produce a perfectly timed, professionally sounding show calls for preparation. Discourage distraction; insist on privacy when you're on the air.

Because the art of timing is an integral part of professional production practices, and because timing is so frequently neglected, the classroom teacher may want to post a copy of A Guide To Good Timing on the control-room wall of the school's campus broadcast station.

A Final Briefing

Now that you know the technological aspects associated with professional air work, you're ready to acquire finesse. To impart to your announcing the sound of self-assurance, the smooth nonchalance, the imperturbability of the seasoned professional (or as close as you can get to it as a beginner), apply the accumulated knowledge, understanding and technical skill you have so far acquired to the readings and commercials which follow.

Because you are now being groomed for professionalism, some mental conditioning is in order. Think of yourself as an artist, an accomplished public speaker, which you **are**. Build up your self-confidence—bolster your ego with thoughts that you already are a working professional on your way up. **Act** like a pro. **Sound** like a pro.

Warning! Perfection is impossible to come by. No one can or should expect to achieve perfection. The seasoned pro knows this; that's why he appears almost jauntily careless and completely relaxed as evidenced in his professional sound. To pressure yourself into a state of perfectionism—to subject yourself to volleys of your own harsh critique—is to expose yourself to tension and its ulcerizing consequences. It's common knowledge that today's highly pressurized commercial environment has produced certain individuals who cannot function properly unless they indulge in the evil and damaging practice of imbibing in barbiturates, scopolamine, or one of the other sleep-producing preparations to drug them into unconsciousness, and to gulp pep pills or smoke grass to stay awake on the job. Guard against the habits of the weak. RELAX! If you do the best of which you are capable, that's enough! Don't cultivate the doughnuts-and-coffee, Coke-and-hamburger routine. **Develop sensible living habits**. Keep yourself physically and mentally fit, so that you may enjoy a long and successful career which demands stamina all the way.

Speaking of keeping fit, let's talk about personal appearance. The DJ most likely to make it to the top is the chap with that healthy, well-groomed look of the professional man; sloppy Joes may well have to pick up the crumbs, settle for mediocrity. To expect to enlist the assistance of the "right people," advertising agency producers and directors, casting agency talent buyers and the others who may further your professional status, your personal bearing should stand paramount. Good grooming never goes unnoticed. Personal neatness is always appreciated. Because the DJ works in a windowless cubicle, removed from public view, is no valid reason for laxity in personal habits. I have known a few deejays who shuffled to work at 6 AM wearing wrinkled and faded jeans, soiled shirts and sloppy loafers. With faces unshaven and hair uncombed they went on the air in disheveled shape—literally—more asleep than awake. One deejay I knew was promptly fired because of his unkemptness. For the early-rising jock, time probably won't permit a morning shower, but then, there's the evening. It's embarrassing to watch visitors inspect the station only to find a deejay slouched in his swivel chair, muddy feet on the highly waxed turntable chomping away on a ham sandwich and gurgling a Coke. Unfortunately, informality is too easily mistaken to mean sloppiness. Of course, it's perfectly allowable—and in proper taste—to remove your coat, loosen your tie and roll up your sleeves while working in a control room. In summertime you may work in a pair of cool slacks and a sportshirt. For the DJ who anticipates professional consideration, personal cleanliness should become law. Good grooming reflects the image of the successful professional. If I may say so again, the tastes of the mod set in way-out proportions are not for professional broadcasting.

A trite phrase holds good here: Be the master of your own fate. All starts are difficult—in any profession, so stay with it all the way. Never permit anyone to discourage you. Weigh carefully the unsolicited advice; it usually comes from uninformed sources. Seek sound opinions from the experienced. Even then, accept only that which you, personally, feel is fitting and proper. Put positive thinking to work for you, and it does work, have no doubts about that. Reject negativism. You'll gain much more by making a mistake than by side-tracking the problem or by burying your head in the sand. Face up to the tough ones. That's the process of education—learning by trial and error. During an interview or in a letter of application, never overrate yourself. Boasting might get you the job, all right, but if you can't make good on your promises, you'll go out faster than you came in.

The groundwork is now laid for your career in professional broadcasting. If you're a high school senior, prepare to use radio-broadcasting to defray the cost of your higher learning. If you're a college student, feel free right now to get into broadcasting near your campus to pay your own way through college. If you're a working adult, this is the time to consider broadcasting as the most pleasant and most profitable way to supplement your regular income. A dozen of my students are doing exactly that. So can you! The college student may already be in broadcasting and well on his way toward his goal.

In the material which follows, the radio scripts were carefully chosen from my personal collection of story material; the commercial announcements were expressly written for this book. What you do with them is up to you. You're now your own teacher. Alternate scripts and announcements if you wish: one story one day, two commercials the next. On playback, when a weak technique is noticed, review the lesson and drills in which the technique appears. As you work on the following material, please consider these important points:

TO COMMUNICATE, project—don't introject. Speak to one listener, never to a group!

TO MAKE IT LIVE, give it characterization. Speak in living color, not in monotonous black and white.

TO SOUND SINCERE, cultivate believability. Be yourself. Develop poise, ease and naturalness.

TO SOUND AUTHENTIC, don't read words, make **word** pictures. Don't read news, become a professional storyteller.

TO BE UNDERSTOOD, Enunciate and articulate clearly. If they can't understand you, all your efforts are wasted.

15 Professional Scripts

Good morning, friends and neighbors. What a grand day for the pigskin classic, brisk and sunny. I'd like to talk about booby traps this morning...I mean a booby trap with a cold nose. The other day I read about an eight-year-old girl who opened the back door of her neighbor's house. A shot rang out. When the child came to in the hospital's recovery room, she learned she had lost her left arm. And mind you, all this happened simply because an overly cautious man had rigged up a booby trap, a rifle with its muzzle pointed directly at the door. The way his story went, he wanted to scare off prowlers, but instead he maimed an innocent child.

In a strikingly similar case, an intruder entered a home and he, too, faced a rifle blast which sent him to the police infirmary. The strange part of this story is that the intruder received a suspended sentence, while the man who had set the trap is being sued by the would-be burglar for $30,000, and, said the intruder's lawyer, the law is on the side of the burglar. It seems that two wrongs don't make a right.

In big city housing developments the cry is a familiar one: muggers, burglars, thieves and other unsavory characters who lurk in dark hallways to panic the lone woman occupant with an unfamiliar knock on the door or stealthy footsteps. Yet, unfortunately, the message is: "No dogs allowed."

When I think about warning devices, my thoughts always turn to the most effective burglar alarm of all...a keen-eared dog with a lusty bark. Believe me, neighbor, those who would brazenly intrude upon your privacy have a profound respect for a watchdog and his bite. To have a watchdog in the home is a great idea, but the animal should not be confined to a short length of chain out in the backyard...we should also consider him a companion. We had dogs as far back as I can remember, and they always had the run of the house.

Come the holidays, and they'll be here before long, helpless puppies and kittens are too freely given to small children as toys, but the tykes are too young and unknowingly cruel sometimes in their treatment of young animals. Their

233

pets are vulnerable and helpless in small hands. Of course, you can't blame the kids. They'll never know any better unless parents teach them how it should be done.

Do you know what happens when a child tires of his toy, the pup or kitten he received as a Christmas present? Well, sir, back to the dog pound it goes until the next time a thoughtless parent decides to try the experiment, and so it goes. Humane societies try to carefully screen all applicants who want to adopt pets, but it seems they can't win 'em all. The way I look at it, neighbor, I wouldn't want to be without a dog. You see, a watchdog carries a big stick—his bark.

(For use on December 25th)

Greetings, friends and neighbors. Here it is Christmas Day again, a day for cheerful giving and happy greetings...for Christmas trees and gay hearts. December 25th is also the birthday of a great woman and famous humanitarian, Clara Barton, who founded the American Red Cross. Very few persons know of the personal circumstances and events surrounding the life of Miss Barton, which had a direct bearing upon and actually influenced the founding of that great organization. Clara Barton lived a life of sacrifices. When the Civil War started in 1861, Miss Barton, then 40 years old, was said to have rushed into the streets of Washington and urged people to help the suffering, to minister to the wounded. A quiet, fearless woman, Clara Barton walked amidst cannon fire to reach the wounded of both sides. She nursed and fed them, always with a reassuring smile which both the North and South fondly recalled. When the war came to an end in 1865, President Lincoln appointed Clara Barton to head a group to search the scarred battlefields for the bodies of 80,000 soldiers reported missing in action. She carried on her humanitarian work until 1869 when ill health overtook her. It was then she decided to go to Switzerland for a long rest. While in the Alpine country, Miss Barton learned about the International Red Cross. Immediately she found a renewed interest in altruistic work and joined that organization in its relief work. At last Clara Barton was truly happy. In 1881 when she returned to America she was personally instrumental in the founding of the American Red Cross movement and became its first president. Clara Barton died in 1912 at the age of 91. Surely the blazing symbol of the Red Cross should remind us continually that Clara Barton, born this day in 1821, passed this way.

Good morning, friends and neighbors. This is the birthday of a great American...and manufacturing automobiles was his business. Henry Ford lived long enough to become the world's most productive manufacturer of automobiles. The famed philanthropist, at the early age of 12, must have found more than mere rhyme and rhythm in the old axiom: Early to bed and early to rise makes a man healthy, wealthy and wise. Say his biographers, before and after school, young Ford worked in a small garage to invent an automobile engine. That was the birth of the old Tin Lizzie—the Model-T Ford. When checking facts and figures, it astonishes one to learn how America's economic system and its standard of living were heightened because men like Henry Ford lived among us. Because of those automotive pioneers, we now have motels, drive-in theatres, service stations, rubber manufacturing plants—over a half million of them—a pulsating industry to provide America with rapid transportation. According to U.S. Labor Department statistics, there are now more than 1,160,00 men employed on automotive production lines, and over 965,000 steelworkers in the nation's mills. What about the oil drillers, and the tire production workers and the others? There's a story about Henry Ford, whose big, black limousine broke down on a lonely dirt road. A farmer chugged up to the big car, hitched a length of rope to it, and towed it to a garage some 10 miles away. When Ford's chauffeur wanted to pay the farmer for the tow, he refused, and drove away in his old jalopy. Some months later the farmer was amazed to find a spanking, new Model-T standing at his front door. Attached to the steering wheel was a note, "Sorry to hear about your Ford, but even Model-Ts wear out in time. Thought you could use a new one." The note was signed, Henry Ford. Henry Ford lived until 87 and amassed a fortune estimated at $200,000,000.

Hi neighbor. This morning I'd like to speak on a subject of current interest...freedom of speech. I'm reminded of a wise man back in the 1770s who was thrown in the Bastille for advocating freedom of thought and speech. Voltaire, called the "laughing philosopher," is quoted as having stated, "My trade is to say what I think." He was an advanced thinker who expressed his candid opinions on religious matters. When

Voltaire was branded an atheist, he penned the following lines:

"Oh God, hear these my final words: If ever I have erred, 'Twas searching for Thy Law; My heart may go astray, but it is full of Thee."

Are those the spoken thoughts of one who disbelieved in the existence of a Supreme Being? As one scribe said of Voltaire, "His faults were many, but he led the age of bigotry into the age of reason." The late, Bishop Pike, too, was accused by fellow churchmen of voicing opinions contrary to established beliefs. Pike was twice accused of heresy for expressing his personal thoughts about religious issues.

We read that during the trouble-ridden period of the High Renaissance, religionists of that trying era crusaded vigorously for church reforms. The modern thinker, too, may be a profoundly religious individual, yet because of his unorthodox opinions, narrow minds with wagging tongues may erringly label him—disbeliever; some may even go so far as to accuse him of atheistic leanings. This may be a changing world, but the process of updating antiquated beliefs and staid customs, reconciling ourselves to new thought, is a painfully slow-moving one. We know that self-expression is the ultimate in human freedom, but how avidly is one's advanced thinking seized upon and grossly misinterpreted. Neighbor, think it like it is, but be careful how you say it. You're not alone.

Good morning, neighbor. Pull in the ceramic lawn ornaments, draw the blinds and put a bright, red collar on the cat! Soon it will be that time of year again—open season. Watch out when trigger-happy Nimrods, with great aplomb, eagerly scamper off to the deep woods, dank lowlands and brush, to cock their rifles, and with almost fiendish delight, take nervous aim and fire at—maim or kill—any creature that walks or flies, crawls, creeps or hops. It's getting rougher every year. Daddy will buy Junior a shiny new gun—no problem—then, as every year, we'll read all about accidental shootings—needless and senseless killings due to the indiscriminate use of firearms—most times because of plain carelessness or ignorance. The morning paper will carry the story about the eager huntsman with an itchy trigger finger, who didn't mean to, but blasted the head off a fellow hunter, a father of four. The 10-year-old lad who lost the sight of his right eye because his pal playfully pointed a "harmless" BB gun at him and pulled the trigger. The weapon happened to be loaded. Then there's the usual bit about the riffleman who cleaned his gun while it was loaded; he paralyzed his neighbor's wife when the weapon discharged itself. And there's always the juvenile hunting enthusiast, too immature to be trusted with a deadly weapon, stalking the brush for small game while his kid brother walked in front of him. The younger boy was fatally injured when his big brother stumbled and inadvertently pulled the trigger.

National Safety Council statistics on accidental shootings continue to mount allarmingly. And what's more, to clear a path for much-needed housing subdivisions, hunting grounds must yield to the bulldozer. And conditions worsen as hunting activities escalate. Why must we sacrifice living matter to enjoy a sport? What's wrong with skeet shooting, or sighting the bull's eye on the rifle range, or downing clay pigeons in the shooting gallery? And toppling a tin can from a tree stump is lots of fun. All these are testing grounds for the sharpshooter's skill.

I know of a kindly man who harbors homeless creatures, lends his wholehearted support to humane causes and argues vehemently against vivisection practices, yet each fall this "animal lover" takes off to bag small game in the woods adjacent to his home. And a bird lover who drives great satisfaction from mending the injured wing of a starling, or placing a miniature cast around the fractured limb of a robin, can hardly wait until his duck stamp arrives. What's the answer?

Could it be that some of us don't actually understand the Lord's Commandment? Maybe that's it. Maybe we should add three little words to God's Law, to make it read, "Thou shalt not kill...any living thing.

(For use on November 30th)

Perhaps the outstanding personality of the day, insofar as famous birthdays are concerned, is the one-time Prime Minister of Great Britain, Sir Winston Churchill. Churchill was already 66 years old when he assumed the grave responsibilities of his important office, at a most critical time when the English empire faced the worst trial in its long history...early in 1940...about one month before the English military forces marched headlong into almost certain annihilation at Dunquerque. At 71, when many folks begin thinking about buying a rocking chair, Sir Winston took over the leadership of the opposition party. Was Churchill ready to withdraw into seclusion? He could have rested on his laurels when he reached 77 but he didn't. I guess it's like the saying goes: A winner never quits...a quitter never wins.

The man who had brought his country safely through the dark days of World War II became Prime Minister for the second time as an acknowledged leader of allied powers. World renowned for his scholarly volumes on history, biographies and memoirs, Mr. Churchill was awarded the Nobel prized for literary achievement. And Sir Winston was then a young 79. Even then the great English statesman refused to quit the race.

Churchill painted beautiful pictures...he wrote volumes on the history of the Great War, which were hailed as brilliant and sweeping accounts of that global conflict. Mr. Churchill lived and labored and produced admirable things up to the day he died. Sir Winston Churchill passed away quietly in 1965 at the age of 91. Other great men in history were born on this date, but outstanding, as I said, we think of the name of Sir Winston Churchill most worthy of mention this morning.

The Brookhaven Concerts Association is happy to announce its coming season's programs. This year's series of symphonic concerts will begin with a recital by the eminent violin virtuoso, Pietre Merini. Mr. Merini will play the well-known Concerto in C Minor by Rebkow, and as a special offering, the Fritz Kreisler classical love song, "Liebesfreud." The featured orchestra on that evening, October 3rd, will be the London Symphony, which will be expressly flown here from London for that performance. The London Symphony Orchestra will again be heard on Sunday afternoon, February 14th, at that time featuring Maria DeSales, former La Scala Milan soprano, in a series of operatic arias. The Brookhaven Concerts Association will proudly present Thomas Wainwright, pianist, in a program of piano concertos, including the renowned Concerto for Piano in A Major by Ludvig Ebsen and the same composer's "Caprice." There will be a series of thirteen concerts, beginning with the October 3rd music festival and concluding with the Boston Symphony concert on April 15th. Among the musical organizations to be heard this year will be: The London Symphony, the Boston Symphony and the Detroit String Quartet. Soloists will be: Maria DeSales, Thomas Wainwright, Walter Brian, and Frank Montaigne. Our special Christmas program of December

22nd, on a Saturday evening, will consist of organ solos and Christmas carols by the First Methodist choir, with a baritone solo by Frank Montaigne. Mr. Montaigne will sing, "O Holy Night." Tickets for all thirteen concerts may be purchased separately at the door, or to reserve a seat at each concert, you may subscribe for the entire series of thirteen concerts by making your check in the amount of $20 payable to the Brookhaven Concerts Association. Now, back to "Music America Loves Best."

(For use on February 11th)

In this morning's birthday corner we honor Thomas A. Edison, who despite his limited general education, is said to have applied for 12,000 patents. According to his biography, those inventions are valued at about $15,599,000. Those who knew Edison spoke of him as a human dynamo, a powerhouse of energy, a tireless worker in the field of applied science, a field in which he stood at the top. When asked about his inventions and their inspirations, he countered with, "2 percent inspiration—98 percent perspiration."

Edison's inventions were many, including, besides a phonograph and the electric light bulb, a typewriter, motion picture camera, and as only few knew, Edison, about a year before he died, was developing a process to produce synthetic rubber from substance extracted from the lowly goldenrod. The inventor labored hard and long in the development of the electronic tube which today functions in radio and television sets and in other electronic devices.

About Thomas Edison's private life, not too much is known. He was married twice...he was the father of six children. One of them, Charles Edison was elected Governor of New Jersey, Edison's home state. Thomas Alva Edison died in his West Orange, New Jersey home on October 18, 1931. The Thomas A. Edison story is a long and very interesting one. I have merely touched on a few highlights in the life of the great inventor who was born on this date, February 11th in 1847.

A good knowledge of new Federal income tax laws could save a farmer many dollars in the next few months, according to a University of Florida press release. Farmers prefiguring their final tax bill for 1970 shouldn't overlook those 1969 revisions in the Federal tax code, many of which went into effect for the first time this year, says Dr. W. W. Cake, economist, Florida Cooperative Extension Service.

The Tax Reform Act of 1969 contains nine provisions which deal specifically with reporting income from the farm, as well as numerous other changes that effect all taxpayers. Producers would do well to consult the new regulations before deciding to buy or sell a particular item between now or December—or whether it would be more advantageous, taxwise, to wait until 1971, said Dr. Cake. The goal of tax management isn't to avoid taxes, but rather, it is to minimize taxes paid by taking advantage of all the provisions of the tax laws as they apply to the farmer's particular operation.

Two of the Act's provisions affect the reporting of income from sales of livestock purchased for draft, breeding, sporting or dairy purposes. Formerly all such income could be treated as capital gains, which are taxable at the lower capital gains rate, explained Dr. Cake. Under the new law, the gain from the sale of livestock is to be treated as ordinary income, rather than a capital gain, up to the full value of depreciation deductions. This applies to depreciation taken from 1969. The purpose of this change is to put livestock on the same tax base as other property used in business, the depreciation of which is normally recaptured at the time of sale.

Vegetable crops in Florida were subjected to a marked change from the abnormally high temperature that prevailed through the 25th to subnormal lows over the week end. Adverse effects will be reflected more in retarded growth than to actual damage to vegetables moving to market, according to G. Norman Rose of the Florida Crop and Livestock Reporting Service.

Tender vegetables along the Lower East Coast were subjected to lows of 34 to 37 degrees, with spots of frost, but a warming trend around 2:00 to 3:00 AM Monday morning brought temperatures up to around 40 degrees by sunrise. In Immokalee it dropped to 34 degrees both mornings in the coldest locations, but most frost was noticed on debris and ditchbanks. The coastal areas of Fort Myers - Naples was warmer. The Everglades mucklands had patches of frost and 30-35 degrees low, especially inland.

Some outer leafburn occurred to hardier type vegetables grown there. Some burn was sustained in sweet corn, in the developing stage, but mature corn came through OK. In center areas temperatures dropped to 28-35 degrees with scattered light to moderate frost. The Hastings area reported a low of 25 degrees, but no damage to cabbage is indicated. All areas of production are expected to continue harvest of most items that were in production prior to Christmas. Most areas of the State continue dry with some type of irrigation used to alleviate the moisture shortage. Showers, where received, were most beneficial.

Shipments of all vegetables during the week of December 20-26 were down 31 percent. 1,799 carlots equivalent reported compares with 2,589 the previous week, the peak for the fall season. Tomatoes led all commodities again in carlots shipped with 457 reported, a drop of 31 percent from that of the previous week's 667 carlots and 37 percent less than the 725 three weeks ago.

For years we've been warned that too much cholesterol and saturated fats in our diet can cause heart disease. Now a University of Florida professor says there's no association between the two.

"There is no discernable association between reported diet intake and serum cholesterol levels," according to Dr. C. Bronson Lane, who is with the University's Institute of Food and Agricultrual Sciences.

He cited a newly completed study by the National Heart and Lung Institute, Bethesda, Maryland, correlating diet with heart disease over a 20-year period for the people of Framingham, Massachusetts, a Boston suburb. The new report, Dr. Lane said, disproves, or at least, questions what the American Heart Association and others have been telling us about diet and heart disease for years. Namely, that food, high in saturated fats, such as, beef, pork, milk, butter, and other dairy products have been responsible for the growing incidence of heart disease and high blood cholesterol levels in the U. S.

Almost until the time of the release of the final report of the Framingham study, its director was telling Americans to change their eating habits to reduce the "alarmingly high cholesterol levels" in their diet. The study directors were also advising us to replace saturated animal fats with polyunsaturated vegetable fats, to eat less meat, and to use corn oil margarine instead of butter. The final Framingham report says the premature allegations against saturated fats just aren't so. "There is no discernable association between reported diet intake and serum cholesterol levels," explained R. Lane.

A symposium on "Pesticides in the Environment—A Real or Imaginary Hazard," is expected to generate controversy in Miami Beach on Monday night, November 30th, as the annual meeting of the Entomological Society of America gets underway. More than 2,000 scientists from across the nation, the largest number ever to attend a national meeting of the Society, are expected on November 30th-December 3rd at the Deauville Hotel.

Over 500 highly scientific papers, dealing with various aspects of insects and their control, will be presented during the meeting, according to D. Richard M. Baranowski, chairman of the program and professor with the University of Florida's Sub-Tropical Experiment Station, Homestead.

Extension entomologists from various land-grant institutions around the nation, who advise growers and homeowners on how to control unwanted insects, will also participate in a panel discussion on the environment. Moderator for the discussions will be Professor James E. Brogdon with the University of Florida's Institute of Food and Agricultural Sciences in Gainesville. Some 50 entomologists from the University, the U.S. Department of Agriculture, the Florida Department of Agriculture, and various other state and federal agencies are scheduled to present cases at the meeting. One of them, Dr. W. G. Eden, chairman of the University's Entomology and Nematology Department, is the Society's president-elect for 1972 when the national meeting will be held in Montreal, Canada.

Good evening. This is George Nelsen with today's report on the nation's business. Activity on the New York Stock Exchange was brisk today, but gains only moderate. Volume sales on the board almost reached the 18-million mark, a 2-million gain over yesterday's 16 million shares sold. The Dow Jones average of 30 industrials showed a gain of 1.65 points to 849.47. The country's largest airline, United Airlines, this afternoon announced cutbacks in its service. A company spokesman blamed the move on the continued slump in United States air travel. By early February, he said, United would reduce the number of its daily departures by 9 point 5 percent below the company's present level. Also in airline news, Trans World said the company, during 1970, suffered a loss in profits of 63 point 9 million dollars. Three San Francisco banks have announced cutbacks in interest on time deposits. Wells Fargo Bank, Bank of America and Crooker-Citizens National Bank initiated the time-deposit cut to 5 percent. The three institutions will continue to pay 5¾ percent on two-year deposits and 5½ percent interest on 1-year accounts until maturity. But all new time accounts, said the banks, would pay only 5 percent interest. To stimulate American loans and investments to the development of foreign countries, President Nixon today signed an order which sets up an overseas investment corporation, comprised of government and private interests. The arrangement will guarantee loans by American companies for foreign development purposes. The corporation was authorized by Congress in 1969. With the increase in available mortgage money, housing developers look forward to much construction activity during the coming year. However, because of investments in new equipment and such, financial returns in 1971 will remain much the same as they were in the past year.

It's like the man on TV says, "Come on down—put fun in your life! Soak up the sun!" Most folks are of the opinion that Florida has summer weather all year long. Well, that's not so. Actually, the four seasons also come to the Sunshine State, but with a difference. Seasonal changes are subtler and the divisions between them more elusive.

Autumn tiptoes into the state and goes virtually unnoticed until mid-October. Autumnal changes are most discernable in North Florida, where the dogwoods turn to crimson and other deciduous trees are transformed into shaggy globes of gold and orange. Never-changing evergreens provide the background for this colorful array. In Central and South Florida, autumn is subtle indeed. The air is crisper, the skies a bit bluer and the billowy white cumulous clouds less numerous. And winter—delightful, with an occasional cold snap.

You garden enthusiasts out there will be interested to learn that there are almost no deciduous trees in the central and southern parts of Florida. And the stolid pines and moss-hung oaks remain impervious to the changing seasons, which flourish in Florida's sub-tropical clime, and citrus trees spend the fall and winter months nurturing the young fruit to maturity, seemingly unaware that the air is cooler and the winds brisker. So far as Floridians are concerned, summer begins in May and lasts into October. The season begins and ends with kids rushing home from school, jumping into swim suits and heading for the lake or beach to catch the last bit of sun.

Most Florida towns have a plentiful supply of fresh-water lakes, and salt water is never far away. So, as you can understand, much of life in this sub-tropical climate, says the Florida State Department of Commerce, centers around the water and outdoor activities. So, come on down for fun in the sun! Come to Florida!

Many a parent bouncing an infant on his knee has thought that the child was worth his weight in gold.

"And, as it turns out, that's almost the literal truth," says Miss Carla Bartscht, Home Management and Family Economics Specialist, Florida Cooperative Extension Service. The Institute of Life Insurance has analyzed what it cost a family to raise a child to age 18, and found that it takes about three years of current family income. In round numbers that comes to about $30,000. Mind you, this figure can vary widely, depending on family circumstances.

How does it break down? Some $3,000 goes for the expenses of birth and medical care, over the 18 years, she says. And food eats up $8,000. Every parent learns that although infants may not consume much, teenagers devour everything in sight. Clothing amounts for almost $4,000, and the child's share of family housing expenses takes another $9,000. Transportation burns up about $4,000, while personal care, recreation and education are responsible for $2,500.

Add it all up and it comes to almost $30,000, Miss Bartscht points out. And that doesn't include the costs of a college education, which can easily run to another $15,000 at a 4-year school. With costs that high, many families put aside money for college over the years through savings of various kinds. But any way you look at it, that little bundle of joy may truly be worth his weight in gold.

20 Commercial Announcements

Now is the right time of year to fertilize your lawns and garden, and the right fertilizer to use is time-tested **Rapid-Gro**, the famous 5-10-5 plant food with a guaranteed analysis in accordance to United States Department of Agriculture specifications. You'll find the entire line of **Rapid-Gro** farm and garden products at JOHNSON FEED STORES, Greenvale county's leading feed and nurserymen for over fifty years. Let an experienced JOHNSON nurseryman advise you on the proper analysis of **Rapid-Gro** to do the most for your garden and its soil requirements. Another thing, at all three JOHNSON FEED STORES there's never a parking problem, because all three JOHNSON stores are expressly located outside the heavily-traveled areas. All three JOHNSON FEED STORES are open from 7 to 7, six days a week. Stop in soon in Williamstown, Cooper or Warren City.

An old saying goes: "An apple a day keeps the doctor away" remember? Here's another: A flower a day keeps the blues away. What I mean is that if you know of someone who is ailing, or observing a birthday, or celebrating a wedding anniversary, you can make the occasion doubly enjoyable or express your sympathies by sending beautiful flowers from the STORE FLOWER SHOP, in the Hotel Astor, Times Square. Whether it's a simple corsage or a massive floral offering, telephone your order, day or night, 24 hours a day to THE ASTOR FLOWER SHOP. Your order, large or small, will receive prompt attention. Call the ASTOR FLOWER SHOP at 765-8900. Call now, if you wish. That's 765-8900.

Whenever and wherever folks gather to enjoy themselves, there you'll find ice-cold...refreshing FROSTY POP. There's a reason for this. Folks prefer FROSTY POP to other soft drinks because FROSTY is light drinking, yet so tasty...the last bottle of FROSTY tastes just as refreshing as the first one. And that's saying a lot, isn't it? Delicious...thirst-quenching FROSTY POP is the favorite beverage of millions from coast to coast, and it has been America's **preferred** soft drink for over fifty years! Buy a carton of FROSTY POP **today**. The **last** bottle in the carton will taste just as **refreshing** as the **first** one. Shouldn't your family beverage be...FROSTY POP? **We** think so!

Have you tried **new** KREEM? No, don't say soap...say, KREEM. You see, KREEM is not a soap. KREEM contains one-third costly cleansing oils. That means that our **new** KREEM leaves your skin so soft...**baby** soft, so **kissable**. The kind of skin men love to caress. Can you say the same thing about your **present** complexion soap? Instead of **soap**, wash with **gentle, mild and beautifying** KREEM. You'll **love** it.

Do you need money fast? Then take your financial problems to HOME FINANCE. There's an office near you, ready, willing and able to lend you the needed cash in the amount of $5 up to $500. HOME FINANCE asks no questions. The only requirement is that you are employed. If you need money quickly...you get it quickly...no questions asked. Save yourself time and effort. Pay all your bills right now, then repay your loan to HOME FINANCE in small, easy monthly payments. It's that simple! And interest rates are low at HOME FINANCE. See the yellow pages of your telephone directory for the address of your nearest HOME FINANCE office. Lending money is their business.

What do you do when a headache strikes? The sensible thing to do is to have a bottle of fast-acting SOOTHALL tablets in your medicine cabinet, ready to relieve that low and miserable feeling...fast! You see, SOOTHALL tablets act quickly to drain clogged sinuses and to reduce swollen membranes that often accompany a common cold. That's because SOOTHALL tablets are like a doctor's prescription. They actually contain four tested ingredients and much more of the pain reliever than is found in other cold tablets. Buy SOOTHALL tablets in the pocket size packet of 25 tablets, or in the larger 50-tablet size. For real economy buy the family-size bottle of 250 tablets. SOOTHALL...on drug counters... everywhere!

One of the best ways you can get a new baby started in life is by buying him or her a United States Savings Bond. And once you're started, keep on with it. As the baby grows, the bonds you buy will keep growing, too. When the baby is ready for college, the bonds will be ready to **pay** for his or her higher education. Yes, United States Savings Bonds pay 4¼ percent interest when held to maturity—and Freedom Shares, sold in combination with bonds, pay a **full 5 percent!** The **extra** interest will be added as a bonus at maturity. Now you can buy the Bond-Freedom Share **anytime** and no monthly committment is necessary. Get the facts where you work or where you bank.

You have to know less than nothing about photography to take sharp, **clear** pictures with a KODAK INSTAMATIC camera. Everything's **automatic.** Insert the film, push the button—**Presto!** You've taken a **perfect** picture, evenly lighted, sharply focused, well defined because KODAK INSTAMATIC does all the work. All **you** do is feed the film, hold the camera and press the button, that's **all!** See the **new** KODAK INSTAMATIC camera at your dealer soon. They start as low as $22! Put an Eastman KODAK INSTAMATIC on your Christmas list!

Are you planning a vacation trip soon? I mean, an **unusual** kind of vacation? Well, how about an **exciting** cruise on the blue Mediterranean...just to be different? Yes, you can make this vacation an unforgettable experience. Just think of it! Thirty-one **glorious** days sailing in utter luxury aboard the flagship Maronia. Laze on deck. Make friends. Go to gay parties. Visit fifteen **exciting** ports of call in exotic lands. Enjoy unusual foods in far off places. Sounds great! Doesn't it? Call your travel agent today, and tell him that **you** want a reservation aboard the S. S. Maronia, sailing from New York on June 30th for the **greatest** vacation of your life! Bon voyage!

Here's an **amazing** invention! A refrigerator that needs no defrosting...ever! That's right! You'll **never** need to defrost again! Unbelievable? Yes, but true! And this **new** FREEZALL refrigerator carries with it an **unconditional** guarantee of satisfaction—not for one year, not for **five** years, but for the life of your FREEZALL. You'll have to see..this unique appliance to **believe** it. See the **new** FREEZALL at your local appliance dealer. Yes, it's amazing! That's what **you'll** say when you put a FREEZALL in **your** home. Remember, happy homemaking starts in the kitchen with a FREEZALL refrigerator!

At last it can be told! We're ready to throw open the doors of Smithtown's largest discount center, a full city block of floor space displaying everything in stock. Men and women's clothing, a complete department devoted to the needs of the small fry, a furniture mart that will thrill you, and for the handyman, a plumbing, electrical and woodworking supply department—everything to make home repairs by yourself. That's not all! Do all your shopping under one roof. Do your weekend marketing in our **super-discount** supermarket. That's right, we haven't mentioned the name of our new shopping center, but you already **know** that...NATIONAL DISCOUNT PLAZA, on Route 50, just outside Smithtown city limits. Grand opening this Saturday starting at 10 AM. Prizes and souvenirs for all...candy for the kids... orchids for the ladies...and surprises for the men...something for everyone at the NATIONAL DISCOUNT PLAZA this coming Saturday morning at 10. Whether you want to buy or not, celebrate grand opening with us this Saturday! Plenty of free parking. Come early...bring your neighbor!

Are you still paying your bills the old-fashioned way...by cash or money order? Well, you don't have to. Go modern with a FIRST NATIONAL SAVINGS AND LOAN personal checking account. Or better still, ask about their new credit card system. Buy anything and everything you need and simply say, "Charge it!" It's that simple. FIRST NATIONAL SAVINGS AND LOAN will do the rest. All bookkeeping is handled for you at a modest rate. Wouldn't you like to be able to buy all the things you've wanted to buy...all the clothes you need right now by saying just two words...charge it? Of course, you would, and you can! It costs nothing to find out about FIRST NATIONAL SAVINGS AND LOAN credit card system. Inquire today. Ask at any branch office in the city.

The coming holidays mean guests and parties. Of course, you'll want to spruce up your home with gay, fresh decor, or perhaps a newly-decorated and tastefully furnished guest room. Say, there's an idea...a new bedroom group! How about HELLER BROTHERS window display this week? You'll see solid hard rock maple furniture in warm, comfortable Early American styling, created by craftsmen, expert in creating that antique illusion that's so desirable in furniture of this kind. See this display when you get to town. HELLER BROTHERS, on Prospect just east of Main Street, in Allendale, will gladly help you with any of your home furnishing problems. They are authorized dealers in Lee and Mohawk carpeting and rugs, and their new enlarged store is loaded with furniture, wall decorations and floor coverings of every description and in every price range. HELLER BROTHERS are open from 9 to 9 Monday through Saturday.

Maybe you don't know one car from the other...maybe you know nothing at all about the mechanics of an automobile. Well, that's reason enough for you to choose your used car from CHEERFUL CHARLIE...Woodlawn's reliable and honest used-car dealer. Every automobile on CHEERFUL CHARLIE'S used-car lot plainly shows a sticker on which is noted the cars age, mileage, condition and price. There's no guesswork at CHEERFUL CHARLIE'S place. Ask the questions...CHEERFUL CHARLIE will come up with the honest answers. Prices are always right! You don't know anything about an automobile? You don't have to. See CHEERFUL CHARLIE, at the Four Corners, midtown, Johnson City. CHEERFUL CHARLIE is open until 10 PM seven days a week.

Want to surprise the family this Sunday? Then, take them out to dinner at WAYSIDE INN on Route 134, in Webster. You know the place, that colonial, white building in a charming country setting? Yes, dine in elegance, yet enjoy the informality of a candlelight and silver feast. Need we say that WAYSIDE INN serves complete dinners from $2.00 up, including beverages? WAYSIDE INN is also open for lunch from noon to 2 PM, Monday through Saturdays, featuring such taste-tempting dishes as German sauerbraten with potato dumplings, Irish style corned beef and cabbage and chicken cacciatore with that old-world flavor. For graceful dining, where your friends meet Sunday evenings for dinner, make it a family affair at the WAYSIDE INN on Route 134, in Webster. For downright good eating, family style, make it the WAYSIDE INN Sunday.

Are you wondering if it's bad breath or something? You can't afford to take chances. Use MINT, just be sure. You see, new MINT mouthwash acts quickly to make your mouth feel clean..your breath fresh. Yes, MINT is guaranteed to kill millions of germs in the mouth on contact, and germs are the cause of bad breath. MINT is long-lasting, too...lasts for hours. When other mouthwashes taste like soda pop, change to new MINT. Yes, new MINT is different. It's America's fastest selling mouthwash! Effective, safe, fast-acting MINT comes in two sizes, the personal size, 8-ounce bottle and the family-size bottle of 16 ounces. The larger size saves you money, too. Get MINT, today!

When children hate to brush their teeth, there's usually a good reason. It could be that your present toothpaste doesn't appeal to them. Taste may well make the difference. That's exactly why we make DENTOFRESH toothpaste with an entirely new, appealing flavor children love...almost candylike, yet it's guaranteed highly effective to fight off tooth decay. If you haven't given DENTOFRESH a try, you should today. Youngsters love to brush with DENTOFRESH and that's important! DENTOFRESH bears the seal of approval of the American Dental Association. What more is there to say about DENTOFRESH? You've just got to prove it to yourself, that is, prove it to your youngsters. Watch them enjoy that daily chore of brushing teeth. Comes in the large family size tube, too. Now, DENTOFRESH, at all drug stores and supermarkets. Oh, sure, adults like it, too.

Who doesn't like homemade soup? But, then, how many working women have the time these days to prepare a steaming pot of delicious soup? That's why MRS. WAGNER'S soups have grown so popular with mothers everywhere. You see, MRS. WAGNER'S chefs prepare over twenty kinds of soups in that old-fashioned way that grandma used to. Delicately seasoned, just right, MRS. WAGNER'S soups are slowly simmered to bring out that old-time flavor and goodness. Just think of it! Creamy cream of mushroom, chickeny cream of chicken soup, hearty mutton soup, invigorating tomato with rice and many other soups can be yours tonight for dinner. See the special MRS. WAGNER'S display in your supermarket. Know what you'll say? It tastes just like grandma's homemade soup. That's because we make our soups as if grandma were watching us. MRS. WAGNER'S soups...Mmmmm good!

For a hair dressing that leaves no greasy film to give your hair that pasted-down look, use HAIRSTAY, the modern dressing for well-groomed men. HAIRSTAY is truly a man's hair dressing. It smells nice, sure, but not like perfume. HAIRSTAY leaves a fresh, clean scent behind. What's more, it keeps your hair in place all day long, even through windy weather. Once you try HAIRSTAY, you'll stay with it for life! Now in two sizes, HAIRSTAY is the most economical hair dressing you can buy. For that well-groomed masculine look, use HAIRSTAY. Get it in the small, trial size or in the big, money-saving plastic bottle. On drug counters from coast to coast!

Say, want to put some fun in your life? Try bowling! Take a few friends for an old-fashioned night of kegling at the PASTIME ALLEYS on Rostrum Boulevard, in Greenlawn. Bowling's not only real fun, but it's also healthy exercise, the kind of invigorating exercise we all need to keep us trim and in good physical shape. PASTIME ALLEYS are open seven nights a week. Make it a weekly bowling fest...take the whole family. Yes, they serve sandwiches, coffee and soft drinks, so how about a bowling party soon at the PASTIME ALLEYS? Bowling puts fun in your life! Try it and see!

TRADE PUBLICATIONS

Broadcast Management-Engineering. Broadband Information Services, Inc., 200 Madison Ave., New York, N.Y. 10016. Publishes monthly. Carries classified advertising section. Issues yearbook.

Broadcasting-Telecasting, 1735 DeSales St., N. W., Washington, D.C. 20036. Publishes weekly. Carries classified advertising section. Issues yearbook.

Billboard, 165 West 46 Street, N. Y. 10036. Publishes weekly. Carries classified advertising section. Available on many newsstands and by subscription.

Variety, 154 West 46 Street, N. Y. 10036. Publishes weekly. No classified section. Carries an excellent pop record section.

Radio-Television Daily, 1501 Broadway, N. Y. 10036. Published daily. Mainly of interest to management. No classified section. Excellent sales material.

PUBLISHERS OF RADIO AND TV BOOKS

TAB (Technical Authors Books) Books, Monterey Avenue, Blue Ridge Summit, Penna. 17214. Catalog available. Also publishes and distributes Gernsback Library Books.

McGraw-Hill Book Company, 330 West 42 Street, New York, N. Y. 10036.

Hastings House, Publishing Inc., 10 East 40 Street, N. Y. 10016. Catalogue of Communication Arts books available.

See also the classified sections of trade journals, **Broadcasting Yearbook,** for other publishers of books dealing with communication, speech, electronics, etc.

SUGGESTED READING

Hal Fisher, **The Man Behind The Mike**, TAB Books, Blue Ridge Summit, Pa. 17214.

Marjorie Hellier, **How To Develop a Better Speaking Voice**, Wilshire Book Company, Hollywood, California.

Harry Shefter, **Faster Reading**, ARCO Publishing Company, New York, N. Y.

David Dary, **Radio News Handbook**, TAB Books, Blue Ridge Summit, Pa. 17214.

Henry Jacobowitz, **Basic Math Course for Electronics**, TAB Books, Blue Ridge Summit, Pa. 17214.

William A. Peck, **Anatomy of Local Radio-TV Copy**, TAB Books, Blue Ridge Summit, Pa. 17214.

Employment Outlook for Radio and Television Broad-casting Bulletin No. 1550-115. Supt. of Documents, U.S. Printing Office, Washington, D. C. 20402 (10c).

Study Guide and Reference Material for Commerical Radio Operator Examinations (75c) Supt. of Documents, U.S. Printing Office, Washington, D. C. 20402.

Vol. 1, FCC Rules and Regulations, Parts 0, 1, 13 & 17. $2.50 ($3.50 foreign) including Commission Organization, Practice and Procedure, Commercial Radio Operators, Construction, Marking and Lighting of Antenna Structures. Supt. of Documents, U.S. Printing Office, Washington, D. C. 20402.

HOLLYWOOD GAGLETTER, A monthly service to the nation's deejays. Available from Edmund Orrin, Boyer Road, Mariposa, Cal. 95338.

THE BROADCASTER'S HOME LIBRARY

Handbook of Radio Publicity & Promotion—by Jack Mac-Donald. Over 1500 on-air promo themes adaptable to any format, and over 350 contests, stunts, station and personality promos. (No. 213)

Modern Radio Broadcasting: Management & Operation in Small to Medium Markets—by R. H. Coddington. (No. 482)

The Anatomy of Local Radio-TV Copy—by William A. Peck. Hundreds of ways to increase station billing with sales-proven copy. (No. T-90)

Managing Today's Radio Station—by Jay Hoffer. A collection of critiques on the art, outlining principles evolved by the author during his 20 years as a broadcaster. (No. 461)

Radio Promotion Handbook—by William Peck. Hundreds of ideas and scores of factual examples to spark new ways to promote a station, its programming and personalities. (No. 267)

Radio Program Ideabook—by Hal Fisher. All the programming ideas you need to build an audience. (No. 268)

Guidelines for News Reporters—by Sol Robinson. A handbook on the techniques of Broadcast Journalism. (No. 516)

Power Technique for Radio-TV Copywriting—by Neil Terrell. How to write sales-producing copy using the author's proven methods. (No. 518)

Broadcast Station Operating Guide—by Sol Robinson. Covers all aspects of station operation from management to programming, sales, and engineering. (No. 467)

Organization & Operation of Broadcast Stations—by Jay Hoffer. An exhaustive examination of the responsibilities and capabilities required in each job classification.

Radio Station Sales Promotions—by Jack MacDonald. 300 merchandise-moving ideas.

The above books, plus three on the suggested reading list, are available from TAB Books, Blue Ridge Summit, Pa. 17214.

Index